Because You Want To Write

About the author

Pearlie McNeill has been a creative writing tutor for the past twelve years for the Workers Educational Association in Devon and London, and for two years at both Lancashire Polytechnic and Liverpool University.

Other publications by the author include: *And So Say All of Us* (edited with Marie McShea), Second Back Row Press, Sydney, 1984; *Through the Break* (edited with Pratibha Parmar and Marie McShea), Sheba, 1987; *One of the Family*, The Women's Press, 1989 (published in Australia in 1990 by University of Queensland Press and awarded a High Commendation in the 1990 Human Rights awards in Australia); *Women Talk Sex* (edited with Bea Freeman and Jenny Newman), Scarlet Press, 1992; and various short stories such as 'The Awakening' in *Despatches From the Frontiers of the Female Mind*, The Women's Press, recently translated into Spanish and Italian.

PeaRLie McNeiLL

Because You Want To Write

A WORKBOOK FOR WOMEN

Scarlet Press

Acknowledgements

Scarlet editor Avis Lewallen has always believed in this book and there are no words that can adequately express my thanks and appreciation for her seemingly tireless commitment and input, resistance to distractions (many of them mine), her willingness to be involved in never-ending debates about this or that idea, and her offering of relevant material to read and things to think about. Thanks are also due to Marie McShea for discussing much of the work with me and particular thanks to her and Pat Heard for their suggestions concerning the science fiction chapter, to Olive Rogers and Linda McGowan for contributing ideas about the imagery chapter and to Liz Tait for helpful feedback on the autobiographical chapter. I must also thank the many, many women I have worked with in classes and workshops over the years. Meg Coulson has given me invaluable support, reading through the evolving draft chapters, and her insights and wisdom have expanded my approach to various issues and how to present them. I trust she will know that her encouragement has been an integral part of the writing of this book. I should also like to thank The Women's Press for permission to reprint 'Women Poets (with your permission)' by Velma Pollard, from *Considering Women*, 1989.

Published by Scarlet Press 1992
5 Montague Road, London E8 2HN

British Library Cataloguing-in-Publication Data
A catalogue record for this book is available
from the British Library
ISBN   1 85727 030 4 pb
          1 85727 035 5 hb

Designed and produced for Scarlet Press by
Chase Production Services, Chipping Norton
Typeset from author's disks by
Stanford Desktop Publishing Services, Milton Keynes
Printed in Finland by WSOY

Contents

Women Poets (with your permission)

the little man
too early home today
surprised me scribbling
while the washer turned
ahaa ... I see you
take your little write
well let me see your book ...
mhmm ... mhmm ... not bad not bad
a little comma here
a period there
that sentence can make sense ...
almost

your friend there scribbling too
and Genie down the road
well well how nice
how triply nice
not mad not mad ...

Velma Pollard, December 1979

Introduction

A vivid memory from childhood haunts me still when I think about the word 'because'. The scene was my primary school classroom and the principal had just walked into the room. There were many good teachers in that school but the principal was a holy terror. Her entrance was greeted by an unfamiliar hush that echoed around the room. We straightened our backs, put our folded hands in front of us and turned respectful glances in her direction. Standing alongside our teacher she began firing questions. I prayed I wouldn't attract attention but when my name was called I sprang to my feet, my prompt action belying the cringing fear I felt, holding on to the desk for support as I tried to take in what was being asked. The question was repeated several times but I seemed unable to hear. The only word I could stutter in reply was: 'Because …'

'Answer the question, child – quickly now, and stop using the word because.'

Was it panic that affected my hearing? How could I do anything to change the situation? I couldn't think. I could hardly speak. I clung to that one word as though the English language had yet to be invented. 'Because' was the only word that made it possible for my tongue and lips to move. Finally, disgusted, the principal told me to sit down. I sank back into my seat choked by shame and tears.

We are taught lots of rules about words: Don't use that one here and never use that one at all. So, 'because' seems a good word for me to introduce into the title of this book, a defiant gesture about breaking the rules. Writers need to know that all rules exist to be broken.

This book also began with a question. The question wasn't mine but that of a woman who'd attended a workshop I'd done in London some years ago. She asked if I had ever thought of photocopying my notes so that participants could use them afterwards. The idea had never occurred to me, though I know how much I have benefited from the wisdom and knowhow passed on by many women in all sorts of ways. I believe in the idea of sharing what we have learned. The question stayed in my head and was followed by others: What issues were important to women writers? What sort of structure should a book like this have? How would it all fit in?

The story now jumps to the 4th International Feminist Book Fair held in Barcelona in 1990. It was here that I met three members of Britain's (then) newest feminist publisher, Scarlet Press. I had a book to sell, an anthology of women's writing which I had worked on with two other editors, Bea Freeman and Jenny Newman. Were the women at Scarlet interested in this anthology? Yes, they were. Months later I was able to talk to them about a second book, a book for women on writing. I'd taken my outline synopsis to one publisher who had, after much umming and aahing, decided it was not for them. A potential co-author on the writing book had dropped out due to other work commitments. Flattened somewhat by both of these events, it would have been so easy at this point to give up but, like bubbles rising in a glass of fizzy water, motivation kept coming to the surface.

A meeting was arranged with Scarlet editor Avis Lewallen, and so on a chilly autumn afternoon I made my way to her house for lunch and a discussion about this creative writing book. I wonder how many books written and edited by women have been conceived around a kitchen table. I was astonished and pleased to find my ideas were understood and well-matched by her observations and perceptions. After further discussion Avis agreed to become a co-writer on the project. She contributed substantial background work to several of the chapters, including the information on the history of the novel in the appendix. Before too long, however, it became clear that her commitment to Scarlet and the work this generated made it very difficult for her to continue as a co-writer, and she subsequently reduced her role to one of editor. The book nevertheless is the result of a very productive relationship between us. Through the ages, books written by women have been innovative and diverse, not only in content and style but also in how they've been worked on and produced. We both feel that it is important to validate and document these practices.

How to use this book

This book aims to be a practical workbook and a guide to women's writing in different genres. These aims are pursued in three ways: first, through giving information on writing techniques and providing encouragement through writing exercises; second, by giving further information in the notes and sources at the end of each chapter to enable the reader to follow up on particular areas of interest; third, by covering the background history of individual genres and showing through examples from the work of women writers the flexibility and variety of approaches possible. In this way the book addresses issues relevant to women today. It can be of value to writers or potential writers, tutors of writing classes and interested readers of women's fiction. The book is also designed to be used in a number of ways. You can follow the exercises by working on your own or by working with a group, or you can use them to supplement material supplied through a writing course.

The opening chapter looks closely at diary keeping with its links to autobiography and it also examines the connected, but often ignored, category of biography. For many writers the place to start is with the self, your own life, your own history and experience. Sometimes the beginning is a random thought jotted on a scrap of paper, or sometimes it's the keeping of a diary, journal or notebook. Whatever form this material takes it's a basis for continuing, either to an extended examination of your life or to fictional explorations. Exercises focused on using your memory provide encouragement to put pen to paper and pursue the past in a more disciplined way. There is also some discussion of the fears and doubts that beset us when we begin to commit ourselves to writing. At times there is a genuine fear of reprisals or repercussions attached to writing something down. Recognising and facing such fears is the first crucial stage of overcoming them. Sometimes we are merely procrastinating – this can be related to writer's block. We often put off something because it's difficult and requires some effort. Writer's block – and strategies for overcoming it – is dealt with in the next chapter.

'Techniques: understanding and practice' gives you information on the basic writing techniques necessary for working through the rest of the book. It covers how to begin building characters, the question of stereotyping, and character settings. There are also details on how to start thinking about plot and juggling all the different components for structuring a novel. This is followed by sections on point of view, the use of dialogue and some common writing problems, concluding with how to go about editing what you have written. It's important to work through this chapter before moving on so that you can begin to use these techniques in the subsequent exercises.

'Finding the right words: women and language' covers the important issue of how language affects us as women. The chapter examines the historical lineage of certain words and shows how the bias of the English language has become an accepted part of speech. It also illustrates how the use of language changes over time. By showing that it is not 'fixed' but open to change it offers us, as women, possibilities for defining ourselves anew.

Following this, 'Making the best of imagery' looks in particular at political imagery to demonstrate how much it is a part of our daily language. This chapter provides exercises that illustrate how the use of imagery can aid meaning and gives information on literary devices, such as alliteration and assonance, with suggestions for how to improve language skills and how to avoid common problems such as the overuse of adjectives, adverbs and clichés.

This is followed by 'Telling tales', a chapter on short stories. The major advantage of short stories is not that they are short but that they can be endlessly reworked. All aspects of fictional writing – from character and setting to plot and theme – are employed in the short story and can provide excellent practice for the beginner. The chapter gives some 'basic rules' about the short story, but the main point to be made here is the scope for experimentation provided by this genre.

The next section of the book covers the different kinds of novel, starting with the very popular historical novel. Where have other writers found inspiration and where have they done their research? Examples from a number of contemporary writers provide practical information about where to begin looking for material. It also addresses questions such as how much licence can you take with historical detail, how do you convey those details, and what are the different ways of telling the story?

We then take a magnifying glass to the genre of crime fiction in 'Piecing the puzzle together: murder she writes'. Women writers have been at the forefront of the crime-writing genre for a number of years. What motives and methods have they used? This chapter takes you step by step through the construction of your own 'whodunnit' by looking at the plot, the narrative, the crime, the investigators, the clues and the suspects. Where do you want to place the emphasis – on the crime itself or on the background motives? What sort of investigator will you choose – a police officer, a private eye, an amateur? How can you use location to good effect? How do you make the plot plausible and keep the reader guessing?

If crime fiction is about piecing the puzzle together, the chapter on science fiction and fantasy – 'What if' – is more about taking things apart. Women writers have used science fiction, fantasy, and sometimes a combination of both to analyse women's position in society and to put forward new ideas about how society could be organised. In this genre the realm of the imagination is explored. How have women writers used time travel, reformulated old ideas, dealt with the question of aliens? Language comes up again too in a genre well-known for providing the means to create a new vocabulary for women.

The final chapter on 'Other information' returns to some of the issues raised at the beginning of the book. How do you overcome those barriers to writing and how do you keep going once you have started? It also offers guidance for working in a group, addressing the question of how to give and receive positive feedback. There's a section with practical information on presenting your manuscript to publishers and there are details of writers' organisations that can provide advice and support.

Finally, the appendix supplies a short history of how the novel developed and covers the very significant contribution made to this development by women writers.

Telling it like it is: diary, autobiography and biography

Diaries and letters

What do we mean when we talk about a diary? Is it an appointment book that reminds you what's happening three weeks from now? Maybe it's that bulging filofax system you carry around everywhere, stuffed chock-a-block with collected bits and pieces. Is yours a sturdy, well-bound notebook that you keep by the bed in which you record faithfully every night the things you've done, thought and said? And what about that jumbled mishmash of scribbled notes, old shopping lists, theatre programmes, outdated catalogues, newspaper cuttings and fragments of thought spontaneously written down on scraps of paper that you keep in a file bound with a strong rubber band in a kitchen drawer? Could that be called a diary?

More important than whether what you write can be thought of as a diary is seeing how flexible the practice can be. For some this private activity is definitely diary keeping; others may prefer to think of it as keeping a 'workbook', an 'ideas-book', or a journal. Entries can be frequent, written as part of a daily routine, or if time is short the diarist might wait until there's a specific purpose, an urgent need. You can experiment with a diary – the potential is limitless. A single entry might be something straightforward and simple – a shopping list for a special dinner perhaps. Or you may want to record events, weaving in people, places and incidents as they come to mind. Sometimes there is a need, a hunger of sorts, that motivates us to confide and seek clarification of thought in the pages of a book. Those first efforts might well be a stumbling attempt to articulate feelings of confusion, and only with practice will skills be developed. The novice diarist continues, knowing that she has to allow time for the habit, and for growing recognition of what she needs, to take hold. Then again the gush of words can burst forth like flash flooding – a sudden release – once the need has been met, followed by an ebbing away of intensity until the next time.

Putting something down on paper can focus our attention, help us to solve problems, allow us to be creative. Calling what we write a diary may be a clear, conscious decision, but it could also be a practical process that evolves over time. I'll have to write that down, you mumble, as you reach for a notebook, knowing how quickly dreams fade once daylight dawns. Another time it could be an upsetting conversation with a friend that you remember. The conversation stays in your mind, certain phrases repeating themselves over and over again. You make a note of who said what, jotting down all that you can recall. Perhaps, in response, you'll pen a letter to this person. Though you may not send the letter, you realize later how much better you feel having found a way of resolving your hurt or anger. It might never have occurred to you to connect this form of activity to diary writing, even though diary-writing techniques have been used.

Loneliness prompted me to start keeping a diary shortly after leaving home the year I was sixteen. I lived in a boarding house when, in November 1956, I wrote my first entry:

> Dear, dear diary,
> It would seem that I have been lonely all my life. There's this huge boulder I imagine seeing on Bondi Beach. Its heavy bulk can't be moved and the bottom half of the boulder has settled well below the sand. At low tide waves thump playfully around the base, revealing sharp corners that warn me to be careful. At high tide the breakers crash with an angry force spraying foam upwards; sometimes like a fountain but at other times it looks more like vomit.

Boulders as obstacles featured in my diaries over the next five years; then I stopped writing altogether. I'd never thought of myself as someone who was keeping a diary – not really, not seriously – and I wonder now how I could have dismissed so easily the value of such writing. Almost two decades later, in 1974, I sat at the kitchen table stealing time from household chores while my children were at school, writing my way out of a breakdown. I couldn't write directly about my experience – I called it fiction and used the main character as the narrator – but in effect this

was what I was doing. The decision to write felt more like a
compulsion than any sort of artistic endeavour. A searing kind
of isolation mixed with frustration, confused anger and, yes,
desperation, was pushing me. I had to do something or I just might
explode. I had no confidence about writing techniques (the very
thought of dialogue was daunting) so I wrote a monologue, using
short sentences. These choices came as Open-Sesame-type
solutions to my inexperience and inadequacies as a writer. Later,
much later, that monologue became a radio play, broadcast in
Australia in 1979.

Each afternoon I'd allow time for re-reading the material,
slashing a line through any words I thought were unnecessary or
repetitive. I knew I was stripping the story down to the barest form
of expression possible. My main character was a woman locked
inside her head. I didn't give her the complications of my life but
I spoke through her. Part of my work involved reading again those
earlier diaries. It was all there – the imagery, the confusion, the
reaching out – but when I wrote them I simply hadn't known that
I could create other possibilities for myself. That ever-present
boulder made clear that I had sensed the problem, but I had
come up with no solutions. Later on, when writing about a
woman who saw herself as mad, things began to make sense. It
was a slow but unstoppable process. Images about water came again
and again; sometimes my head felt so full of them I couldn't write
fast enough to transfer them on to paper.

> My thoughts drift and waver. I lay quiet listening to the wind.
> A beach. Gaping. Bare. Straining away from the outgoing tide.
> I was standing on a cliff. The beach lay open and vulnerable
> at the foot of the cliff. The waves would rush against those
> rocks, bursting their strength in angry, wasted violence.
> They had been ignored by those cliffs for a long, long time.

But now there was visibility – of myself, to myself. I could see me
in the picture.

> I wanted to smash myself against those rocks. Yet I knew I
> could not. I could only be mad. I had stood on that cliff and
> yelled and yelled. Only the echo of my voice came back to
> me. Echoes. Echoes. My echoes. I was talking to myself. I was
> talking to myself.

I grew up in the Sydney suburb of Bondi Junction, not far from
the beach. As a child and as an adult I went there often. I liked

the beach in the early morning with the sun looming over the horizon, beaming optimism upon sand, sea and foam. Boulders and cliffs were my way of talking about my father. He was hard, violent, cruel. I felt weak and vulnerable in my responses to him. The usefulness of keeping the early diaries was that they not only allowed me to express my feelings at the time but also provided invaluable source material that I could subsequently use.

There are as many reasons for keeping a diary as there are for writing a book. Some writers purposefully and diligently use a diary or journal to track a process or to record events as they happen. Beatrice Webb was the eighth daughter of an aristocratic family. She was born in 1858 and grew up in a mansion in Gloucestershire. Embracing socialism as an adult, she came to despise many of the values of that wealthy, Victorian background, while at the same time acknowledging arrogantly that she 'belonged to a class of person who habitually gave orders' (Webb, in Austin, 1965, p. 2). Beatrice met her future husband Sidney Webb (a well-known socialist) when she was working on her first book, *The Co-operative Movement in Great Britain*, which was published in 1891. They married in 1892 and worked on several writing projects together before setting out on a long journey to America, New Zealand and Australia in 1898.

It was a common practice in those days to keep a diary, much more so than now, and Beatrice used a diary to record her thoughts and observations during that trip, dividing the material later into sections headed 'America', 'New Zealand' and 'Australian' diaries. *The Webbs' Australian Diary 1898*, edited by A. G. Austin, was published in 1965. Here is Beatrice's opening entry dated September 1898:

Sydney, New South Wales

> Arrived here (Australia Hotel, American in its prices and pretensions) after a detestable voyage.
> September 8th, disembarked late at night rather than stay another hour on the dirty steamer and among the noisy Australian commercial travellers and squalling colonial babies – the scene of our misery.
>
> Sydney, in spite of its exquisite harbour and lovely Botanical gardens, is a crude chaotic place. It is seemingly inhabited by a lower-middle class population suddenly enriched; aggressive in manners and blatant in dress ...
> 　　　　　　　　　　　　　　　(Webb, in Austin, 1965, p. 22)

Presumably Beatrice Webb did not anticipate the publication of this diary when she wrote it.

Another famous diarist who did not expect an audience was Anne Frank. On her thirteenth birthday, 12 June 1942, Anne was delighted to receive a blank-paged notebook with a stiff, cardboard cover and she began writing in it two days later. She had no experience as a writer and would probably have been surprised to think of her diary being published at all, much less as early as 1947. She would have been even more surprised by the fact that it has become the best-known diary of a female writer this century.

Anne's parents were German Jews who migrated to The Netherlands in 1933. They lived in Amsterdam where, before the invasion of the Nazi army, one-tenth of the population was Jewish. A few short weeks before Anne's thirteenth birthday the family went into hiding in the two upper, back floors of an old building overlooking a canal. This was the office of her father's firm, which was now run by two Dutch men who were courageous, loyal and willing to help hide Anne's family and others.

Early entries show an easy, chatty style. On 20 June 1942, for example, she explores her reasons for keeping a diary:

> It's an odd idea for someone like me to keep a diary; not only because I have never done so before, but because it seems to me that neither I – nor for that matter anyone else – will be interested in the unbosomings of a thirteen-year-old schoolgirl. Still, what does that matter? I want to write, but more than that, I want to bring out all kinds of things that lie buried deep in my heart. There is a saying that 'paper is more patient than man'; it came back to me on one of my slightly melancholy days, while I sat chin in hand, feeling too bored and limp even to make up my mind whether to go out or stay home.
>
> (Frank, 1989, p. 14)

Later on, she writes:

> And now I come to the root of the matter, the reason for my starting a diary: it is that I have no such real friend.
>
> (Frank, 1989, p. 14)

Anne called her diary 'Kitty' and the last entry was written on Tuesday 1 August 1944. On 4 August German Security Police accompanied by Dutch Nazis raided the building, arresting Anne's family and other Jewish occupants who were hiding with them. A cleaner in one of the building's offices found the diary amid a pile of papers a few days later and it was handed over to Anne's father when he returned to Amsterdam after the war. Anne's mother died on 5 January 1945.Two months previous to that Anne and her sister Margot were sent to Bergen-Belsen. In February 1945 both sisters caught typhus. Margot died first, and then Anne died in early March. Although Anne Frank wrote this diary for comfort, she provides us with a unique historical account of a tragic experience.

The diary can also be a therapeutic tool, a self-help method that is undeniably powerful. Audre Lorde's *The Cancer Journals* makes use of diary entries as well as first person narrative:

> Last month, three months after surgery, I wrote in my journal:
> *I seem to move so much more slowly now these days. It is as if I cannot do the simplest thing, as if nothing at all is done without a decision, and every decision is so crucial. Yet I feel strong and able in general, and only sometimes do I touch that battered place where I am totally inadequate to any thing I most wish to accomplish. To put it another way, I feel always tender in the wrong places.*
>
> (Lorde, 1985, pp. 18–19)

Here is a powerful stripping down of description to a minimum, avoiding any overstatement yet conveying feelings poignantly. This diary is telling it like it is.

While some women may find the privacy of the diary its greatest attraction, others might prefer instead the communication that is possible in a letter. Letter writing can have the same exploratory benefits as diary writing, and can come in the form of a conscious choice to direct exploration towards another person, or even towards several people. Of course, diaries can be the basis for a letter, and letters might stir up feelings and/or thoughts that will later be explored in a diary.

For me, the link between diaries and letters is a close one. Letters are a means of communicating to others how we are feeling, what we are thinking, what we've been doing. Letters might also begin as a means of processing recent events, clarifying issues.

The diaries and letters of two women, Ruth Slate and Eva Lawson, became important resource material for drama teacher and director Tierl Thompson when she used the then unpublished material for a stage play called *Dear Girl* (co-devised with Libby Mason and performed in Britain during 1983–84). The same material formed the basis of the radio dramatization *Friend to Friend*, broadcast in 1984. The book, *Dear Girl – The Diaries and Letters of Two Working Women 1897–1917*, edited by Tierl Thompson, was published in 1987. Ruth was a clerk in a grocery firm, Eva a legal secretary. Both women recorded personal feelings in their diaries as well as first-hand accounts of important events – some of the great suffrage rallies, for example. Ruth was self-effacing, dismissing her diaries as 'full of detail and self-interest', but she also noted that 'the habit of recording the outside details of my life has a wonderful hold upon me' (Thompson, 1987, pp. 2–4).

Do you keep a diary? If you do, do you feel the same way about diary writing as Ruth Slate did? If you haven't kept a diary before, are you thinking now that you might like to? If you feel there's a big commitment in keeping up with the recording of events on a regular basis, you could begin by keeping copies of any personal letters you write. It's a good idea to keep carbon sheets handy, the kind intended for handwriting as well as for a typewriter. You never know how useful it might be to have copies of the letters you've written. A folder filled with copies takes little time to organize. Those letters may contain important information about you, and reading through them at a much later date can be illuminating, entertaining, embarrassing and full of surprises. *Did I really think that? Say, that's not bad, I'd forgotten that I'd written that. How interesting, I didn't realize I knew so much about that incident at the time.*

Our personal, intimate writings, intended for a small audience only, may show that we did have some idea of what was happening to us even if we didn't uncover all that we knew at any one time. These writings can pinpoint the chronology of events, can give greater accuracy about how we felt and can provide rich resource material for other writing.

Autobiography

My first short story was autobiographical, about a daughter (me) attending her mother's fifth wedding. Guests were not invited to the church but were asked instead to turn up in the evening for a celebratory meal. A scene in the ladies' room at the reception had the daughter seated in a toilet booth listening to a conversation between two older women. She learns that her mother isn't married after all – the wedding plans were simply an attempt to deceive family and friends into thinking that the supposed bride and groom had tied the knot.

Reading that story aloud in a creative writing class, with shaking knees and pounding heart, was a first step towards thinking of myself as a writer. I made mistakes with that story (for one thing, I never did get the daughter out of the toilet), but what I understood almost immediately was that my own life was the place to start – it was the prime source of what I needed/wanted to write about. This may not be true for everybody. The decision to write about personal experience is an individual choice. Keeping a diary may be thought of as something separate; indeed diary enthusiasts might even insist that diary writing doesn't count as writing in any literary sense and might not consider themselves writers at all.

It's possible that something written factually may later become fiction. Personal experience can also be written in the third person and thus mask the connection between the author's life and her work. We may write to unlock inner secrets, using written expression as a form of self-help therapy, exploring memory and feelings. The decision to delve deeper may not feel like a decision at all, more like a commanding force, a quest in search of something. We're all used to hearing (or telling) life experiences in anecdotal form – stories about relationships (past and present), work, childhood, events, incidents and people, all talked about in ways that suit the occasion. Some of us relate the dramas of life with great skill and timing, embellishing a story with humour and/or insights gleaned in retrospect. Maybe you are one of those people. Are there friends who tell you often that 'you ought to write that down' or 'that would make a good book'? And how many times have you heard someone say: 'the things that have happened to me, well, I tell you, I could write a book'?

One major difference between talking about experience and writing about it has to do with feedback. When talking about an incident we can be encouraged by a smile, a nod of sympathy. If laughter greets our jokey style we might add overstated gestures, stress certain phrases, roll our eyes in merriment, and so encourage more laughter, a warm approving atmosphere. Then there are the serious moments, the intimate sharing of a secret, the opening up to a friend about past pain, prompted perhaps by stress, or grief, or something that echoes through our mind recalling that long-ago event.

Let's say you have an experience you want to make into a story. You make the time, sit down with pen and paper and set to work. You hear the clock ticking, the sound of a car. Silence envelops you; it echoes round the room. You read what you've put down. What to say next? You write a few more words, then doubt creeps in. Striving for the perfect opening sentence, and failing to achieve it, could undermine your sense of purpose. This whole idea is pointless, you think. Who am I kidding? Who'll want to read this rubbish? Perhaps you begin well, maintaining a momentum for several paragraphs before the sentences start to falter and become bogged down with too much detail. The story you were writing in your head takes on a dreamlike quality when you compare it with this turgid, heavy-going reality.

To write, to want to be a writer, we have to learn to do without immediate feedback. We can find ways of getting what we need later, once we have something written down to share. Facing this challenge is important for most writers, but the implications for a potential autobiographer who does not recognise the challenge sufficiently can be the postponement, perhaps forever, of a truly valuable process of self-discovery. Be prepared. Expect to feel self-conscious when you first write about yourself. As you continue, a workable flow will be established; you'll become caught up in the process and you'll notice an increasing desire to get back to the work.

Fiction writers can juggle plot, characters and settings at will; they can take real-life situations, jostle them this way and that, then place them on the page in cleverly camouflaged fashion. The autobiographer has to remain within the limits of fact, truth and memory. A lie, once told, distorts the telling of experience. Truth is, of course, a subjective matter. Two children reared in the same household may have completely different childhoods to talk about, so it isn't a question of seeking approval from another person who was there, wanting to have her agree with your interpretation. It is more a reaching for authenticity, an assembling of facts clustered around the author's memory and perhaps around other people's recollections too. This is the autobiographer's aim, and beyond it there is a more personal motive, a motive that can vary considerably from one writer to another.

Choosing to write about yourself means coming to terms with inevitable feelings of vulnerability and responsibility. How will you feel, knowing others (significant others among them) might read what you have written? And how can you write about people you know or have known?

I believe there is an ABC of writing:

A   for ability
B   for bluff and
C   for courage

All writers need ability, bluff and courage, but writers who draw directly from their personal experience need to develop sustaining amounts of bluff and courage as part of their craft. You know you have to tell the truth. You want to tell the truth. But what if so and so reads it? Maybe you blush at the very thought. You may feel uncomfortable at the idea of being so exposed. I did. Yet the marvellous truth about exposing vulnerability, really exposing it, is that you begin to feel free, even though you can have no way of knowing what will follow.

Alexandra Kollontai struggled with these issues. She wrote about her life in 1926 in a book entitled *The Autobiography of a Sexually Emancipated Woman* (published in complete form in 1972). Kollontai's opening sentences illustrate the discomfort a writer can feel when turning the spotlight on to self:

> Nothing is more difficult than writing an autobiography. What should be emphasized? Just what is of general interest? It is advisable, above all, to write honestly and dispense with any of the conventional introductory protestations of modesty. For if one is called upon to tell about one's life so as to make the events that made it what it became useful to the general public, it can mean only that one must have already wrought something positive in life, *accomplished a task that people recognize.* [original emphasis]
>
> (Kollontai, 1972, p. 3)

Writing as a political activist, and in a country where most of the women among the Marxist revolutionaries came from the upper class, Kollontai's autobiography, understandably, centres around the changes in Russian society. She does talk about her childhood but the comments are few and hasty, as though she were anxious to get it over with quickly in order to get on with the *real* story. This split between the political *out there* self and the personal inner self can obstruct a writer's introspection and the problem can be one that continues to echo down the years.

An enjoyable way of getting started can be to begin with information about your childhood. The age you decide to work with will depend on how much you remember, how far back you can go. Maureen Duffy began her story, *That's How it Was*, immediately *before* her birth:

> Lucky for me I was born at all really, I mean she could have decided not to bother. Like she told me, she was tempted, head in the gas oven, in front of a bus, oh a thousand ways. But there I was, or nearly. She'd done the washing in the afternoon. 'You shouldn't be doing that, my dear, not in your state,' the landlady said. 'I'll be alright' and she reached up to the line, stretching her guts on every peg. About two o'clock she woke and the bed was brimming with blood.
>
> (Duffy, 1983, p. 13)

Writer and poet Maya Angelou, in the first volume of her autobiography *I Know Why the Caged Bird Sings*, chooses a particular moment that summarizes for her the dominant feeling of her childhood. It is a scene from a church ceremony:

> 'What you looking at me for?
> I didn't come to stay ...'
> I hadn't so much forgot as I couldn't bring myself to remember. Other things were more important.
> 'What you looking at me for?
> I didn't come to stay ...'
> Whether I could remember the rest of the poem or not was immaterial. The truth of the statement was like a wadded-up handkerchief, sopping wet in my fists, and the sooner they accepted it the quicker I could let my hands open and the air would cool my palms.
> 'What you looking at me for ...?'
> The children's section of the Colored Methodist Episcopal Church was wiggling and giggling over my well-known forgetfulness.
>
> (Angelou, 1984, p. 3)

This is a scene containing strong feelings of humiliation, anger and frustration, with a keen sense of not belonging to the community that the young girl has found herself in. These feelings are finally summarized at the end of the section before she moves into a more straightforward account of how she and her brother ended up in Stamps, Arkansas:

If growing up is painful for the Southern black girl, being aware of her displacement is the rust on the razor that threatens the throat.

It is an unnecessary insult.

(Angelou, 1984, p. 6)

It is obviously a moment that has remained vivid in Maya Angelou's mind.

Val Wilmer in *Mama Said There'd be Days Like This* tells about herself as an adolescent:

I was about twelve years old when I walked into the Swing Shop in Streatham, south London, and asked if they had any jazz records. I remember what I was wearing: a navy-blue windcheater and pleated grey flannel shorts, the tomboy outfit I put on to play football and cycle around the common, smoking cigarettes stolen from unlocked parked cars.

(Wilmer, 1989, p. 3)

You may wish instead to begin with a straightforward statement about your name and background. The autobiography of MumShirl, an aboriginal activist and social worker who wrote with the assistance of Bobbi Sykes, is a good example:

My full name is Colleen Shirley Perry. I am the daughter of Isabel Agnes Perry and Henry Joseph Perry of Erambie Mission, West Cowra, New South Wales. But I am better known as 'MumShirl'. This is my story.

(MumShirl, 1987, p. 1)

(Incidentally, Bobbi Sykes, poet and writer, now more formally known as Dr Roberta Sykes since completing a Harvard doctorate in the early 1980s, was thrown out of her convent school in Townsville, Queensland, on her fourteenth birthday because she was black and not considered a suitable candidate for further education. She proceeded to educate herself and was the first Australian to be invited to Harvard. Her latest book, *Black Majority*, was published in 1989.)

Wonderful Adventures of Mrs Seacole in Many Lands was first published by James Blackwood in 1857. I picture Mary Seacole writing these next words with a broad smile on her face:

I was born in the town of Kingston, in the island of Jamaica, some time in the present century. As a female, and a widow, I may be well excused giving the precise date of this important event. But I do not mind confessing that the century and myself were both young together and that we have grown side by side into age and consequence. I am a Creole, and have good Scotch blood coursing in my veins.

(Seacole, in Alexander and Dewjee, 1984, p. 55)

To disclose something about yourself in the opening paragraph of a book can be very powerful. Here's how Germaine Greer did it in her book *Daddy, We Hardly Knew You*:

It is silly of me, a middle-aged woman, to call my dead father Daddy. It's not as if I were some giddy heiress antic-ipating the next instalment of my allowance or little Orphan Annie learning to get what she wants out of Daddy Warbucks, or yet some southern belle refusing to be her age. My brother and sister called my father Reg, but they knew him better than I did and could permit themselves such familiarity. I always called him Daddy, and much mockery did I take from Mother for doing it. Daddy is a baby's palatal word; the word *mother* on the other hand is admirably adapted for saying through clenched teeth.

(Greer, 1990, p. 1)

The use of the first person narrative, the 'I' of my own ex-perience, provides a frank clarity, strengthening the communi-cation between woman as author and woman as reader. Daring to use 'I' might seem at first like a bold, brave adventure, scary even to contemplate, but if you think of it as an assertive act for self then you may come to feel better about the idea in a remarkably short time. The next question is whether you will write autobio-graphically or choose instead to alter existing facts/details/names of people in your life and write fiction that is based on your life. A third choice is to use the strength of the first person narrative to write fiction that has little or nothing whatsoever to do with your own experience. As I have explained, I had to use fiction as a necessary prerequisite before I could reach a later stage of claiming for myself the 'I' voice of my own experience, telling it exactly as it was. Once that stage had been reached I was able to begin writing *One of the Family*, an autobiographical book that talked about my childhood and growing up.

Memory

How reliable are your memories? Do you really recall your seventh birthday with such clarity – that birthday when something out of the ordinary happened at your house? Have your recollections perhaps been overshadowed by an older relative replaying the scene countless times so that you cannot distinguish your memories from her repetitious accounts? It is true that we can be affected by other, older people's viewpoints and perceptions. Their opinions on what did and did not happen may have more weight than your own as a child. Is it true that your Uncle Walter never liked you? Have you perhaps been told this so often that you now accept it as an unexamined fact?

Children are powerless and dependent on the adults around them. A child's mind can be manipulated to such an extent that sorting out the truth once adulthood comes may be a difficult task. How do you strip away passed-on versions of truth to reveal an unpolluted perspective? I'm not suggesting that there is malice or perversity in your upbringing (though there might be), but there are many, many reasons why parents and others subtly affect the way children think. If we begin with an acceptance that memory is not infallible, that we have been influenced (and we may never know to what extent), then we can proceed with a willingness that allows more flexibility in our work. Here are two distinct ways to get you started.

Exercises

Episodic and chronological

Write in episode form about things you can remember: schooldays, funny or embarrassing incidents, your first job, etc. Work with the intention of making each episode a story, devising a beginning, a middle and an end for each episode. As the writings accumulate, place them in an appropriate order to create a collection. This process will help you to expand on what you know, and could excite your interest sufficiently to lead you to 'flesh out' the material, using what you have done so far as starting points for separate chapters.

You might want to think about an autobiography right from the start. The chronology could work via the years from your birth, but you can choose how far back you wish to go. You need not follow a direct line from birth to adulthood – you could think of imaginative ways of weaving in various events and incidents according to an alternative structure that you devise for yourself.

The five senses

We all know the five senses: sight, hearing, smell, taste and touch. Read through the following paragraphs for each of these and then choose one to work with. The material here may seem very dense or concentrated so you could first copy out sections that interest you and work with them a section at a time. Alternatively, you could record the sentences on to tape and play them back, stopping the tape while you are writing, beginning it again when you are ready to move on to the next sentence. In this way you'll have control over the flow of your responses.

Sight

Returning to places we have known well in the past can evoke memories about earlier times. You may note certain features of the landscape that you had forgotten and that you are able now to describe more fully – a house, a street, a village. There will also be material you can look at without leaving home – photo albums, postcards, letters, diaries. What items do you have in your wardrobe (or that of some older relative) – shoes, dresses, flared pants? Are there prized possessions handed down through the family – a feather boa, a picture hat, a gold watch and chain? Maybe you have items in the kitchen – handed-down crockery, cutlery, teapots?

In our family there was a set of handmade saucepans that one of my uncles had fashioned from stainless steel with three stainless steel rivets attaching the handles. The handles were hollow, slightly flattened tubing, and not once did any of those handles come loose. The very sight of one of those saucepans could transport me back in time to the mid 1940s. What items would send you back? Perhaps you know someone who kept a box of buttons that children played with. If you have none of these things, browse in antique shops, check out jumble sales and car boot sales. You don't have to own any of these things, you simply want them to work for you as 'triggers' to jog your memory.

Hearing

Music can wring the heart with sharp feelings of loss, or it can irritate you dreadfully if it's noisy, next door and not your taste, but what about those special songs you've hummed and sung and gone a bit silly over? We can be filled with delight when a special tune starts up on the radio, reminding us of romantic moments with such poignant clarity it almost takes our breath away. I'm stunned many times by the uncanny accuracy with which certain songs flood my mind with people and events I'd thought were left behind. Particular songs may remind you of particular people. When you've done with the radio and your old record collection turn to the outdoors and listen to the birds, the laughter of children, the sound of the sea pounding on rocks, rain drumming on an old tin roof. How did your parents shout your name when it was time to come inside? Do you remember?

Smell

Have you got a keen sense of smell? What comes to mind if I mention castor oil, newly baked bread, a school corridor? What about blood, dirt, smoke from a fire, baby powder? The list is endless: things like camphor and cloves; fruit such as mangoes, bananas, oranges; hot tar; petrol; bleach … How memorable is the smell of a house where someone you have known or loved has died? Smells can take us by surprise – the whiff of a lilac tree, peanut butter, old books, the wonderful smell of small children and babies as you snuggle against their tiny necks. What else can you think of? Organize a smelling session, either from memory or from things you happen to have around you. Without thinking too much, simply write whatever comes into your head.

Taste

Once you go beyond food and drink, think about things you might have put into your mouth as a small child: the ear of a much-loved teddy bear; the corner of a pillowslip. Did you suck your thumb? What sweets did you like? Imagine one of those sweets in your mouth. Did you savour it slowly, making it last as long as possible? Did you crunch it hurriedly, anxious to get another one from the bag on the table before everyone else had finished theirs?

Touch

You may find it works better if you have your eyes closed while touching the items you choose to work with – leather, crushed velvet, an animal's fur (assuming you have an obliging pet), the newel post of a staircase. Staircases can stir many an adult – those times when you sat on the top step, slid down the banister, ran up the stairs two at a time, peeped through the railings to see what you could see. Each item will need to be handled for several minutes. Allow yourself to stroke and rub the texture.

It is worth bearing in mind that you don't want to overwhelm yourself with too much at any one time. A few items chosen at random might elicit more than a pile of stuff that swamps you with so much emotion you wind up crying instead of writing.

Writing for yourself

Decide early on that there are benefits, as yet unknown, that you will derive from this process. An exploration period is called for. How long? At least two years. Buy a separate, special folder or notebook and make the purchase a private ritual, selecting exactly what you feel is right after careful thought about the way you are going to work. An expensive notebook is not the aim, but you will need to decide whether you are going to keep a number of sheets (typed or handwritten) in a folder that will allow you to file extra sheets in one section or another, or whether you will use a notebook. The advantage of the first option is that you have a simple system that allows you to add further information exactly where it's needed. The second option may be easier to keep hidden if you feel the need for strict privacy. Before you begin to use your folder or notebook, write on the inside cover a short statement that makes clear this is something you are doing for yourself. Simply, *I am doing this for myself* may be all that's needed. Each time you begin this work remind yourself of your intention by reading that statement first, preferably aloud.

There are traps that will become familiar as you get underway – some traps are simply distractions and will crop up no matter what it is that you are writing, others are more specifically linked to autobiography.

- Will I hurt so and so?
- Can I bear the thought of someone else reading this?
- Ought I to be writing this down?
- Wouldn't it be healthier or kinder to forget the whole thing?
- What will other people think of me when they see this in print?
- Why am I *really* doing this?
- Are my motives suspect?

The danger of getting bogged down by questions such as these means that your thinking becomes circular – you go through the list of questions without finding any satisfactory answers and then, when you come to think about writing again, you go straight back to those questions and work your way down the list, as before. To pull away from the problem we must come at it from a different angle. Telling it like it was or is does present us with challenges, complexity and the odd contradiction or two. There may be other people we are worried about. Feeling protective, even unwillingly, can inhibit the desire to express our truth fully. Perhaps a book like this ought to be urging you to fight against such weighty distractions but I know only too well how wracked with anxiety many of us are by such concerns to dismiss them lightly, or to pretend that they have little bearing on our decision to speak out.

Issues of privacy, responsibility, risk, and the right or need to speak out can be placed along an imaginary spectrum, stretching from the prominent, urgent issues at one end to smaller concerns that have more to do with simple procrastination than any outside factor (or person) placing undue pressure on us. It would be wrong to suggest that matters of concern positioned at the worrisome end of the spectrum can be overcome by this or that exercise or strategy or a change in your attitude. There will be some of you who know that the risk is too great, the timing not right – the reasons best known to you and you alone. Nothing written here is intended to sway you from any strong feelings you have, except to say that if a situation or a relationship is so bad that you cannot think of your needs without fear of reprisal, then knowing that, facing that truth head-on, might be crucial in changing those circumstances for a better, safer, freer future. At the other end of the spectrum it is obvious that allowing procrastination to have its way will mean that no suggestion, no matter how good it is, can ever be truly effective until you make up your mind to get started.

Let's say, though, that you've placed your concern somewhere between these two ends of the spectrum. If what you are wanting to write about is painful you have to know that the first stage is helpful to you, a form of self-help therapy. You have that right, the right to take care of yourself. If, after writing out the pain and the hurt and the anger, you have achieved some resolution, further understanding, and insights, then that's when you ask the questions about what happens next.

Write with emotion – edit with reason

Once the material has been written you will have shifted emotionally from that earlier starting point and may, without further ado, be able to make a clear decision about what you want to do with it. If not, set up a working session on the issues with a friend or a group. It may be a series of conversations with different friends. I'd recommend, though, that you leave this discussion phase until after a good deal of writing has been done. View the writing as therapy, a healing process. By postponing the discussion phase you may find that you've resolved the dilemma in any case.

Biography

Writing about our own lives, fictionally or autobiographically, is very often where new writers begin. However, Evelyn Waugh suggested that writing about the life of another was an ideal project for novices seeking to launch themselves on a literary career. His article 'Careers for our sons: Literature' stated: 'If you want to make a success of it, choose as a subject someone very famous, who has plenty of books written about him quite recently.' He goes on to say:

> You will not make very much money by this first book, but you will collect a whole list of kindly comments which your publisher will be able to print on the back of the wrapper of your next.
>
> (Bennett, 1991)

Journalist Catherine Bennett details at length (including Waugh's comments above) 'the fiercely competitive world of biography' in an article in the daily newspaper, *The Guardian*:

> ... But much biography is more like DIY (Do It Yourself) – a tin-tack here, a glob of Polyfilla there, a bit of sticky tape where no one will notice.

Further on in the article she says:

> Biography is one of the great forms of literature, but it is no easier to do well than any other. How could it be? It involves understanding a life, almost always a life of greater signifi-cance than the biographer's own. Yet it looks like something any drudge could do. You just start at the beginning, bung in the research, and carry on until the end. Talent is optional. Again and again, biographers reduce their subjects to their own level: make us feel that we've mastered the life, and with it, effortlessly, the work.
>
> (Bennett, 1991)

Evelyn Waugh gave no thought to women as writers; nor does Catherine Bennett's pithy article mention women – either as subjects or biographers. Does the idea of investigating someone else's life appeal to you? As you will see in the chapter 'Researching the past', biographical material has often been the starting point for fictional works. The subject does not necessarily have to be someone from the past. How important is it that we write about our own lives and other women's lives?

Louise DeSalvo and Mitchell A. Leaska edited the book *The Letters of Vita Sackville-West to Virginia Woolf* (1984), and in 1989 DeSalvo alone published another book, *Virginia Woolf: The Impact of Childhood Sexual Abuse on Her Life and Work*. This important book, fascinating and very well written, was taken up by two publishers and copies appeared in the United States and Britain. Reviewed in a British Sunday newspaper, the book was dismissed in scathing terms by the reviewer. As if that was not bad enough, the book's details positioned immediately above the review – the title, author's name, publisher and price – were printed with errors, as though the book was of such little importance that it should not be taken seriously by any prospective reader. Review space for women writers has always been limited, but seeking recognition for biographies about women by women is an important challenge and an issue of serious concern to both women writers and readers.

Some of the dilemmas involved are illustrated by the story of Mrs Jean Harris, convicted in 1980 of the murder of her lover Dr Herman Tarnower, known as the 'Scarsdale Diet doctor'. After a fourteen-week trial that ended with her being sentenced to fifteen years to life, a biography written by Diana Trilling hit the headlines. Some years later Jean Harris published her autobiography. She recalls her feelings when she read about Diana Trilling's book in an article in *Vogue* in which she was discussed by the biographer:

> Now I read that a woman named Trilling has written a book around her theory that I lived out my life motivated by a burning desire to go to dinner with the right people ... to climb socially. When will people like Trilling learn what 'society' is?

A bit later on she comments:

> The same sloppy little woman I had seen each day at my trial – the same one I had seen stretched out, full length and

shoeless, on one of the court benches quietly snoring – the
same woman who kept repeating what a bore the whole thing
was, and if it didn't end soon she wouldn't be able to meet
her publishing deadline.

                                                    (Harris, 1988, pp. 352–353)

This description may seem unkind, cruel even, but it must be
remembered that Diana Trilling's account benefited from all the
topical interest the court case had engendered while the autobiography appeared without fanfare or media hype, for by the
time it was published Jean Harris was yesterday's news.

Nicole Ward Jouve wrote her book about a man, and it's
unlikely that she asked *his* permission before starting her work.
The man's name? Peter Sutcliffe. Known in the mid 1970s as the
'Yorkshire Ripper', he had murdered thirteen women and maimed
a further seven before he was finally caught. Ward Jouve is rare
among women writers in exploring the life of one man and the
society that spawned him. So many male writers, particularly journalists, seize on a murder case, attend the trial, follow every
possible lead that will give them more information and detail, and,
in a remarkably short period of time, publish a book about the case.
Such books capitalize (in sales) on the inevitable publicity
generated by the media attention. This area of crime writing
needs more attention from women writers and the thorny
questions about the rights of the individual under scrutiny will
require careful consideration according to the issues involved.

For her book *Scotch Verdict*, published in 1983, Lillian Faderman
looked at the lives of two Scottish women, Miss Woods and Miss
Pirie, who met at an art class in Edinburgh in 1802. Both women
were hoping to add art as a subject to those they were already
qualified to teach. Their friendship blossomed, indeed they
became passionate friends in an era when romantic friendship
between women was more of an accepted social institution. Some
years later, in 1809, they set up a school together and rented a
newly constructed property at the west end of Queen Street,
Edinburgh. By the following spring there were five day students
and nine boarders. By November the next year all of the students
had left. No one explained why, and when parents and servants
came to collect individual girls they refused to give any reasons
for such a sudden, momentous decision. It soon became clear that
one of the students had said *something* to her influential grandmother (who was also the girl's guardian). This grandmother

had been instrumental in making the school a success, recommending the establishment to other families and furthering the good reputation of Miss Pirie and Miss Woods. In a similar fashion, she had now let her displeasure be known, influencing those same families to remove their daughters from the school.

What had this pupil told her grandmother? Could Miss Pirie and Miss Woods have been incautious, indiscreet or improper in some way? We can only imagine the torment and anguish they must have gone through – their school was now but a shattered dream, future work prospects as remote as paying the bills that were piling up fast. Initially, they wrote beseeching letters to the families, and when those were ignored they made personal visits, asking what complaint had been made against them. When these persistent efforts failed they made a surprising move, an action that showed courage and perhaps desperation as well. They sought the services of a lawyer, telling him they wished to sue for libel.

John Clerk agreed to represent them, deferring his charges until he won the case for them. Lillian Faderman writes vividly about the resulting trial of Miss Pirie and Miss Woods v. Dame Cumming Gordon, combining precise and complex detail with an easy, accessible narrative style. She also puts herself in the story, giving us details of how her interest was sparked, how she carried out her research and including, too, her own diary entries showing the unfolding of her discoveries.

In a way it is very easy to understand the appeal of biography, but what does it really involve in terms of research? British journalist Brenda Maddox chose Nora Joyce as her subject. Her book *Nora* is dense with revelations, information and insights about this most remarkable woman. Previously portrayed (usually in academic footnotes) as illiterate and coarse, Nora Barnacle (born 1884) grew up in Galway and left home for Dublin the same year she met James Joyce, 1904. She was working in a Dublin hotel then, and, later the same year, left Ireland with Joyce for Trieste, Italy, knowing that he had no intention at that point of ever marrying her. She was already a woman of determination and spirit when she met Joyce, and her influence on him has been conveniently obscured by the myth that this male genius had bedded down with a woman of little brain or consequence. Brenda Maddox explains in her introduction how many questions about Nora arose for her after reading Richard Ellman's biography of

James Joyce (published in 1982), and how those questions persisted, fuelling her intention to write this biography:

> Nora Barnacle is a reporter's dream: an unexplored corner of the Joyce story. She has, I quickly found, a legion of admirers, people, like me, who always wanted to know more.
>
> (Maddox, 1989, p. 2)

So where did Ms Maddox find the research material she needed?

> ... the great mass of unpublished letters in the Joyce collection at Cornell University and in the Harriet Shaw Weaver papers in the British Library ... public documents. I am indebted to the record officers of Trieste, Paris, London, many parts of the United States, Dublin, and above all, Galway, for answering my requests for documents.
>
> (Maddox, 1989, pp. 3–4)

She reveals a little about her process of writing in the next paragraph:

> This then has been a work of excavation ... I have not invented any quotations, I have written 'Nora thought' or 'Nora wondered' only when I had evidence that she did so. Where I have speculated on her thoughts and feelings I have tried to make that clear to the reader. I began this book liking Nora. I finished in awe of her.
>
> (Maddox, 1989, p. 4)

When writers tell us of their working process they also inform us about their integrity and the issues that have concerned them while writing about others. Each book you write or read has stories to tell, not only the one that lies between its covers but also the one about how it came to be written, what the author intended, and how the work was done. In addition we can learn a great deal about integrity and ethics by reading what women writers have said about their books. In the 'Researching the past' chapter there are further details of the research process and an exploration of writers' sources of inspiration.

As you can see, we can use the personal beginnings of writing in various ways: for comfort, for self-exploration, as a kind of therapy, for the recording of memories, and to chart our thoughts, feelings, and ideas. We may wish to use this material further and explore our lives more deeply through autobiography, or investigate through biography the life of another, or we may use this material as a springboard into other kinds of fictional writing.

Sources

Alexander, Ziggi & Dewjee, Audrey (eds.),*Wonderful Adventures of Mrs Seacole in Many Lands*, Falling Wall Press, Bristol, 1984. First published by James Blackwood, July 1857.

Angelou, Maya, *I Know Why the Caged Bird Sings*, Virago, London, 1984.

Austin, A. G. (ed.), *The Webbs' Australian Diary 1898*, Sir Isaac Pitman and Sons, Melbourne, 1965.

Bennett, Catherine, *The Guardian*, 21 November 1991.

DeSalvo, Louise & Leaska, Mitchell A. (eds.), *The Letters of Vita Sackville-West to Virginia Woolf*, Hutchinson & Co, London, 1984.

DeSalvo, Louise,*Virginia Woolf: The Impact of Childhood Sexual Abuse on Her Life and Work*, The Women's Press, London, 1989.

Duffy, Maureen, *That's How It Was*, Virago, London, 1983. First published in Britain by New Authors, 1962.

Faderman, Lillian, *Scotch Verdict*, Quill Press, New York, 1983.

Frank, Anne, *The Diary of Anne Frank*, Pan, London, 1989. First edition, Contact, Amsterdam, 1947.

Greer, Germaine, *Daddy, We Hardly Knew You*, Penguin, London 1990.

Harris, Jean, *Stranger in Two Worlds*, Futura, London, 1988.

Kollontai, Alexandra, *The Autobiography of a Sexually Emancipated Woman*, Orbach & Chambers, London, 1972.

Lorde, Audre, *The Cancer Journals*, Sheba, London, 1985.

Maddox, Brenda, *Nora*, Minerva, London, 1989.

McNeill, Pearlie, *One of the Family*, The Women's Press, London, 1989. (Also published in Australia by University of Queensland Press, 1990.)

MumShirl, *MumShirl – an autobiography with the assistance of Bobbi Sykes*, Heinemann Educational (Australian Writers' Workshop Series), Australia, 1987.

Thompson, Tierl (ed.), *Dear Girl – The Diaries and Letters of Two Working Women 1897–1917*, The Women's Press, London, 1987.

Ward Jouve, Nicole, *The Street Cleaner – The Yorkshire Ripper Case on Trial*, Marion Boyars, London, 1988.

Wilmer, Val, *Mama Said There'd Be Days Like This*, The Women's Press, London, 1989.

Further reading

Milner, Marion (Joanna Field), *A Life of One's Own*, Virago, London, 1986. First published 1934.

Milner, Marion (Joanna Field), *An Experiment in Leisure*, Virago, London, 1986. First published 1937.

Milner, Marion (Joanna Field), *Eternity's Sunrise – A way of keeping a diary*, Virago, London, 1987.

Rainer, Tristine, *The New Diary*, Angus & Robertson, Sydney, 1978.

Techniques: understanding and practice

This chapter gives information and offers exercises over a range of techniques essential to writing. It includes: characterization, plotting, writer's block, point of view, dialogue, structuring the novel, editing, a short section on play writing, and discussion of some common problems. It would be advantageous to work through this chapter before moving on to the chapters on specific genres.

Characterization

For my understanding of characterization I have to credit Shirley Temple, who first gave me an interest in footwear. This was during the 1940s when I was six years old. I would have given anything for a pair of those white, ankle-high, Shirley Temple boots, but when I pleaded with my mother she told me that I was not to feel sorry for myself and should think instead about the man, somewhere in the world, who had no feet. I failed to see the connection, though I would never have said so. After that time I noticed that my mother judged people by their shoes and how well they looked after them. A man with dirty shoes, she insisted, was not a reliable person. As I got older I noticed how often my mother referred to feet and footwear: if you were in my shoes; pull up your socks; I wouldn't be in her shoes for anything. These were the sayings (among others) by which she lived her life.

It wasn't until a few years ago that I remembered how powerful an image shoes can be. Walking past a second-hand shop, I caught sight of a pair of high-heeled shoes in the window. The pointed toes, the cracked patent leather, the thin strap at the back of the heel, were similar to a pair I'd owned in the late 1950s. Unexpectedly, tears prickled at the back of my eyes. I had to have these

31

well-worn substitutes – not to wear but to write about. Back
home I placed them on a stool near the kitchen window and stared
at them. That was how I learned how to use shoes to create
characters.

Have you noticed how shoes are shaped by the feet that wear
them? Do you know someone who treads down the back, or
walks in a distinctive way, so that if you come across their shoes
kicked off in a hurry you can immediately recognize who they
belong to? I have one friend who leaves her slippers with one half
covering the other, and where those slippers rest there's a sense
of expectancy that works like a note reading 'Back in half an hour'.

Exercises

Shoes

In this first exercise I'm going to ask you to look at shoes and to
imagine the person who might wear them. You don't have to rush
off to jumble sales but the exercise will work better if the shoes you
choose are not your own. If the exercise is done in a group, each
person could remove one shoe and place it in the centre of the
room. Choosing at random and without looking is preferable to
selecting deliberately. Examine the shoe closely. Was it chosen for
comfort? For walking? For a job interview? For a special date or
outing?

You will also need an assortment of about twenty items to spread
out on a table or on the floor. My list would include such things as:
a scarf, jewellery (maybe a ring, a watch, a necklace or a bracelet),
bicycle clips or pump, a screwdriver, a hammer, a penknife or
compass, a few paperback books, a record or cassette tape, a fan, a
candle, a pair of sunglasses, a hat or beret, a bunch of keys and one
or two handwritten letters discreetly poking out of an envelope. The
intention is to have a broad selection. If you can get hold of a few
larger shoes or boots, a child's Wellington boot or maybe a discarded
sandal or baby's bootie, that would be an advantage. I always include
a walking stick to represent disabled people (on one occasion I had
the loan of a crutch), as shoes suggest mobility and not all of us are
mobile. Include the walking stick with the shoes and either pass it on
with one particular shoe or have some discussion about how it will
be included. If working alone, think about how you would want to
work with the issue of disability with any character(s) you create.

Now think about the character of the person who might wear a
shoe like this and write something down as soon as you can. Write

whatever comes to mind and give your character a name quickly. It doesn't have to be a life or death naming occasion, you can change it later on if you wish, but providing a name will help you 'firm up' the character in your mind. Having done that, now inspect the array of displayed items, mentally selecting no more than three that you think will go with your shoe. Why have you chosen those items? What connection did you make and how can you add the items to the characterization you have started with the shoe? You'll need to leave the display complete in case someone else wants to use those items too. If you choose too many items you can become distracted from your purpose. You might want to set a time limit for the exercise or you might want to write for a lengthy period while the flow is with you.

When you have a sense of familiarity about the character, put the shoe aside and repeat the process with another randomly chosen shoe. Maybe you'll choose the walking stick this time round. What you are seeking now is a connection between your two characters. Do they like each other? Could there be some tension between them? Are they neighbours? Friends? Schoolmates? Lovers? Ex-lovers? Mother and daughter? Husband and wife?

If the exercise works for you then you can use shoes as a valuable resource. Let the characters live in your imagination and keep them in the foreground by allowing yourself time to develop them further. Providing yourself with enough time to think is essential. Don't try to force anything; simply let the connection between these two people grow.

Sometimes, if I am having difficulties with someone I know, my feelings will surface when I do this exercise. If that happens to you, work with that 'material'; do not push it away. Some interesting things have happened since I first began to use this exercise in creative writing sessions with groups. It's not unusual for one writer, working with another's shoe, to describe the owner with a measure of accuracy, often to the surprise of that shoe's owner. Some people may be reluctant to take off their shoes – it might be the day they're wearing a sock with a hole in the toe, or perhaps they suffer from cold feet. If you are organizing the session, having a supply of shoes avoids this problem. You could also arrange the session in advance, so that participants can bring slippers on the day and/or wear their best socks or tights.

Inanimate objects as characters

Look around your kitchen. Choose any item. It might be a wooden spoon, a bowl, a gadget, a dishcloth. Think of this object as a character and give it an identity, habits, likes, dislikes, perceptions about the people in the household. A name is not really necessary but please yourself. Write from its point of view. How does the world look from the kitchen sink? The cutlery drawer? The broom cupboard? Avoid note taking, just dive right in and be spontaneous.

This light-hearted monologue exercise is useful if you are getting back into writing after a spell of other work. You can use it to create humour or an unusual point of view. The same exercise could be done using animals as the narrating voice. Does your dog or cat have a lively personality? Express that with a quirky sense of humour. Is there a neighbour's pet you dislike intensely? Use it. The tension you have can work in wonderful ways if you use it to see the funny side of things. If you giggle and break into laughter as you're writing, make much of that enjoyment to expand your ideas further. This is the time to be silly, sarcastic, foolish, whacky, gleeful, mean, sharp.

Drawing on who you know

This next exercise has two parts. To gain the most from it, don't read the second part until you have completed Part one. Cover up the rest of the page if you feel tempted.

Part one

Write a description of someone you know, but *not* a close friend or lover – a neighbour would be ideal. Don't worry if you have no neighbours, or have some but don't know them; fiction does not depend on that kind of accuracy. You could use an acquaintance and pretend that person lives close by. What about someone you work with? Would she make a good neighbour? Neighbours often see more than they let on. You don't have to like them – in fact, it might be better if you don't.

Part two

Now you've done that, switch the narration from yourself to the neighbour and have her write a description of you. Will you feel self-conscious? If so, aim for humour and then, when you feel more used to the process, work on being more introspective.

Did you find your self-description accurate, unfair, harsh, tongue-in-cheek? Were you conscious while doing it of an audience reading over your shoulder? There could be a rich vein here and you'll know soon enough if you wish to tap it or avoid it until some future time. Later on, you could make this exercise more challenging. Have you ever been involved in a complex triangle? It may have been a personal, heart-wrenching matter. Was your triangle between friends, or was it centred around a work situation? We can, in isolation, fantasize a number of possible scenarios, and it's likely you'll have experienced some feelings of paranoia in the process of those imaginings. If you have the need, the strength and the willingness to know more about your responses, you can create a dialogue between the two other people in the triangle or use what you know with two fictional characters. Dialogue may seem an obvious form to use and by all means do that if it feels right, but don't overlook the value of letters exchanged as a means of interaction. These two real (or imagined) people will express their feelings and thoughts and need not be sympathetic or caring about you at all. It would be more courageous and fruitful, perhaps, if you make them suspicious of you, even nervous about how you might respond, what you might do next. *Don't undervalue your own position and strength in what you write.*

What you learn may help you to move away from feelings of hurt while at the same time teaching you something about characterization, plot and motive. You may want to create characters that begin as children and grow up, that make dramatic life changes, or that evolve slowly through a number of years or events. Much of fictional writing is about people living ordinary lives that become complicated, even messy, as they act this way or that, respond to situations or initiate changes that turn out to be more than what was expected.

Once you become proficient at moving between one character and another you will have developed an ability to relate directly with those imagined people, and this is of great value when things are not going well. You can then write letters to them and seek to have their answer(s) come to you in the same way. This strategy can also be used when a personal decision has to be made and you feel at odds with yourself as you are pulled to and fro by conflicting arguments in your head.

Two types of characterization

We can rely heavily on physical appearance or lay the emphasis instead on the human qualities of our characters. For the most part, characterization combines a mixture of both. To understand this further, I am dividing this exercise into two parts, calling one the *external* view and the other the *internal* view. I will ask you to write about the same character *twice*. Each description will be different, so avoid any temptation to overlap the two types. Read through the two sections first and then decide on a character to write about.

External view

Write a description of a character referring only to those things that can be observed externally: height, colour of eyes, body language, way of talking, laughing, facial expressions, moving, walking, gestures and mannerisms. What clothes and colours does this character favour? Casual onlookers would not know the background story of this person but they could glean information from things said and done and from *how* they were said or done.

Internal view

Now write a second description of this character that tells us about the things the eye cannot see. A narrator might well speak with vast knowledge of a character and/or a close friend could tell us of motivating factors that have had some impact on this person. What is pertinent to our understanding of this character – family background, education, religion, politics, attitudes, feelings, the way she thinks? Did something happen to this person a few years back that has changed her dramatically? What endearing qualities does she have? Maybe those qualities are hidden. What habits and interests could you mention?

Before continuing, look at each description carefully and decide if there is anything further you want to write before comparing the two.

Which description did you prefer? Look again at your external description. Did you mention the eyes? What colour are they? Have you written this physical description as a reflection of the people you see around you every day? Comparing the two descriptions, what could a reader conclude about *you* if reading either/or both descriptions in a book? How including/excluding would your descriptions be for a broad range of readers?

Stereotypes

As outlined in the chapter 'Making the best of imagery', there is a distinction between a cliché and a stereotype. A cliché is a word, phrase, clause or sentence that has become so overworked that it has ceased to be effective; a stereotype is an identikit picture of a person or group of persons; it is usually negative and the public view of that person or group is likely to become diminished or narrowed as a result. As women writers, as feminist writers, it is particularly important for us to think about this. How would you describe the media view of a feminist, or feminists in general? What is the media view of disabled women? Working-class women? Black women? Lesbians? Of course one woman might be all of those.

Here are two very different examples to show how stereotyping operates. When Alice Walker visited Britain following the publication of *The Temple of My Familiar* the media was unable to ignore her popularity and the success of her earlier book (later a Hollywood film), *The Colour Purple*, but the coverage of her tour was dismissive, treating her work, in effect, as marginal to the mainstream of male writing. Unable to deny the fact that huge crowds (men as well as women) were queuing up at London venues in order to hear Alice Walker talk about her books and her life, they chose to speak of her as a 'messiah of the feminist movement' and those wanting to listen to her were referred to as 'disciples, hanging on to her every word'. In this way the importance of a contemporary black feminist writer can be lessened through media presentation.

At a time in the 1980s when England's Greenham Common was consistently in the news, a group of people who lived near the air force base took exception to the number of women living outside the gates. This group of locals got together with the intention of getting the women out of the area. They produced a single-page leaflet that was widely distributed, stuffed into letterboxes and handed to passing motorists. As well as a call to action in the text of the leaflet, much space was given to a drawing showing a woman seated astride a nuclear missile. The woman was wearing dungarees, an old jumper with holes at the elbows, and army-type boots. Her face was far from pleasant. The words on the leaflet were hostile and threatened violence. What those locals wanted to convey with their hatred was that *all* the women living at Greenham Common were vile and nasty lesbians, presumably manhating, and therefore had to be got rid of. There was no mention of *why* the women were camped on the common, and this imposed stereotype avoided any acknowledgement that nuclear weapons are a source of concern to a great number of women, and many men, from every type of background and from all walks of life.

The use of a stereotype to isolate and condemn a group of people has been used time and time again. It is probably this aspect of our writing that will present the greatest challenge in our characterization of people who are different from us – whatever 'us' means to an individual writer in the way she thinks about her identity and how close that identity is to what she is writing about.

Description of clothing, shoes and accessories is the usual way by which writers create or reinforce a stereotype. A character dressed in a certain way can convey a great deal to an audience. On radio it will have to be the character's way of speaking that does the trick. Think about how you describe the following: a male estate agent; a female estate agent; a 'man about town'; a 'woman of the world'.

Can you avoid thinking about what these people might be wearing? If you mention facial features alone, the strength of the description is at risk. One word that has become too firmly associated with a particular kind of stereotype is the word *eccentric*. What immediately comes to mind when you read that word? If you were to write about an eccentric, rich, elderly person you might well convey a fondness for, and perhaps tolerant appreciation of, this unique kind of independence, but try using the word about a down-at-heel person and the meaning can change instantly, and most often negatively. 'Eccentric' at this end of the spectrum can add an unsavoury meaning, suggesting madness or unacceptable anti-social behaviour.

By compiling a list of possible stereotypes for yourself along the lines of those suggested above (and this kind of exercise works very well with a group), you can discuss various ways in which stereotypes are used and perceived. Your list could be drawn from any aspect of life, related to home, to work, to family relationships and so on.

It may seem to you that working on this aspect of writing is best avoided – after all, you might ask, who wants to create stereotypes anyway? Creating characters who represent groups that have suffered from media distortion brings with it a challenge that is similar to kicking a ball through two goal-posts, one marked *cliché* and the other marked *stereotype*. What can you say, avoiding the cliché, that is new? What can you say, avoiding the stereotype, that is different?

There are occasions when writers would want to keep physical appearance – this person is black, that person is white – because it's crucial to the story being told. These are deliberate decisions forming part of an overall purpose in the writer's mind. It is not my intention here to dispute such decisions. The point I'm making is about accessibility and raises the question *who are you writing for?* Description of characters can have a lasting, powerful effect on readers, and with thought and effort we can make our characters more believable and relevant to a greater number of readers. I'm not suggesting uniformity, but I am saying that this aspect of characterization is often a neglected area in a writer's consciousness. If you read that a young girl has 'eyes a thousand years old', is that a better, more accessible, description than knowing what colour those eyes are? In choosing our descriptions we need to be aware of the implications of inclusion/exclusion. We want to be read, and we want what we write to be relevant to and inclusive of as many women as possible.

Character settings

Exercises

The following illustrates how to think about character settings. Let's say, for example, you are visiting a farm. The owner, a woman struggling to make 'a go of it' with two friends, is giving you a guided tour around the farmyard. You look here and there eagerly, trying to drink it all in. What can you see? What can you hear? What can you smell? What can you touch? Shopping-list style, write down each separate thing you notice. When you've done that, divide your list into categories, placing a category label beside each item mentioned.

Your list may look something like this:

Items	*Category*
Trees	Objects
Cows	Animals
Barn	Object
Two friends	People
Clouds	Weather detail
Sunshine	Weather detail
Dog	Animal
Dog barking	Sound
Laughter	Sound

Did you stroke an animal? Did you taste fresh milk? What smells did you detect? What about the mood involved with that setting? Is there an air of mystery about this farm or its owner(s)?

Settings encompass objects, people (usually the minor characters in the story), animals, the five senses, weather details, climate, even the time of day. Emotion and mood are also included. We could think of these last two as atmospheric detail. That sense of mystery – did you feel it most intensely in the barn? This would certainly place it within the setting. Perhaps a sad, grim tale from the dim, distant past is about to be told. Or was it the owner who acted mysteriously? Is she burdened by a secret that threatens to overwhelm her? If so, that mystery is contained within the character.

Our characters can be cast within matching or contrasting settings. Creating a fictional woman who is thinking of ending her life and then providing her with a wet, gloomy day (matching) may seem appropriate, but bright sunshine, blue sky, children playing in the park (contrasting) may be more effective in emphasizing her pain and distress.

Matching and contrasting

Here are five different exercises for you to work with, *matching* character and setting in the first exercise and then *contrasting* character and setting in the second exercise. Your intention here is to explore the merits of each method and to get a feel for settings and their intrinsic value in characterization. You may not want to use all five, but make sure each one you use is worked with twice.

1   A child is handed an ice-cream. She might be a happy child or confronted now with a situation that is difficult for her to understand. Where is she?

2   A man looks at his watch. He is waiting for a friend who is already twenty minutes late. He hadn't wanted to come, but on the phone this morning his friend had insisted. Impatient and annoyed, he's torn between worry and concern. Where is he and what's the weather like?

3   A woman is cleaning her teeth. She has just this moment decided to leave her partner. Is she at home? Has she gone away for a few days? How is she feeling?

4   It's moving day tomorrow and this young woman will be leaving home. She has in her arms a battered old teddy. She walks across to the window, tears running down her face. What can she see from the window? Why is she leaving home?

5   It's late at night and this man is driving down a narrow country road. He's very tired and he knows he should stop somewhere but

there are no lights to be seen, nor can he find anywhere to park his car. Why is this man driving so late at night? Where is he going? Why?

Character and plot

Here are two lovers – Character and Plot. Although they are more likely to be found together than apart, it is not wise for us to take their togetherness for granted. In some novels and stories they are intimately entwined, feeding tidbits of nourishment back and forth as the story unfolds. Tales of suspense and crime fiction are good examples of the happy couple's blissful moments. Then there are stories where Character insists on having greater autonomy, choosing other friends to be with as well as, and sometimes instead of, Plot. I like to think that Plot is off somewhere reading a book at such times, or building a boat, and is not bothered in the slightest by Character's funny moods. A recent appearance of Character without Plot is Jeanette Winterson's *Sexing the Cherry*. The chapters of the book fit together like a mosaic of writings, a sequential collection, unlike a plot-revolving story where the plot can act like a whirlpool pulling the characters and the narrative down into its depths.

Some writers believe that characters create plot. English novelist John Galsworthy said that character *is* plot. This suggests that ideas about plot come from creating characters, getting to know them well and then allowing those characters to act in ways that produce a storyline or plot. Soap operas work in this way. *East-Enders*, the long-running BBC television series set in the East End of London, came about when the writing team went away together with the express intention of creating a number of characters to appear in the first series. It took twenty-two days to create twenty-one characters. Imagine how much detail was needed: background, beliefs, habits, mannerisms, likes and dislikes, as well as predictions about how they might behave in any number of situations. Each was given a 'family' and more could be invented (if needed) later on: long-lost aunts and uncles, ex-lovers, friends, and the odd enemy or two. In this way characters influence and direct the plot. Each episode moves with slow but believable momentum, with intermittent crises to create added tension and cliff-hanging drama.

Characters need not necessarily come first. A crime fiction writer might ponder first on ways to get rid of a body *before* she thinks about *who* will appear in her book. A science fiction writer may be concerned with how females in her planned utopia could possibly procreate without using male sperm. Another writer might want to explore a work setting she is familiar with, making use of what she knows, and only when she has the setting worked out will she consider the cast of characters. Ideas about a plot may come from a variety of sources. I remember reading about flamingos at a nature reserve in Lancashire, England, a few years ago, that had forgotten how to mate. These tame birds had been there a long time and the numbers were dwindling. Wardens had to bring in some wild flamingos to teach the tamer birds what to do. What a statement about learned behaviour! I mean, aren't we all, birds, animals and humans, supposed to know 'naturally' what to do? Transferring this thought to the human condition, I wondered what might happen if a child was not informed, or was misinformed, about something crucial? What if a girl grew up believing she was a boy because no one told her otherwise? Similarly, what if a boy grew up never realizing he was a boy? If some new thought or idea gives you something to ponder, perhaps that will be the beginning of your next story.

Two plotting types

We can talk about the plotting process in two ways. I label these as 'structural method' and 'organic method'. The structural method is where writers may need to have everything worked out and well planned before moving beyond the note-taking stage. Let's say the writer begins with an idea for something that might happen on a train. Gathering information about likely journeys, the type of train, how many carriages, what amenities it has, and time schedules for different months of the year could be a fact-finding mission that takes some time to complete and is the obvious first stage in the plotting process. The writer could decide that a train journey is a necessary part of the research. The file of notes and related material gets thicker and thicker as time passes. A notebook may be tucked in there somewhere. Turning the pages we can see lots of headings, possible starting points, for example. This way of working is a form of brick-building and there'll be something solid behind the writer when she is ready to move beyond this planning stage.

The organic method may have appeal for those writers who begin with a character or an ending that persistently comes to mind, and there might be three drafts of this ending in the writer's file along with suggestions for linked events that she thinks could happen in, say, chapter three. A strong character moving in and out of a writer's mind could become the first focal point, but just when you think you've got her contained on the page she twists out of your grasp as if saying, 'Oh no you don't, I'm not that easy to pin down'. Will you try to grab hold of her or will you let her lead you wherever she wants to go?

These two plotting methods are not as separate as you might expect, nor is there any suggestion here that one is a better way of working than the other. You might switch methods in the space of one story or book. It is not unusual to have a mid-way crisis, with characters refusing to budge, or finding that the well-planned strategy has gone awry because some contradiction shows up and won't let you off the hook.

Plotting genre

Although I think the following exercise is ideally suited for writing within a genre – crime fiction, science fiction, suspense (such as a ghost story), mystery and so on – you may, after you have done the exercise a few times, adapt it in any number of ways to suit your needs. Some exercises are difficult to explain with the written (rather than the spoken) word so I'm using a recent workshop experience here to give you more information on how this exercise can be used.

Exercise

The following list could be varied each time you do this exercise and you could find it valuable to have someone else collect and arrange the items for you. This would avoid any distracting association being made with any of the items before you begin.

- Small bottle of tablets
- Bottle of distilled water
- Protective dust mask (the type used when sanding wood)
- Pack of tarot cards (on the occasion of the workshop referred to I used a cup and saucer marked with astrological symbols instead)
- Telephone number written on a scrap of paper and made to look as though it had been ripped from an address book
- Dressing gown

- Walking stick
- Two wine glasses – one with a small amount of wine,
  the second empty but obviously having contained some wine

Think of this exercise as a recipe for which the list above serves as one ingredient only. From what has been explained throughout this chapter so far you'll know that we need characters, a setting and a plot. We also need to ask ourselves some questions. Where have these items been found? Later you will want to decide what significance to give to each item, but the questions concerning significance need to come from you, so I won't ask them here.

In our workshop session it had been agreed in advance that the group wanted to work with elements of horror and mystery, with no clear direction in mind. This had come about because one woman wanted to work with the fear she felt when left alone in a large, rambling house all week because her partner had to work in a city and only returned home each Friday evening for the weekend. We had first discussed her fears and had concluded that the size of the house, in a semi-rural position, felt 'too big' for her to feel secure. It was hoped that this writing workshop would give her more insights about the situation, and that she would then want to think about her fears and what she could do to change the situation. With this in mind the following questions were designed to fit with horror and mystery. However, one of the women in the group suggested that this same collection of items could have been used for other types of plot. What do you think? You may already have decided which genre you are exploring, though you could also decide to leave that decision for a time.

Were the items listed found in a room that might later be called 'the scene of the crime'? What would that room look like? Would it be of value to isolate the house in some way to further the creation of a situation similar to that of the woman who was working with fear?

The following notes consist of what was written on the day by various participants, and I am indebted to those women for allowing me to include their contributions. I have collated all that was written and put it together rather than show separate entries. It was agreed we would invent no more than six characters, but that more background characters could be created as part of the setting.

What associations could we make if thinking of horror/violence/ murder?

Blood and gore? Missing fingers (maybe other parts of the body?), blood-stained clothing left in such a way as to suggest that havoc has occurred. This could also include blood-stained walls and other surfaces. Vomit, piss, fire, water, lit candles, grandfather clock, saw, knives, axe, raw meat, old pieces of furniture.

Are there things you would add to this list?

Animals/insects? Cats, screech of an owl, dog growling or howling, maggots, cockroaches, large spiders.

Other people? No near neighbours, footsteps, rustling that could be a person moving about, door knocking, screams, shadows in the moonlight that could be human.

Weather details? We had agreed on a matching setting. Night, with or without a moon, wind, storm, pounding waves below the cliff edge, firelight.

Atmospheric detail? Dim lighting, chilly feelings outside, spooky feelings inside. Large spaces underground, maybe a cellar that seems to be the source of the fear, creaking, unexplained noises.

Anything else? Stuck record, ticking clock that seems to grow louder, gnarled trees, masses of fallen/falling leaves. Water: dam, creek, lake, pond, the ocean nearby. A strange silence at odd intervals.

Remembering that this is a recipe, what other ingredients do you think we need?

To help with the plotting here I'd suggest a series of maps. The first could be done to illustrate the position of furniture in a room of the house. You may need separate maps for different rooms. The house could be drawn (a rough sketch will do) in the middle of a large, poster-sized piece of paper or cardboard. Positioned around that house will be other details, for example, where do those footprints in the snow lead – away from the house at the back? If the weather remains bad they could disappear in no time. So taking the weather into account as part of the story may be a necessary aspect of the narrative. (Make note when reading crime fiction or mystery novels how often weather details are used as part of the plot.) Will you need a wall for your house so that someone can lie unobserved? Where will it be? How close to the house? Questions to puzzle over can be written on one corner or on an attached piece of paper. They might read something like this:

- What is the distance between the house and the village post office?
- Could there be an ancient wooden gate positioned in the wall and cleverly disguised by ivy, that only a few people know about?

To conclude the information taken from that workshop I include here a definition of horror, written by Liz (the woman who had suggested the workshop as a means of dealing with her own fears). For 'your' and 'you' read 'I', 'me' or 'my'.

> Horror is something written about the commonplace
> gone wrong (uncontrollable) which is so scary that
> your spine tingles and you breathe fast. It begins to
> colour your own reality and you have to stop reading,
> or dare to go on. It stays in your mind long after, and
> has a horrible way of becoming part of who you are,
> seated deep inside your body cells, now indelible, and
> exorcism your only escape. You took a risk in reading
> that book, that story, listening or watching the news
> even, but you didn't escape its power, as you had hoped
> you would, and you are, now, somehow, smitten.
> Good luck.

Using maps can help us to look for plot weaknesses. Pin yours where you can look at it often so that you'll be reminded each time you pass it. A notebook kept nearby can be used for adding further detail. There is no predictable method of working with this recipe. The displayed items from the list might serve as a springboard only, and not be referred to again. This doesn't mean that the items weren't useful but it does suggest that the writer needed something (other than a blank page) to get her started.

A stop called block

Imagine that this plotting business is like a train journey, the destination being the finished story or novel. Having taken that journey a few times, I'd like to tell you about some of the station stops along the way. The train does not always take the same route to arrive at its destination, so you might not pass through these stations stops in the same order as someone else. I refer to these places as *write, think, block* and *plan.* Block is not a pleasant place to visit but it does help if you accept it as part of the route and not as a detour or as an end in itself. You may find that the order comes in a different sequence at different times and perhaps there are other stops you'll want to add.

When the writing is going well you soon find that there's a rhythm apparent in the way you work. But what if Block lurks around every corner, a shadowy figure looming over your fragile attempts to maintain a momentum? Block may simply herald the end of a stage, suggesting that your momentum has faltered and that further thinking and planning is required. Now's not the time to gnash your teeth with worry. In order to effect a much needed shift in your approach do something physical (if possible) to give yourself a break. Virginia Woolf was known to have walked the streets of Richmond, south London, muttering to herself, seemingly unaware of the people around her. Doing something physical worked for her; it could also work for you. Later, when you feel ready to pick up the threads again, don't go back and stare at the same blank page. Come at the material from a different angle. Here are some suggestions you might want to try.

1 Seek out a setting that fits with what you've written so far. Your task might be to explore the setting with atmospheric detail (or some other aspect) in mind.
2 Spend a few hours in the library looking up reference books that are relevant in some way to the period you're writing about.
3 Compile a list of details that need checking out and systematically work through the list, establishing that the information you obtain is accurate for your purposes. Your list might include the road/rail distance between two cities, the geographical location of a building that has long since been pulled down, the exact date of some well-known world event that you intend to time-link with the formative years of one of your characters.
4 You might want to imagine that you are acting the part of one of your characters, using her senses to move in the world. Arrange a journey with a destination resembling a scene she has to work through in your story. It doesn't have to be the same destination but you could strive to work with her emotions. How would she be feeling? Write sentences in your head as you go along, stopping at convenient moments to make notes of this process.
5 Write letters to yourself and/or your character(s) and then work on the replies with spontaneity and not too much deliberation about what you think ought to be said. This practice can be extremely valuable, a means of uncovering insight and ideas for how to proceed.
6 When I'm feeling exhausted but still determined to keep at it I use music to give me that feeling of uplift. Sometimes it has an almost miraculous effect. What kind of music would you choose?

Structuring a novel

If you have not written a full length book before, the most
daunting aspect is likely to be length. If you are writing a novel
for the teenage market an acceptable length is around 40,000
words. Depending on the size of print used, this will provide
around 150 pages. Adult novels are not easy to pin down for an
average word count but something around 280 pages could be the
aim. Chapter planning is another concern. Publishers may ask for
a chapter plan after receiving the synopsis of a book and it will
help if you've done some of the preparatory work beforehand. The
following exercise is designed to help you understand how to
structure material into chapter sections and then, once you've
given each chapter section a heading on separate sheets of paper,
to make notes about what things you'd want to cover in each.

Exercise

Think of the break-up of a relationship. I'm not asking you to draw
on your own experience here, or on that of people you know. The
aim is to get a more general overview of what couples go through,
pinning down the various stages from a starting point you'll define
and tracing that process to the final resolution. You can approach this
from any point of view: from the point of view of the person being
rejected, or from that of the person doing the rejecting. Or you can
also take the third person point of view, seeing the relationship from
the outsider's standpoint.

Let us assume that there are twelve stages. As you define each stage
you'll give it an appropriate title. The starting point won't be the same
for any two couples, but there might be some similarities along the
way.

Diagram one shows how these twelve assumed stages fit along a
horizontal line. What you need to do now is to place a heading (using
as few words as possible) against each number.

The first heading for one person could be disbelief; for someone
else it might be suspicion. Is the process likely to be the same for the
person who is being rejected as for the person doing the rejecting?
What words will you use and where will you put them?

The second diagram is how one woman described a break-up
process. Use this diagram only as a guide, and work to put down what
you think is appropriate. You might want to discuss the work with
friends or talk it over as part of a group exercise.

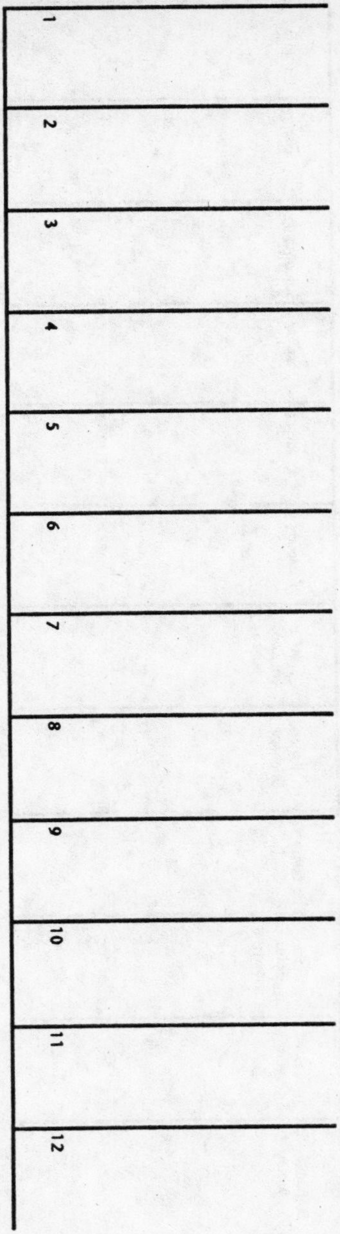

Diagram 1

1 Suspicion	
2 Shock	
3 Questioning	
4 Anger	
5 Hate	
6 Surviving	
7 Feeling sorry for myself	
8 Meeting THEM	
9 Getting on	
10 Almost myself again	
11 Inner strength	
12 A new beginning	

Diagram 2

Once you have defined your twelve stages, write each heading on a separate sheet of paper and then jot down all that you think goes with it. You might finish up with a list of questions, a few sentences or lengthy notes.

In this way you can provide the basic structure for a book with each of these sections becoming the chapters. Additional chapters, such as setting the scene before the break-up and a chapter beyond the break-up, could be added. Alternatively, you may decide to combine two or more of the chapter headings into one chapter. The final number of chapters you have is up to you. Any material, whether based on personal experience, researched notes or fictional writing around a particular theme, can be applied in this way. Part of the challenge of working on a full-length writing project is deciding how you will structure it. Once you have devised a number of suitable headings you can then shift them around. You are not restricted to telling the story in chronological order and may wish to begin the story at the point when it's all over and work backwards in time. Such a structure was used for a recent film entitled *Betrayal*. The film begins with two characters, a woman and a man, ending an affair that they are quite certain their respective partners know nothing about. They pride themselves on being clever, thoughtful and kind. Their affair ends amicably and the plot weaves from the present back into the past. We see the same couple five years earlier, at the height of the affair. Returning to the present, however, there's a surprise. Not only does it become clear that their partners have known what was going on, but they too had been having an affair – with each other. The shock and outrage experienced by the first two characters who had thought themselves so clever is fascinating to watch and the structure of the film gives the story a number of dramatic twists.

Component juggling

Now you are at the circus. Sitting in the front row you watch a clown juggling four balls, each one emblazoned with a different word: character, plot, setting and theme. Can you see them? The clown has spotted you leaning forward, intent on getting a closer look. She takes your hand and gently leads you into the spotlight. She tosses the first ball towards you. Which one is it? Can you see? Here comes the second ball. You're doing well with those two, but can you manage a third? How amazing, you've really done it, three balls in the air. Are you sure this is only your first time? Oh, come on, you can't manage this fourth one too, can you? Well, look at you, I'm dead impressed. Oh. Oh. Ohhh. One of them has dropped but you're still managing to keep the others in motion. What a superb effort. 'Ladies and gentlemen,' shouts the juggler in a loud, ringing tone, 'put your hands together and give this woman a great round of applause.'

No matter which component you begin with there's always the possibility that juggling with all four will be tricky. What if they fall around your feet like deflating balloons? The answer to that is that writing is the same as juggling – practice, practice and more practice. Luck can often lend a hand too. There's no magic formula; writing is work, and hard work at that. Giving up too soon is often the problem. I don't accept that there is such a thing as 'bad writing', only a series of 'early drafts'. This is particularly true of plotting. Characterization appears to many as a well-trodden path, while plotting is a game without any rules. It can be scary, but it can also be challenging and fun.

Point of view

Point of view need not be fixed. Although it is more traditional to tell the tale using first- or third-person narration, other options are possible. For example, the narrating role can be passed on from one character to another, like a relay team passing the baton in a marathon. Andrea Freud Lowenstein, who set her novel *This Place* in a women's prison, had four of the characters, including two inmates, share the narrator's role, each with a very different voice and style.

Using the terms 'first', 'second' and 'third' person can be confusing. I've noticed when working in schools and with some groups how easy it can be to assume that what is meant is one, two or three voices relating the story. I feel it is important, therefore, to stress how the three categories work.

The first person, *I*, tells us *I was there, I know about it, this is my point of view*. The opening paragraph of Kitty Fitzgerald's book *Marge* is a fine example of first-person narration:

> I have to keep the light on in one of my rooms all the time. Day and night, I've always been prepared. It hasn't happened yet, the thing that's supposed to happen, but I know if I wait and watch I'll be alright.
>
> (Fitzgerald, 1984, p. 1)

The second person *you* voice, speaking directly to another person, is a little-used strategy but Gloria Naylor's book *Mama Day* proves how effective it can be when used with skill and confidence:

> I had been making a list of what would have to happen before I'd ever speak to you again: a cold day in hell, a heat wave in Siberia, a blue moon (I scratched out a red sun – I'd seen plenty of those here), a winter Olympics in Antarctica, the Super Bowl in Havana, your left ear rotting off followed by your right toe followed by your middle finger (either hand) followed by ... – when one of Carmen Rae's children brought me a note from Miss Ruby.
>
> (Naylor, 1990, p. 244)

This is Mama Day speaking directly to George. In other sections of the book he speaks to her. This strategy allows the author to use the narrative as a pliant instrument. It is possible to shift between the first-, second- or third-person voice.

Third-person narration, the *she* voice, can seem more objective than the other two but this is an assumption rather than a fact. All three points of view can be used subjectively or objectively. Here the narrator's voice is saying *this is what happened, here's how they felt, thought and acted but I am not personally involved, am more like a fly on the wall, seeing, recording.* When using the third person we are talking about something or someone. Bengali writer Mahasveta Devi, in her short story 'The Wet-Nurse', begins with a rhyme about her aunt before telling the reader more directly about the character Jashoda:

> My aunt who lived in the thicket
> My aunt who lived far away,
> My aunt never called me fondly
> To give me peppermints or candy.

> Jashoda cannot remember whether her own aunt treated her as badly as the one in the children's rhyme, or looked after her well. More likely, right from her birth she had just been Kangalicharan's wife and the mother of twenty children, if you count the living and the dead.
>
> (Devi, 1987, p. 1)

Exercises

For you to work with 'point of view' I've chosen four scenarios and included food in each (a neglected area in fiction anyway), so give yourself over to wild fantasies of luscious fruit, frothy desserts or thick wholesome soup being consumed by your characters as part of the exercise. Work with as many of the four scenarios as you can, trying out first one type of narrating voice and then another.

1 Two people meet (their first date?) in a restaurant. They offer samplings of their chosen dishes back and forth, across the table.
2 Another restaurant. This time rejection is on the menu. Who will reject whom? Will the dishes chosen be appropriate? How will the rejected person respond?
3 Reconciliation. It's been a long time since these two met. They meet unexpectedly in the street. Shyly, with a mixture of embarrassment and wary confusion, they go to a nearby café. What connected them in the past? What have they got to say to each other now?
4 This is a group of people who may be friends, workmates or relatives. Perhaps it is a sporting team having a meal together after the match. How many of them are there? Everyone arrives close to the arranged time, but something unplanned is about to happen. What might that be?

It may seem obvious to use one of the involved characters to tell the story, but think about what other options you have. The food can be used as props and can add to the storyline, a strand that is woven into and becomes part of the unfolding tale.

If you look back through earlier work (perhaps work written before you began to use this book), are there other ways of narrating that you might now reconsider?

Dialogue

Many new writers express fear and trepidation about writing dialogue. The biggest challenge is of course to avoid the unnecessary repetition of she said/he said indicators. Second to this is how to convey the *way in which* a character says something without resorting to adjectives all the time: '... he repeated thankfully' or '"Of course I've heard of you Mr Thatcher," he said in a level voice.' You can use the words of the dialogue itself to convey the feeling or attitude: 'I can't do that. Not here. Not just like that.' Or you can use physical description: 'She spoke, tapping her fingers on the glass ...' If you feel hesitant or would like more practice the following exercises may prove useful:

Exercises

1   Something has happened. You must decide how devastating that something is. Could it be the end of the world or are these two people simply stuck in a lift? Place your two characters in a confined space. Will it be a rocket ship? A train? If so, they would need to be the only two passengers in the carriage. They might, of course, be in a car. They have no names but can refer to each other, if necessary, as A and B. You need to work through the piece with beginning, middle and end in mind. The use of A and B could make this a suitable exercise for science fiction, but the genre and what you do with the characters is up to you. Remember that the only device you have for moving the story on is the dialogue itself.
2   Here you are asked to write about an argument between two people. Would you choose an argument between two adults or a more obviously unequal relationship, say between an adult and a child? As with the previous exercise, the dialogue is the only means of carrying the story along. You can use names for your two characters if you wish, but try not to over-use them.
3   This time it is a telephone conversation. Will it be two lovers? Two friends? One of those odd calls that turns out to be a wrong number? Will it be a personal call? Could it be about work? Telephone conversations have a built-in formula – we say 'hello' at the beginning and 'goodbye' at the end. For this reason you may find that this particular conversation has restrictions as well as certain advantages.

Here's how Gillian Hanscombe uses dialogue in a story entitled 'Ebbs and Flows', published in a collection of short stories called *The Reach*. The differing viewpoints of the two characters is clear to the reader and, wisely, the author gets out of the way, allowing the exchange to take place in a freer context. This is particularly valuable when writing dialogue for more intimate settings:

> 'June?'
> 'Yes.'
> 'What about now? It's dark. Night-time. We could just have a cuddle here. Don't have to wait till we go to bed. No-one'll see. No-one'll know. And we've worked hard all day.'
> Looking distressed.

'I can't do that. Not here. Not just like that.'
'Why not?'
'It's too – sudden.'
'But I've been talking about it all the time.'
'Yes. Well, you know that doesn't help either.'
'Well?'
'What?'
'Can we?'
'No. You shouldn't keep on at me. It just makes it worse. Harder.'
'But I really want to.'
'And I don't really want to.'
'Don't you love me then?'
'Of course I love you, you silly cow. That's nothing to do with it.'
'That's everything to do with it.'
Silence.
'Eve.'
'Yes.'
'Are you going to wash up then? Or shall I do it?'
'No. I'll do it.'

(Hanscombe, 1984, pp. 120–121)

Another exercise would be to write a passage (or rework a section of material you have written previously that includes dialogue) in which, again avoiding 'she said' and 'he said', you work to include different indicators for who is saying what. You will no doubt find numerous examples in books you already have, but to get you pointed in the right direction:

I reach for the first lie: 'Mother, I'd like you to meet ...'
'Oh yes,' she beams. 'We've just been talking about my African violets. Daniel's mother grows them too.'
'Oh?' I smile at Daniel in genuine appreciation as I reach for the whopper: 'Father, I'd like you to meet ...'
Still in a rage over our quarrel he grunts from behind his newspaper, held between white fists.

(Fraser, 1989, p. 80)

The quote comes from *My Father's House* by Sylvia Fraser. An autobiographical book, subtitled *A Memoir of Incest and of Healing*, it illustrates the point that non-fiction can be as compulsive and accessible to the reader as fictional plots and characters.

This next quote comes from a crime fiction novel, *Banking on Death*, by Emma Lathen. Note how the details of movement, eye contact and gestures move the story along:

> 'Roy!'
> Stan Michaels lumbered to his feet. 'Roy,' he repeated thankfully. 'My God, it's good to see you. I'm going crazy.' He glanced at Thatcher, and hurriedly added, 'Paul Reardon and I have been on the phone to Beloit half the day. Oh, this ...'
> Again John Thatcher identified himself. Roy Novak exchanged salutations with him; he did no more than glance at his wife with a cold 'Hello, Jeannie.' She watched him through narrowed eyes as he turned back to Thatcher.
> 'Of course I've heard of you, Mr. Thatcher,' he said in a level voice. 'What's your interest in BIP?'
> Again Thatcher explained that he was acting in the interests of Robert Schneider's children ...
>
> (Lathen, 1983, p. 168)

I'm not advocating that you throw away the word 'said' and never allow it to darken your door again; what I am suggesting is that you broaden your understanding and practice of dialogue so that more options for its use will be open to you. Dialogue can then become a great asset and a more integral part of the narrative.

May Sarton's book *Crucial Conversations*, published in 1975, consists mostly of dialogue, though it uses narrative and letter writing too. Poppy Whitelaw has decided to leave her husband Reed after twenty-seven years of marriage. Is this a play? Yes and no. The reader supplies the necessary emphasis for the crackling emotions in the dialogue – it is like listening to a play being performed in your head – but interspersed with the dialogue is third-person narrative that teases out complex strands of information, insight and self-realization.

There is one further way of using dialogue or, rather, *not* using it but appearing to do so. Strictly speaking, this device would be described more accurately as narrative, though the impression conveyed to the reader is one of dialogue. Here's an example from my own autobiography, *One of the Family*, where my friend Claire and I are having a conversation about kids on the evening before my wedding:

> But what about Claire? Had she thought about children? What would she like? Claire said she didn't know. She

couldn't see herself as a mother, wasn't even sure if she wanted to be a wife. The truth was she liked her life just the way it was.

I was stunned. She'd never said anything like this before. That might be all right now, I said, but what about the future? Would she still feel like that in ten years' time? Claire was amused at my confusion. She'd still have friends then, wouldn't she? Or did my getting married mean that I intended ending our friendship? Of course it didn't, I rushed in to reply ...

(McNeill, 1989, p. 250)

Some common problems

Over-writing

In effect, this asks the reader, did you get that? I'm not sure you did, so I'll add a few more words, sentences, paragraphs, pages, to make sure you do. There is a positive side to this tendency. The more you write the more you'll be informing yourself about characters, description and plot, and possibly you'll be constructing a fair few good sentences too. It is not too difficult to overcome the habit, but you'll have to learn *not* to be too attached to what you write: 'Oh no, not that sentence, that's my favourite' will not help you to prune excess. If you are using a typewriter use double spacing (so that you can work with a pencil between the lines), and type up a few paragraphs of material that you think is over-written. Imagine each sentence has to work as a brick in a wall, carefully distributing the weight. If there are sentences that are not adding to the story, cut them out. Begin by reading each paragraph through without the first sentence, then without the second and so on, right through to the end. Can you do without any of them? What has happened to the meaning? Has it become sharper? More direct? Too diluted? Confusing? Think now of each sentence as a separate brick that can be moved around. Experiment. Once you have done this with sentences, do it with each word in each sentence.

Do a few exercises using short sentence structure all the way through. With a highlighter pen mark out the sentences that you think are working well. Now eliminate the rest. What has happened to the material? If you feel you have lost something, introduce the other sentences, slowly, one at a time. Or maybe you've come up with a new sentence to try. Flexibility is your aim.

Be honest; be brave. Your work will benefit from these efforts sooner than you think. Ask for feedback from others. Try more than one version and see what other people think, but *always* see your own opinion as being just as important as anyone else's.

Under-writing

This is like the person who whispers a message, a secret, but feels it inside as a shout. The writer may need to gain a more accurate perspective and this may prove difficult to do alone. There are times when we cannot trust our own judgement. If you know you find it difficult to write very much – to elaborate, describe or explain – simply recognizing that this is a problem is the first step to solving it. Feedback from another trusted writer friend can help enormously. You might have someone in mind who can help you work towards a broader understanding of what you are *not* saying, or explaining, or making clear. Try to expand the number of sentences you use in a paragraph. Set yourself exercises where you aim to use three or four sentences in place of your usual single sentence. There is a place for economical writing: emphasizing a point dramatically; conveying information subtly. You'll need to decide, later rather than sooner, if this is your writing style (maybe up to now you have written poetry), or whether it is an unwanted, chronic habit – perhaps a symptom of your own reticence.

Repetition

You'll find in this book that many words or phrases appear quite often. Due to language limitations – having insufficient words to describe similar things – some repetition is unavoidable and needs to be accepted as inevitable, up to a point. Beyond what is reasonable, the challenge has to be met. Finding original ways of saying what we mean is an essential part of the craft of writing. Writers need to work with high standards and to make sure those standards remain high. How strict do you need to be?

Check your adjectives regularly. You've said it was a 'wonderful' day on page four. Do you really need to use that same word three paragraphs further on? What about those personal pronouns *her, him, she, he, they*? I see you've used *her* twice in one sentence. This is sometimes appropriate, but not always. Does the sentence need to be shortened, rearranged, reworked, reversed? Longer sentences can be viewed as two halves of a whole. Reversing the order of the two halves may give more clarity, or allow you to cut out a few unnecessary words. Here's another sort of problem, similar but not exactly the same. *He* appears in two sentences close together. Would it be wise to use the person's name the second time round? (Writers often make use of surnames, nicknames or name variations to get around this problem.) If you are working with a friend or a group, what about a feedback session designed to weed out small editing faults?

Endings

Poor or unresolved endings can be an indicator that a writer ran out of steam well before the end was in sight. What's the use of strong description, believable characters and workable storylines if the ending falls with an unsatisfactory plop? Perhaps the ending needed more time, more drafts. If you wish to be published, reworking has to be preferable to sending off a manuscript that may later be rejected. You could hope that a publisher/magazine will see the strengths in the writing and encourage you to work for a better story resolution, but it would not be wise to rely on this. Impatience will have to be seen for what it is, and you'll learn so much more if you accept that there will have to be a number of drafts before you can call a story/novel finished. This may not always be the case, miracles do happen, but they don't happen every day. Seven drafts is (usually) what I need to finish a project; the last three are concerned more with grammatical-type editing than with structure or content.

If you feel that your endings are a weak point you could devote several working sessions to plotting the end separately. Work on the story up to the point *before* it will end, then begin the next session from that point onwards. Alternatively, you could begin a new project having devised an ending as the first priority. You could also aim to have more than one ending, choosing, say, three options and working with each as though you were creating a different story each time.

Editing

My motto, which I frequently quote on creative writing courses, is 'write with emotion, edit with reason'. By getting down that first draft, going full pelt with the motivation, keeping every note you write, trying not to censor yourself if you can't get the right word, and so on, you can make the most use of your flow. Later, you can look at the work with a more critical eye.

Have you ever seen those drawings in children's books and magazines in which the reader is asked to find things, perhaps animal faces hidden among the branches and leaves of a tree? If you had not been told they were there would you have missed them? Similarly, editing requires a special way of looking at writing. You can't expect to grasp the techniques as quickly as you can spot the tree animals. It takes time to learn, and being open to feedback from others could speed up the learning process.

Spread out what you've written, bearing in mind that maximum flexibility is the best approach. Lack of flexibility is a common problem for inexperienced writers who may feel that writing is a linear process, a straight line drawn between A and B. You can develop the habit of lateral thinking (which means looking at situations in unorthodox ways) by the cut-and-paste method of rearranging paragraphs. This assumes that you are working on paper, not on a word processor. It is wise to have made two copies of the original draft before you begin with the scissors, because you might not always remember the exact order of the original draft and may wish to refer back to it from time to time.

Cut each paragraph into a single, separate section and then rearrange the sections randomly, changing the order to see if there is a potential improvement with a bit more work. A dramatic new possibility might now occur to you, or you might see that a particular aspect of the work needs more attention. You can also use this method with single sentences. I find a stapler quicker and less messy than glue, and I attach the paragraph sections to a back page (usually sheets of paper I recycle from earlier discarded writings). If I do come up with an alternative satisfactory arrangement a photocopy will show the staple marks, but they can be erased with white-out very easily. I also number each paragraph to ensure that I don't lose any of them. It can be annoying later to find a stray paragraph on the floor! Numbering helps me to keep track of the process. If I do decide to reject paragraphs (and they may contain writing that I think is worth keeping), I'll save these passages on file for possible future use. Of course, if you have a word processor the editing becomes much simpler as you can easily reshuffle pieces of text on screen.

Editing can be difficult to understand fully, and uncomfortable to accept in practice. It might be one of your strengths; more commonly, it is an aspect of writing that develops with experience and a commitment to learning. An editing exercise I strongly recommend is to analyse someone else's work. The aim is to learn how to look more intently and to find the hidden techniques and strategies. Use short stories to begin with and then move on to lengthier material, such as novels. The following questions are a useful guide for analysing material. You may have others. If so keep them in mind as you read through the story and make notes as you go along.

- Opening sentence ... does it work for you? Arresting? Inviting? Dramatic? Gently leading you in? How would you describe the opening sentence? Is the material making use of short or long sentence structure? Does it describe the setting, or the characters or events, or is the emphasis on action and movement?
- Is the plot strong? Is there a feeling of momentum?
- Is the writing accessible?
- Is it first-, second- or third-person narrative? Does it work for you?
- What about imagery? If it's there does it work?
- Do the images add meaning to the text?
- How would you describe the work – reflective, action packed, introspective, analytical, descriptive?
- Do you feel compelled to read on?
- Does the storyline drag? (Often an indication of poorly edited material.)
- What about dialogue? Is it realistic? Is it believable?
- What format has the writer chosen – letters, diary entries, other styles?
- Does this format work for you?
- What techniques do you observe?
- How original are the techniques?

Play writing

For a fuller understanding of playwriting it would be advisable to look for a specialist book such as *Writing for the BBC, A Guide to Possible Markets*. The details of this and other books are given at the end of the chapter.

Research

You will not be able to write a play for radio, television or the theatre if you never listen to them or watch them. It's no use having a vague notion that you'd like to write something if you haven't studied how it can be done. Television 'soaps' are good for learning purposes. If you have a video recorder, tape a few consecutive episodes of the soap you've chosen to work with. If you don't have one, perhaps you have a friend who'd allow you to visit her at home and make use of her equipment. Replaying the material several times will help you to understand, in a layered way, how the scenes are put together in a sequence to make one episode. Before you begin the first of your selected episodes make a list of all the characters you can remember. You'll need to update this list as you go along if there are one or two you've left out, or as new characters are introduced. Here's how to proceed.

Each time a character appears, write down the name. With each scene change, make a note of the new setting. How many scenes are interior? How many are exterior? What action occurs in each scene? What information is conveyed? How many characters appear in each scene? Have different points of view been expressed within one episode? Is the storyline passed from one character to another? Excluding commercial breaks, how long did the episode last? What else have you learned?

Later, with your updated cast list and having watched the episodes a number of times, you can tidy up your notes and be prepared to work out answers to the questions above. You may have added questions of your own as you watched the unfolding stories. You'll soon know how often each character has been used and in what way. There may be varying groups, of two, three, four and more, and in some episodes certain characters will be dominant while others will appear as part of a background story. This position can be reversed at any time as soon as another story-line develops. Each story-line will have a different time-span; some will be resolved in one or two episodes, and others will go on and on.

Seldom do any of the characters have long speeches. Have you noticed how frequently they are interrupted, or fed lines or questions, or given supporting 'ah-has', 'mmms' and body-language feedback from other characters?

How much has happened in the episodes you have watched? Were there moments where the visual scene says it all, without words? Has there been an emphasis on action or conversation? Can you detect any formula in this sort of writing?

Return now to the exercises that focused on food on p. 54. Use any/all of these to write one or more scenes. The food can work as props and you may be able to transfer your previously written work to a visual medium such as television.

What about writing for a stage play or for radio? For information about stage-play writing, make time to browse in your local library and don't be afraid to ask the librarians to help you. Check out books on how to write, as well as volumes of previously performed plays, books on stage design, and any other related subject. Maybe you could ask a local amateur dramatic group to let you sit in on rehearsals. Preparing yourself in this way will allow you to feel steeped in the craft. Don't pressure yourself to write; simply go through the processes and allow yourself to respond to the excitement and stimulation.

Don't forget that it costs money to get a play on to the stage, television or radio. You'll have a better chance of a sympathetic hearing if you limit your cast to around six characters or less. (Usually it is only the well-known, successful writers who are commissioned for extravaganza-type productions that call for huge casts.) An advantage of radio plays is that you can have more than six characters, and you can rely on the first six to play more than one part if necessary. Similarly, it's true that radio is more like the 'big screen' of the cinema than television. Sound effects can be used to create a grand impact on both radio and film. The smaller television screen at home has obvious size limitations. You will have noticed when watching a 'blockbuster' movie at home that you've already seen at a cinema how limiting the small screen can be. An avalanche, for instance, can be given the full 'treatment' on both radio and film.

Although I would stress that *all* rules about writing are there to be broken when the right occasion comes along, the following guidelines may prove helpful while you are gaining experience and developing skill and confidence.

1 Understand what your characters are on about – their motives, what they say and do, need to be clearly understood by you. You may be asked to explain or justify your characters. This need not be alarming if you know your characters well enough to speak confidently. Copious notes on each character will never go to waste.

2   The essence of drama is conflict. Almost always there will be a building up of tension, small or large-scale, at the centre of your material. You have to consider what will happen, what will change.
3   Avoid unbelievable plots and situations. If you force your characters to act or speak in ways designed to cover up an inadequate plot you will strain credibility.
4   Aim for a logical, satisfying ending.
5   Be ruthless when it comes to cutting away irrelevant or weak dialogue.
6   You will need to create curiosity, mystery or suspense in the first sixty seconds.

The dialogue used in plays may sound like everyday conversation but this is, in part, an illusion. Have you ever noticed how at the end of some scenes one character asks a question that remains unanswered, left hanging there as the last word before the scene fades out to be replaced by another? Verbal habits can be included in play-writing dialogue to give authenticity, but subtlety is the keynote rather than accuracy. You probably know a number of people who over-use certain words – *actually, you know, you know what I mean* – but you won't find such over-use reflected to the same extent in dialogue between actors.

You can learn to strip conversational speech by working purposefully with conversations heard around you. It would be advisable to begin with two characters and to expand the number slowly once you get the hang of the exercise. Write down exactly what you heard, word for word, or use a tape recorder and transcribe the material in the same way that you'd write a play. Count the number of words used each time a person has spoken. How many of those words could be removed without changing the meaning? Put a line through the last word in each piece of speech and then keep running lines through the last single word till you have only one word coming from each speaker. Now, build up the dialogue, slowly, weaving in small interruptions, comments, questions from one person to another.

What about gestures, facial movements, mannerisms? What part can these play in communication, particularly in television scripts? Keep the connection between the two people moving back and forth but don't rely simply on long speeches, or indeed on words at all. Refer back to radio, television, stage and screen when new questions arise and you will learn more and more as you go on. *Remember to be ruthless when it comes to cutting away irrelevant or weak dialogue.*

Sources

Devi, Mahasveta, 'The Wet-Nurse', Kali for Women (eds.),*Truth Tales*, The Women's Press, London, 1987.

Fitzgerald, Kitty, *Marge*, Sheba, London, 1984.

Fraser, Sylvia, *My Father's House*, Virago, London, 1989.

Hanscombe, Gillian, 'Ebbs and Flows', Mohin, Lilian & Shulman, Sheila, (eds.),*The Reach*, Onlywomen Press, London, 1984.

Lathen, Emma, *Banking on Death*, Penguin, London, 1983.

Lowenstein, Andrea, *This Place*, Pandora, 1985.

McNeill, Pearlie, *One of the Family*, The Women's Press, London, 1989, and University of Queensland Press, Brisbane, 1990.

Naylor, Gloria, *Mama Day*, Vintage, London, 1990.

Sarton, May, *Crucial Conversations*, W. W. Norton, London, 1975.

Winterson, Jeanette, *Sexing the Cherry*, Vintage, London, 1990.

Further reading

Drytryk, Edward, *On Screen Writing*, Focal Press, London, 1985.

Gator, Dilys, *How to Write a Play*, Alison & Busby, 1990.

Horstmann, Rosemary, *Writing for Radio*, A & C Black, London, 1992.

Longmate, Norman, *Writing for the BBC*, *A Guide to Possible Markets*, BBC Publications, 1989.

Yegar, Sheila, *The Sound of One Hand Clapping*, *A Guide to Writing for the Theatre*, Amber Lane Press, 1990.

Finding the right words: women and language

Origins

We inherit words with invested meaning and very often we use them without appreciating their origins. To illustrate this point I would like to tell you the story of Cassandra. She was the daughter of Hecuba and Priam, who were the king and queen of Troy. Legend has it that the god Apollo promised her the gift of prophecy if she would sleep with him. Cassandra decided to accept Apollo's gift, but once this had been bestowed she refused to fulfil her side of the bargain. Divine favours could not be withdrawn and Apollo was angry. He begged for just one kiss and as Cassandra leaned forward to comply he breathed or, according to some, spat into her mouth, vowing no one would ever believe any prophecies she made. What a fate – to predict disasters before they happened and yet be unable to do anything to prevent them because no one took any notice. Her father Priam claimed she was mad and imprisoned her. Cassandra foresaw the downfall of Troy and told the Trojans that the Greeks would be hiding in a wooden horse, but they would not heed her warnings. After the fall of Troy, Agamemnon, who had led the Greek forces, claimed Cassandra as booty and took her home to Mycenae as his mistress. Drawing near to the palace Cassandra became wary, sensing danger, and refused to enter. She cried out that she could smell blood. Yet she could not avoid her fate – Agamemnon's wife, Clytemnestra, was to take her revenge for her husband's sacrifice of their daughter, Iphigenia, by beheading him and then using the same axe to kill Cassandra.

Cassandra's story is not simply another Greek myth, for it has been used since the beginning of recorded time as a means of viewing hysteria as a disease of the womb. The term 'hysteria' comes from the Greek word *hystera*, meaning womb. According to Plato (c. 429–347 BC) hysteria was a symptom of a woman remaining barren too long after puberty. The unfulfilled womb was said to wander about the body as though lost, causing all sorts of 'diseases'. This condition was said to continue until the woman started to procreate.[1]

Words are important here. The history of the word 'hysteria' has been traced by Laurie Layton Schapira in her book *The Cassandra Complex, Living with Disbelief*. She recounts the story of Edward Jorden, who wrote a book about hysteria in 1603 and who, acting as an expert medical witness in a witchcraft trial, diagnosed as 'hysterical' the supposed witch's victim. He ascribed a 'choaking in the throat', a sensation then known as 'globus hystericus', not to witchcraft but to a physical disorder of the womb. It was around the time of Jorden's book that the word 'vapors' (the vapours) came into use. Later this came to be used synonymously with 'hysteria' (Layton Schapira, 1988, pp. 40–41). It is also noted by Jane Mills, in her book *Womanwords*, that Jorden was the first to see hysteria as a disease of the brain rather than of the womb and that he was the first to detect hysteria in men.[2] Nevertheless, hysteria continued to be viewed as a woman's ailment.

In the eighteenth century Wilhelm Griesinger attributed to women suffering the symptoms described (and still referred to as hysterics) an 'inclination to deceive and to lie, traits of decided envy, smaller or greater nastiness' (Layton Schapira, 1988, p. 43). Medical historian Esther Fischer-Homberger has been quoted as saying, 'Where hysteria is diagnosed, misogyny is not far away' (Layton Schapira, 1988, p. 41).

My purpose here is to show how words are handed down century after century with invested meaning that goes beyond our conscious understanding. Take as another example, the origin of the word 'trivia'.[3] The goddess Trivia was the goddess of small things, but her name and what she stood for has been diminished over time. A dictionary meaning today links 'trivia' and 'trivial' with insignificant or unimportant matters. We even equate trivial with 'petty'. Such biased meaning is frequently contained within the words we use. Without a concerted effort to find out more about language we can unwittingly perpetuate a meaning that we might not wish to be part of.

The English language is full of borrowed words taken from other languages. During its long history Britain has been conquered by a number of different peoples, most significantly by the Romans, who at that time (around 43 AD) spoke Latin and whose influence still lingers. French words are also quite common: 'en route', 'boutique', 'de luxe', 'faux pas', 'cul-de-sac', 'a la carte'. Cedric Astle in his book *How Good is Your English?* tells us that 'Nearly sixty per cent of the words in an English dictionary are of Romance origin (i.e. derived from Latin roots)'.

Many borrowed words have been altered but retain a link with those earlier origins. 'Amphibious', 'biography', and 'biology' all have different meanings yet remain connected to the common Greek root *bios*. The following list serves as an indication of how borrowed words have become so much a part of English usage that their origins are obscured or forgotten:

- Chess is Spanish
- Banana is African
- Souvenir is French
- Typhoon is Greek
- Waltz is German
- Alcohol is Arabic
- Oasis is Egyptian
- Balcony is Italian
- Marmalade is Portuguese

Biblical words have been passed down through the ages: 'Babel', 'Jezebel', 'maudlin', to mention just a few. Aristocrats have made their contribution too: a filling placed between two slices of bread is called a sandwich, a word linked with the Earl of Sandwich – though he was unlikely to have been the first ever to eat a filling in bread this way; a woollen, long-sleeved waistcoat was favoured by the Earl of Cardigan and so the cardigan came into being; and the Earl of Chesterfield gave his name to a type of couch. And there have been words invented for modern technology: 'X-ray', 'television', 'laser'. With the rising popularity of computer technology we now have words like 'user-friendly'. When we use the word 'palace' we are talking about a stately mansion, but the original palace was a hill in Rome upon which Augustus built his house. Limerick, a kind of nonsense verse, was named after the town in Ireland. If we talk about a spoonerism – the transposition of the opening sounds of words, as in 'shoving leopard' instead of 'loving shepherd' – we are using the name of Rev W. A. Spooner, warden of New College, Oxford at the beginning of this century, who was famous for his tendency to confuse words in this way.

Language can change a great deal too. 'Pagan' and 'heathen' were once words that described people living outside cities and towns, country people. Now the meaning and use of these words have altered. Words can be appropriated and given different meanings. The word 'gay', for example, has been adopted by homosexual men and has become generally accepted as a definition of homosexuality in the English language. 'Faggot' is another interesting word, with a changed meaning from past centuries, revealing a close connection between gay men, heresy and witchcraft. Both witches and heretics were subject to death by fire (hanging and drowning were alternative methods) and the bundles of sticks used for the fires were called 'faggots'. At the time of the burnings expressions such as 'to try a faggot', 'fire a faggot' were common, suggesting that the victims were called 'faggots'. The word 'faggot' comes from the Latin *fagus* which means beech tree and the Greek *phagos* or *phegos*, which originally meant any tree bearing edible fruits or nuts.[4]

Very often we have to struggle against the language we inherit and its fixed definitions to try to find new ways of expressing ourselves. It is undeniable that there is a bias in the English language (and other languages too) and that this bias works against you and me. To establish our own viewpoint and analysis from inside the experience of being a woman has to be preferable to having a viewpoint imposed on us from outside our experience and understanding.

Man-made or man maid?

Let's look at insults used about men. The following lists are not meant to be comprehensive. There may be other words that you know of that are not listed here, so making your own list might be a good idea.

- bastard
- son-of-a-bitch
- mother's boy
- hen-pecked

All of the words above, if used to insult a man, are directed at the women in his life, past or present, and are not linked directly to the man at all. The following words are used as insults about women: crumpet, whore, trollop, tramp, tart, harlot, bitch, floozy, slag. As you can see, most of the terms used to degrade women

are about naming a woman as a prostitute. It's clear that many
insults about both men and women have the effect of damning
women directly, and damning men by association. Terms used to
describe women can often be interpreted in two ways. The same
cannot be said of terms used to describe men:

Madam	Sir
Mistress	Master
Lady of the house	Man of the house
Landlady	Landlord
Hostess	Host
An honest woman	An honest man

Then there are the words used to describe a position in life, or
a job role. Often, these words are changed in both the spelling and
meaning when used to describe women.

Governor	Governess
Mayor	Mayoress
Usher	Usherette
Major	Majorette

And what about these?

King	Queen
Brave	Squaw
Wizard	Witch
Patron	Matron
Grandfatherly advice	Old wives' tales

Good things to eat, is that what women are? Honey, sugar,
cheesecake, sweetie pie. How many do you know? We can be
described as having cherry lips, peaches 'n' cream complexion,
delicious, good enough to eat, a dish, a tasty bit, a sweet young
thing, ripe, fresh, crumpet. Men may be referred to as a bit of a
hunk, a fine hunk of a man. Is there a difference in these descriptions?

Then we come to the animal kingdom:

stud	kitten	bitch
wolf	bunny	shrew
buck	bird	cow
lion-hearted	chick	nag
fox	lamb	sow

Women can be referred to as cats. To describe a woman as 'catty' means that she is malicious and unkind. A man can be defined as a tomcat, meaning that he is sexually on the prowl.

And then there are the flowers: wallflower, clinging vine, poison ivy, deflowered maiden, and we all know what it means if a girl or woman loses her cherry or is called a shrinking violet. Men are probably thought too active to be defined as plant life. The exception is the word 'pansy' which is applied to a man who is considered to be less male than other men.

Only a woman can be a battle-axe, a gossip, an hysteric, an old hag, a bathing beauty or a flirt, yet there is no logical reason why these words could not be used to describe men. We immediately think of them as being exclusively descriptive of women. Why?

Women's names are often inspired by flowers or jewels or even virtues that are considered desirable: Rose, Lily, Ruby, Pearl, Faith, Hope, Charity, Patience. I searched in vain for a boy's name that comes from a plant. Do you know one? There are names like Chris, Jo, Terry and Pat which could be used when naming either girls or boys, but the tradition in English is much the same as calling a girl a tomboy, i.e. the name is assumed to be a boy's name and either the spelling might be changed to denote its female use or the underlying assumption is that it's OK for a girl to take a boy's name but its not OK the other way round. There is no acceptable alternative for calling a boy the equivalent of a tomboy within the context of acting like a girl except negatively through the terms 'pansy' or 'sissy', used to remind a boy that he's lowered his status in the opinion of other boys.

The word 'misogynist' is defined in the dictionary as a man who has a hatred of women (the word comes the Greek word *miso* meaning to hate and the Greek word *gyne* meaning woman) but there is no corresponding term, apart from man-hater, for women who hate men. The word misogynist has been in use for many years and the assumption would appear to be that it is acceptable for men to hate women, so much so that a word is used to describe that position, but that women, bless them, would probably never have cause to hate men in general or any man in particular. It wasn't until those 'man-hating' feminists came along that the term had to be invented. It would be of interest to know if any dictionaries contain the term 'man-hater' or 'man-hatred'. None of mine do and I own several.

Other omissions from the dictionary:

bunny boy	tea man	nightwatchwoman
fish-husband	au pair boy	sugarmummy
bit-of-trouser	mid-husband	washerman
she-woman	chairwoman of the board	

The diagrams on pp. 78 and 79 offer two ways of looking at language, first as an oppressor, then as a challenge. You may wish to add to these or decide instead to create your own diagram.

The London-based poet and feminist Astra has kindly given permission to include here her previously unpublished poem on language:

i speak/you speak/she speaks

here and there and everywhere
men as a class
are allowed/encouraged/programmed to be
audible/visible/credible/original/responsible/knowledgeable

women as a class
are allowed/encouraged/programmed to be
none of these
except for a few
token women   from time to time

this process begins at birth
when women   in our patriarchal culture
(that is institutions we take for granted as
desirable/natural/normal/inevitable/unchangeable
i mean: families schools marriage religion governments)
all yearn for boy babies
who are then allowed/encouraged/programmed to be
active   assertive   independent   inventive
while little girls are allowed/encouraged/programmed to be
passive   compliant   dependent   submissive
and of course smiling
even today
even in parts of our 'civilised' world
even within our families   our classrooms our workplaces
                our fun places our jokes   our literature
                our art forms   our psyches

why is this so?
it need not be
and was not always thus

why are so many many women
in mental hospitals/on tranquillisers or anti depressants/
undergoing psychotherapy or marriage counselling?

why are terms like
effeminate/mama's boy/mother's darling/petticoat/powder
puff/
pouffe/queen/old woman/sissy/weak sister/womanish
considered by men and even boys
grave insults?

why are terms like
baggage/bawd/bitch/broad/cat/chick/concubine/cow/
crumpet/crone/dame/dog/doll/drab/dyke/filly/fishwife/
floozy/frail/goat/goose/harlot/harridan/hellcat/hen/
hooker/hussy/hysteric/jade/jailbait/jezebel/lamb/lay/
lesser man/lesbian/loose/madam/minxmoll/mouse/
mutton/nag/nymph/paramour/pick up/piece/pussy/
scarlet women/sex pot/shiksa/shrew/skirt/siren/slag/
slattern/slut/sow/spinster/street walker/strumpet/tail/tart/
tease/temptress/tomato trollop/vamp/vampire/vixen/
victory girl/virago/wanton/weaker sex/wench/whore/
witch/and many many more used contemptuously
towards women
when they might be
accepting   affirming   affectionate epithets?

why must male pronouns
speak for all of us:
            brotherhood of man/manliness/mankind
            chairman/craftsman/and many many more

and be taken so seriously they indicate
all humankind
yet if we said,
            sisterhood of women/womankind/herstory

we'd be laughed at/ignored/labelled
            eccentric
            frivolous
            frustrated
            humourless
            menopausal
            neurotic
            over sensitive
            perverse

> relentless
> rigid
> sick
> stupid
> twisted
> unstable
> warped

or just plain crazy

when can we break our
   silence   invisibility   passivity
and try to de condition ourselves
though we'll risk
rejection   revilement   isolation   incarceration
by most men
and many many women

how soon?

Astra, 1985

Exercise

This exercise has to do with naming. You might want to think about parts of the body, or words used to describe your relationships with others, or perhaps the invisibility of those relationships. Many of us feel uncomfortable with words like 'vagina' and though some women find it a simple matter to use the word 'cunt', others do not. 'Blood related' is a term that describes the connection between one family member and another, but what if you have a close relationship with a child or another adult that falls outside the usual categories of mother, sister, aunt, cousin, daughter or niece? How are you then described? If you live with someone you love and that relationship is sexual how do you define that other person if you are not husband and wife? These questions create much debate among women when talking about language and how it affects us.

To explain further I will tell you about one workshop I did with a group of women where one whole day's work was devoted to women and language. Participants worked in four small groups having first defined an area of interest. This meant that two groups worked on main parts of the body and the other two groups sought to come up with words to describe their relationships with 'significant others'.

The first two groups came up with one word each to replace 'vagina'.

Group one chose the word 'coombe'. As many of the women came from Devon they were familiar with this local word meaning deep-sided valley and thought it a positive word to use. It took two hours to settle on this word.

Group two chose the word 'yoni'. Although I've been told since that this is not a new word, I have yet to find it listed in an English dictionary, though the *Concise Macquarie Dictionary* (produced in Australia) does mention a similar word, 'yonnie', defining it as a stone, especially for throwing. Group 2 also spent two hours settling on their chosen word.

Group three explained their process as more like a 'consciousness-raising' discussion. They found the sharing of experiences and conclusions drawn helpful but admitted they felt daunted and unable to come up with *any* words to satisfy their purposes. 'Co-parent' was a term they agreed was in common usage and some women in the group said that they did use this word but found it lacked a vital, undefined 'something'.

Group four set themselves the task early on of finding a word to replace 'lover'. They felt 'partner' was too businesslike and 'lover' had a sexual meaning that was not always applicable. Amid much laughter and pooh-poohing of suggested words they reported back, with broad grins, that the word they had come up with was 'attaché'. The members of the group agreed unanimously that none of them would ever think of using this word.

It can be a tall order to rename things. Don't expect it to be easy or quick. If you have not done anything like this before it may also be preferable to work with a friend or group. Discussion about words and about life experience of language terms is useful and if you get pleasure out of this sort of challenge science fiction is a genre where there is unlimited scope for the invention of new words.

There is one other word I heard for the first time on the day of the Women and Language workshop. A woman told us of her invented word 'perp', which she used especially with her children to describe *any* sound or smell that came from *any* bodily orifice. In polite company she felt quite able to ask whether they'd *perped* without feeling concern or embarrassment about what others might think. I was so delighted with 'perp' that I adopted it immediately. Do you have any words that are unique to you and yours? Sometimes a 'family' word can be a misspelling or mis-pronunciation of another word. My mother would often say to one or other of her daughters, 'Don't you act obstropolis with me, young lady.' It was only a few years ago that I realized the word my mother thought she was using was 'obstreperous'. Comparing the two I think I prefer my mother's version.

Monique Wittig and Sande Zeig, in their book *Lesbian Peoples, Material for a Dictionary,* comment on the word 'dictionary': 'The dictionary is, however, only a rough draft' (Wittig and Zeig, 1980, p. 43). That's a good thought, isn't it?

Notes

1 For a fuller account see Jane Mills, *Womanwords,* Longman, Harlow, Essex, 1989, pp. 123–27.
2 Jane Mills, ibid. p. 124.
3 Barbara G. Walker, *The Women's Encyclopaedia of Myths and Secrets,* Harper & Row, San Francisco, 1983, p. 378.
4 From Arthur Evans, *Witchcraft and the Gay Counterculture,* Fag Rag Books, Boston, 1978.

Sources

Astle, Cedric, *How Good is Your English?* Elliot Right Way Books, Surrey, England, 1979.
Layton Schapira, Laurie, *The Cassandra Complex, Living with Disbelief,* Inner City Books, Toronto, Canada, 1988.
Wittig, Monique & Zeig, Sande, *Lesbian Peoples, Material for a Dictionary,* Virago, London, 1980.

Further reading

Adams, Carol & Laurikietis, Rae, *The Gender Trap,* Virago, 1976.
Goldfield, Bina, *The Eman(fem)cipated English,* Westover Press, New York, 1983.
Haden Elgin, Suzette, *Native Tongue,* The Women's Press, London, 1985.
Kramarae, Cheris & Triechler, Paula, *A Feminist Dictionary,* Pandora, 1985.
Miller, Casey & Swift, Kate, *The Handbook of Non-Sexist Writing,* The Women's Press, London, 1981.
Spender, Dale, *Man Made Language,* Routledge & Kegan Paul, London, 1980.
Zimmer Bradley, Marion, *The Firebrand,* Michael Joseph, London, 1988.

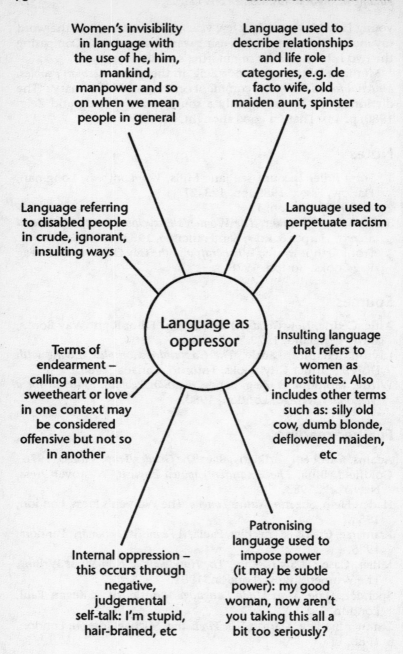

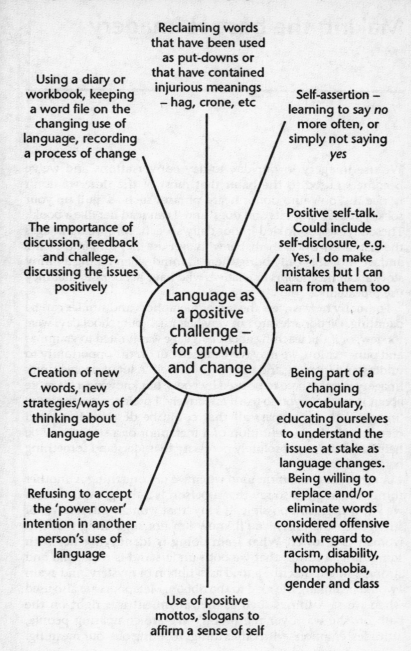

Reclaiming words that have been used as put-downs or that have contained injurious meanings – hag, crone, etc

Using a diary or workbook, keeping a word file on the changing use of language, recording a process of change

Self-assertion – learning to say *no* more often, or simply not saying *yes*

The importance of discussion, feedback and challege, discussing the issues positively

Positive self-talk. Could include self-disclosure, e.g. Yes, I do make mistakes but I can learn from them too

Language as a positive challenge – for growth and change

Creation of new words, new strategies/ways of thinking about language

Being part of a changing vocabulary, educating ourselves to understand the issues at stake as language changes. Being willing to replace and/or eliminate words considered offensive with regard to racism, disability, homophobia, gender and class

Refusing to accept the 'power over' intention in another person's use of language

Use of positive mottos, slogans to affirm a sense of self

Making the best of imagery

We use imagery in our day-to-day conversations and we've become so used to the habit that most of the time we don't notice it. You've no doubt heard phrases such as 'pull up your socks', 'it's raining cats and dogs' and 'I can read her like a book'. These sayings, sprinkled in our daily speech, conjure up images the first time we hear them, but with over-use they turn into clichés and we probably only bring them to mind when telling a funny story about neighbours or relatives who have pet phrases that they use repeatedly.

For many new writers the use of metaphors and similes can be daunting. Dictionaries are not very helpful. If our school days were too few, or if the teaching about language was limited to grammar and punctuation, we may have missed out on the opportunity to understand imagery and how to use it well. A lot of people think imagery is only there to be used by poets, but knowing a bit more about it can help you to use it effectively. I prefer to use the word 'imagery' to encompass all that could be described as word pictures. Having a definition of a metaphor or a simile may be helpful but it isn't absolutely necessary to understand something before we use it.

A *metaphor* is the term used when we say one thing is another thing. We might also say that a person is a thing, even though we know that isn't possible. If I say 'that woman was a tower of strength in the crisis' you'll know I'm not suggesting that this woman is a tower. What I am doing is identifying her with something, a tower, that we both understand is rock solid and strong. I might describe a road as 'a ribbon of mystery' and again I would be linking the road to the ribbon. Metaphors are also used when we says things such as 'her argument was right on the ball' or 'she was over the moon'. We are comparing people, attitudes, emotions with other things to 'bring out' our meaning.

When we use a *simile*, which is a type of metaphor, we are directly comparing a person or thing with something else: 'The small child hung her head like a gas balloon on its string.' Here, the child is being compared with a gas balloon. Similes are inevitably preceded by the words 'like' or 'as'.

- She was as fierce as a lion
- She acted like a bull in a china shop

An *idiom* is best described as a word or group of words where the intended meaning is different from the words used. *How do you do?* is an idiom. We might well ask 'how do you do what?' The words are not really asking a question about how we do something, they are used as part of an introduction ritual, particularly when meeting someone for the first time in situations that tend to be more formal than informal. The media is fond of creating and using idioms. In the early 1980s, at the time of riots in England, various council estates in both the north and the south were referred to as 'no-go' areas. Here, the meaning conveyed is not specific but we get the intended message just the same.

The rhetoric of state

Politicians use imagery to make their meaning understandable to a greater number of people. We have become so used to hearing metaphors and similes on radio and television and to reading them in newspapers and magazines that we tend not to notice how often they are used. I've listed a number of sentences here that have been collected from newspapers over the last decade. Many of them are sure to be familiar to you.

- We are fighting the war against inflation.
- We're experiencing a new bout of inflation.
- We have to fight unemployment but let me tell you, we are winning.
- Recent figures have shown a healthy trend.
- Let us resolve to heal the wounds of a divided nation.
- Our economy is weathering stormy waters.
- Some things will get worse before they get better. We did not promise you instant sunshine.
- The British government has zeroed in on unemployment as its number one target.

- He believed Mrs Thatcher could be persuaded to step aboard
  the European train of monetary union.
- Last month he criticised the PM for not being in the 'driver's
  cab' but still loitering without intent at the ticket office.

What do you think we can learn from this use of imagery? What
if we were to divide the types of image into different categories?
How many categories would there be? 'In sickness and health'
might be one category. The idea of seeing the nation as a body
and the well-being of the state in terms of sickness and health is
not new. Shakespeare's plays, for example, are often littered with
metaphors about the nation as a diseased body. Metaphors about
violence and war are also favourites for political rhetoric. What
others would you wish to make?

If we are asked to think of inflation as an illness then we are
being invited to view the government as a doctor who can make
a diagnosis and come up with a cure. If their treatment works then
perhaps they'll tell us that the economy is recovering and can now
sip a little soup? If, on the other hand, we are asked to see
inflation as *the enemy*, a foe that must be fought, then we are being
asked to accept the government as our defender, standing between
us and that much hated enemy, inflation, who is out to get us all.
Will the government be able to protect us? Either image suggests
that we, the public, are powerless to do anything about anything.
Our role would appear to be that of anxious observers, waiting on
the sidelines and hoping the politicians can do what they say.

The implications of such imagery are wider than the simple communication of ideas. If we accept these conveyed messages too
readily we can be conditioned to accept violence, war and hard
times as inevitable. By developing an awareness of how imagery
is used in the media (by politicians in particular), I have been able
to stand back from the implied meaning, having more control over
my own responses. This has been both useful in my work and
entertaining – it's amusing to note how fantastic and bizarre
some of the images can get.

The mixed metaphor can also be a source of enjoyment. A
mixed metaphor is when two images that do not fit together well
are used in the same sentence or paragraph. Here are a few taken
from *Mix Me A Metaphor* by Jeremy Lawrence:

> We've got the ship of state moving and have now set it on
> its feet.

Along the untrodden paths of the future I can see the footprints of an unseen hand.

If those strikers were alive today they'd turn over in their graves.

Mr Speaker, I smell a rat. I see him forming in the air and darkening the sky. But I'll nip him in the bud I assure you. (Said in Parliament)

(Lawrence, 1972)

Get the idea? Keeping a collection of metaphorical quotes can be of great value. Not only will you gain insights about their widespread use but you will also become knowledgeable about where and when to use them yourself. If you wish to divide into different categories the types of imagery used, this is best done right from the start. You will note how the same images turn up again and again. Sometimes an image can be expressed in the strongest terms – often inappropriately to what is being discussed. For example, this quote came from a Tory MP in the 1980s: 'That notion will have to be laid to rest. The government will have to drive a stake through its heart, the country needs to know exactly how the PM feels about it.' The Conservative government was in trouble and scoring poorly in the opinion polls. The Deputy Prime Minister had resigned a few days before and the question of greater involvement with Europe was said to be dividing the party 'right down the middle'. In keeping with that uncertain mood, the statements of Tory politicians became fierce and hostile. I wondered if the 'stake in the heart' was meant for a *specific person* rather than a general criticism of the government's policy.

Critical examination of the political use of imagery increased during the years of Margaret Thatcher's premiership. Melanie McFadyean and Margaret Renn wrote a book, *Thatcher's Reign – A Bad Case of the Blues*, pointing out her adeptness at using metaphors:

The difficulty is when one department is a good boy and keeps within its spending and others don't then the department who are being good boys have to suffer for those who aren't. *(The Director,* November 1980)

We will not tolerate Britain becoming the poor relation of Europe. *(Sunday People,* 3 June 1979)

Our country is weathering stormy waters. We may have different ideas on how to navigate them, but we sail the same ocean in the same ship. (Conservative Party Conference, 17 October 1981)

Iron entered my soul. You need a touch of steel. Otherwise you become like India rubber. (BBC Radio 4, 12 November 1980)

There is no safe corner where the inefficient can shelter. (Hansard, 12 November 1981)

(McFadyean & Renn, 1984)

Homely metaphors, such as a description of government departments as 'good boys' convey a sense of practicality and good sense with a headmistress's authority. Perhaps this use of metaphor partly explained Margaret Thatcher's populist appeal. Metaphors make speech memorable.

Creating our own

George Orwell once said 'By using stale metaphors, similes and idioms you save much mental effort, at the cost of leaving your meaning vague, not only for your reader but for yourself too.' Below is a list of metaphorical quotes from women, taken from a variety of sources. I don't think you'll find the meaning vague in any of them:

It is better to die on your feet than to live on your knees.
(Dolores Ibarruri, Anti-Fascist Spanish leader)

How can I fight an enemy who has outposts in my mind?
(Susan Griffin, American writer)

Lift and climb.
(Motto used by the National Association of Coloured Women which had its founding conference in 1896)

Revolution is the festival of the oppressed.
(Germaine Greer, Australian writer)

Our child will not be raised in tissue paper! ... We don't want her even to hear the word princess.
(Juliana, Princess of the Netherlands)

Wit has truth in it; wisecracking is simply callisthenics with words.
(Dorothy Parker, American writer)

The courage of men is an intoxication of high temperature, but women's is a deliberation of cold blood, and the more deadly.
(Miles Franklin, Australian writer)

I've come to realise that in my own life astrology is not a crutch or a cop-out, but rather a safety belt that helps me get over the bumps of life.
(Tiffany Holmes, astrologist)

Singin' about a Revolution, because we're talkin' about
a change
It's more than just air pollution
Well, you know, you got to clean your brain.
The only way that we can stand in fact
Is when you get your foot off our back.
Get. Off. Our Back.
(Nina Simone, American singer/songwriter)

A woman without a man is like a fish without a bicycle.
(Gloria Steinem, American writer)

War is menstruation envy.
(Australian T-shirt quote)

What women do is survive. We live by ones and twos in the chinks of your world-machine.
From the story 'The Women Men Don't See' written by James Tiptree Jr (alias Alice B. Sheldon))

I haven't known any open marriages, though quite a few have been ajar.
(Zsa Zsa Gabor, American actress)

Exercise

With this exercise I distribute cards to group participants, the sort that are used as business cards. This requires each person to write small and to limit her words to the space provided. Both sides of each card are used. The cards are placed in a paper bag or some other suitable receptacle. From here they can be distributed, one to each member of the group, and read anonymously. If you are doing this exercise at home you might wish to limit the space on which you're permitted to write. If it's a group exercise mark one side of the card A, the other side B.

On the A side write the words *I am* . Now use a metaphor to write about yourself and/or how you are feeling right now. There is no need to reveal anything about yourself that you'd prefer not to – each person can choose the level at which she wants to express herself.

The second side of the card can now be used to describe a place where you were brought up, where you have lived for a time, or where you live at present. If you lived in Glasgow, say, you'd write down 'Glasgow is ...' and from that beginning go on to describe the city you know in your own way.

I come from Sydney and this is what I have written about the city in which I grew up:

Sydney is a bawdy lady spreading her large generous figure around the harbour, along the coast, up into the hills, in the most brazen fashion. Unmindful of those who'd point or stare, she's a real shocker, I can tell you.

Having used the metaphorical image, now work with similes. This time you might choose to write about yourself at some past period of your life, or to write again about a place where you have lived or are living now. Your opening words will begin,

'I was like ... ',
'London is like ... '.

Confining yourself to limited space can be helpful in two ways: first, if imagery is new to you and your confidence still hesitant you will feel more willing to attempt the exercise knowing that you are not required to write very much. Second, the limited space can have the effect of making you want to go further, to see more and more words beyond what will fit on the card. Resist this temptation if you can, at least in the beginning, for to extend the image requires skill that will come with greater experience of using imagery frequently. If you share what you have written anonymously within the group you will be able to trust the feedback more. At the end of the exercise each person can choose to say what she has written, if that has been part of the agreed contract at the beginning.

From these exercises you can go on to use the same principle to write about other people in your life, other places you have known. Keep the beginning of each piece of writing as simple as possible:

Perth is ...
I am ...
Life is ...
Perth is like ...
I am like ...
Life is like ...

The following quotes were written by a group of women attending a creative writing course in Liverpool, run by a local writer and playwright, Linda McGowan. I was invited to visit the group for one session on imagery. It was agreed beforehand that any material produced during that session would be written anonymously:

- I am a hedgehog full of prickles; on the defensive and inclined to hibernate.
- I am a sandwich filling.
- I am other people's tower of strength and my own worst enemy.
- I am a mixed metaphor – a contradiction in terms.
- I am a play in three acts; Child me, Alice me, Mountain Girl, fair and free. Grown-up now, facade of professional woman ... child lurking within.
- I am a balloon full of gas, never knowing when to stop, and also full of air. I go up in the sky. Some people like to ride on my Uncle Wobble who is a barrage balloon. But we always come down with a bang.
- Liverpool is the muddied pool of life, where oily rainbows float and glide, and innocent wonder slips and slides in the minds of watchful wastrels, on wishy-washy days.
- Liverpool is like your favourite chair, comfortable and cosy.
- Liverpool ... mother of multitudes, tired sometimes, even wicked, but still able to put on the glad rags and party with the best of them.
- Liverpool ... a long way from the cottage loaf: prim and proper, incestuous place of my birth.

What other things can you describe in this way? Friendship? Love affairs? Countries?

I do feel it is a good idea to share what we have written with others and to have them share with us. There are positive benefits in having and giving feedback though this is not so true of other subject areas in writing projects. You may be surprised at how powerful or poignant your material is in the eyes of others. You can have the immediacy of knowing what else you could have done. Here's an example from Monica Baldwin, describing a Belgian convent in which she was a nun for twenty-seven years:

> Built originally round a small open courtyard, it had grown with the centuries till it lay like a long, grey, sleeping lizard, clutching two other courtyards and a cloister garth between its claws. In winter, the cold cut into you like a knife. The pale light crept in through deep-silled, leaded windows and

was frozen immediately into the same wan blue as the white-washed walls. You might have been standing in the heart of an iceberg, so strange it was, so silent, so austere.

(Baldwin, 1987, p. 36)

Exercise

Animal imagery

This exercise can be useful not only for writing but also in a therapeutic sense, for thinking about relationships. Think of a person you know and then think of an animal with which you could compare that person. Then think of a second animal for yourself. What is the relationship between the two animals and what does this tell you about the bond between you and the other person?

Two women who were part of a group I worked with in Devon over a period of years came to this exercise with unexpected relish and excitement. Our workshop session was about mothers and I was using the exercise to further our exploration of mother/daughter relationships. The first woman saw her mother as a hedgehog. When I asked her what she saw herself as, her answer was prompt – she was another hedgehog. The second woman thought her mother was as stubborn as a donkey. She described herself as a snappy little dog, barking at the heels of the donkey, trying to get it to move. You can see immediately that there are insights to be gained from doing this exercise – it can provide another way of looking at relationships, with the added possibility of working to improve them.

Later extend your imagery to fill a whole page and use diary entries to say how you are feeling and what you would compare yourself to right now. Do you feel as deep as a river? As lonely as a mountain climber on a solo trip up a high cliff face? Or perhaps you feel like a gurgling stream? As vulnerable as a soufflé? As wary as a young deer drinking from a pool in the early dawn?

A sustained metaphor occurs when a collection of connected images, usually under one heading or theme, continues for several paragraphs or pages. The following piece, called 'The Characteristics of a Rock Pool', makes use of the sustained metaphor. It was written by Emma Milliken who attended a writing course I taught a few years ago at Silver Moon Bookshop in London. Emma kindly gave her permission for an extract to be included here:

Do you see that rock pool over there – yes, that one. That's me. Really it is – well it could be. If I stand over it I see myself reflected in it. No, don't come too close, not yet.

All that clear moving water is me, rushing down those little waterfalls, cascading over rocks and stones, dripping from those jutting-out bits. Even that there in the corner – the part that doesn't seem to be moving, that doesn't seem affected by the movement.

See how beautiful it is. It looks like it hides a thousand secrets in its depths but on top it glistens. Look – where the sun hits it – it dances with the coming of spring. It's muddy on the bottom – don't disturb it. It spoils the clarity if you stir it up. There are probably all sorts of nasty things under the mud.

Feel it, it's very cold just now, but in summer it is warm enough to paddle. In summer if you should touch it then it would caress you with warmth.

It's not empty you know. It's not just a rock pool. If you look you can see all those different things – they're part of me. Those minnows there, the tiny ones. They're always there – darting around, in and out – just where you don't expect them …

Finding new ways to see and express ourselves can seem daunting at first. I sometimes begin a session with this analogy: I ask students to imagine I have invited them to my home for a buffet meal – in Australia we would say smorgasbord. On the table in my imagined dining room they will see a variety of foods, some of which they may never have seen or tasted before. In such situations we act politely, a few spoonfuls of this and a little of that on to our plates, and we would not dream of spitting out the food or making ill-mannered comments about how strange the first taste might be. We know that some foods demand an acquired taste, while others may be enjoyed and savoured immediately. This, I explain, is the way I would like them to think about the work we are about to do, only it won't be food that's on offer but ideas, different ways of looking at things, using imagery, allegory, and so on.

An allegory is a story or tale that is understood symbolically rather than literally, like biblical stories, fairy tales and fables. In one of Sylvia Plath's early poems, 'The Lady and the Earthenware Head', the speaker wants to get rid of a clay model of her own head. She cannot find a safe place to put it. She thinks of the ash heap but no, it might be stolen; she drops it in a lake but it comes to the surface 'lewdly beckoning'. At last she wedges it in the branches of a tree but this turns out to have haunting consequences for her. The head will not be done away with and the more the woman struggles to be free of it, the more it returns. As Jacqueline

Rose explains in her book, *The Haunting of Sylvia Plath*, 'The effigy haunts the original. It loves and terrifies the very being it was intended to represent' (Rose, 1991, p. 2). Was Sylvia Plath writing allegorically and using the head as a means of talking about her conflict with herself? Can you think of a story that might be told more effectively via a description of something else?

Other useful bits of language

Alliteration

Alliteration is another way of facilitating meaning in a very immediate way. Newspapers frequently rely on alliterative headlines to attract attention. When a number of words, each beginning with the same letter or sound, are used in a phrase, sentence or paragraph, this is called alliteration. It can be difficult to involve every single word, particularly as a sentence gets longer and longer. In Australia in the 1930s, with divorce rare and new, spicy stories appeared in disreputable newspapers with headlines similar to this one:

Blonde Bombshell from Bondi gets the Boot

Recently, a British writers' magazine, *Writer's News*, held a competition in which readers were invited to enter the longest alliterative sentence they could create. To whet their appetites, readers were challenged to beat the length of this one:

Brilliantly building breathtaking breaks, Bernard brought both billiard balls briefly before the baulk.[1]

'She sells seashells by the seashore' is another example. You'll note that there are two words here that do not begin with 'S' but the sentence is still alliterative. It's common to find two words used close together beginning with the same letter: 'trick or treat' and 'stem to stern', for example. I use an alliteration exercise with groups in opening rounds, and always stress the importance of having fun. I would not use this exercise the first time the group met, but once people have had a little time to get to know each other it can have great value. I have found that it raises the energy level and makes for a relaxed atmosphere, as well as providing an opportunity for a good chuckle. Participants can use their own names (or someone else's if they prefer) as the starting point. I could introduce myself like this: 'I'm Pearlie and I pick pink petunias in the park by the pond.' Try it out for yourself using your own name. Again, I stress the importance of seeing the funny side of things for it makes light work of the task and reduces any pressure to perform or to 'get it right'. The discreet use of alliteration can be very effective in emphasizing both the words and the rhythm of language, as can assonance.

Assonance

Though not as widely known, assonance is a technique similar to alliteration. It uses the repetition of vowel sounds that are close to each other, such as: 'The sound resounds around the icy water underground.' Let's look again at *Blonde Bombshell from Bondi gets the Boot.* Not only is this alliterative but it also uses assonance – the middle sounds of the words, 'on', 'om', 'on' – to stress the point. It is worth mentioning here that one of the best ways to hear the rhythm and effect of your writing, as well as to check that your punctuation is right, is to read it aloud to yourself.

Onomatopoeia (on-o-mat-o-pe-a)

Lastly there's onomatopoeia, which is a tricky, long-winded word for the simple meaning of words that *sound* like their meaning: 'whispers', 'rumble', 'crash' and the most obvious 'buzz'. Again, their use emphasizes meaning.

Take any piece of writing you have done and look to see how often you have used any of these effects and you will probably be surprised to find that you use them frequently.

How to improve language skills

You might want to work on broadening your vocabulary or generally improving your language skills. There are lots of fun things you can do to help. Crosswords, for example, help to increase the vocabulary and so do other games, such as Scrabble, particularly for those high-scoring words. A thesaurus is handy for finding synonyms (a word or phrase with a very similar meaning to another word or phrase in the same language) for when you want to say the same thing but in a different way, and it's always useful to have a dictionary close by to check on precise definitions.[2]

I use more than one dictionary as a means of cross-referencing definitions. I also refer to more recently published wordbooks compiled by women, such as *A Feminist Dictionary* and *Womanwords.* Other dictionaries I use frequently include *A Dictionary of Australian Colloquialisms, Webster's Treasury of Synonyms, Antonyms and Homonyms,* and *The Penguin Wordmaster*

Dictionary that combines the elements of thesaurus, usage guide, lexicon and historical survey. Despite the fancy titles, these books are not expensive. Seasonal and special sale prices, jumble sales and bargain basements are rich sources of such books. Don't limit yourself to the English language either – look out for books that list the words of other languages such as Gaelic or Yiddish, or phrase books that will introduce you to other languages. My collection includes Gaelic, Spanish, German, Italian, Yiddish, Cockney and Australian slang, and two valuable books written by A. W. Reed: *Aboriginal Place Names* and *Aboriginal Words of Australia*. Then there are the odd books that defy simple categories. My most recent 'find', *Surnames as a Science*, was published in 1884 and written by an MP, Robert Ferguson. I bought it at a very cheap price in a second-hand bookshop. It gives a comprehensive list of surnames and details about the root origins of names from around the globe. I also have books on punctuation, quotations and proverbs. It's worth checking out books aimed at older children, and if spelling or punctuation is a weak area of yours, books directed at this age group have an uncomplicated, no-nonsense style that makes them easier to use and understand than the adult versions. Ward Lock Educational publishers have a good series of educational titles and I've listed three relevant books from that series at the end of this chapter.

Word association exercises, using an unfamiliar randomly chosen word as a starting point, and/or writing a small story about that one word, can be fun and a helpful way of expanding your vocabulary further. For many years after I left school I borrowed copies of the *Reader's Digest* monthly magazine from the local doctor's surgery, eager to read and puzzle over the regular feature that was headed 'Towards More Picturesque Speech'. Newspapers and magazines may include small items about word meanings and there are word-game books, with titles like 'Test Your Word Power'. The use of language is an ongoing process of challenge, but if you love words, the sound of them, if you delight in using them differently, making few do the work of many, finding ways around repetition of certain words and phrases, then it's all just a part of the joy and excitement of writing.

What to avoid

When we first start to write we can tend to over-describe everything through the use of adjectives and adverbs. And there are some adjectives and adverbs that always seem to go with certain things: 'sparkling eyes' and 'crumbling ruins', 'sleeping soundly' and 'groping blindly'. An instructive first exercise in self-editing is to rewrite a piece taking out all the adjectives and adverbs and then putting back only those that are absolutely necessary. By leaving things out you can achieve a clarity that is quite different from the original. If you would like a further description of editing, see the chapter 'Techniques: understanding and practice'.

Clichés

Some adjectives and adverbs have become so over-used that they are now clichés. Despite the number of times we toss the word 'cliché' around, there seems still to be some confusion about the difference between a cliché and a stereotype. The word 'cliché' comes from the French verb *clicher* meaning 'to stereotype'. I have looked more closely at stereotype in the 'Techniques: understanding and practice' chapter. A cliché is a word, phrase, clause, or sentence that through over-use has become ineffective. Our daily conversations and those of other people are inevitably going to be sprinkled with clichés, some of which are unavoidable, inevitable and now acceptable. The word 'incidentally' is a cliché; so is the phrase 'a matter of fact'. When was the last time you heard someone say 'by the way', 'on the other hand', 'by the same token'? Last week? Yesterday? An hour ago? It isn't hard to see why clichés become overworked, is it?

None of us can hope to avoid clichés altogether. We rely on them to make things easier. Here are some more:

- I was 'hot under the collar'.
- I thought going to see her was 'a step in the right direction'.
- In 'her heart of hearts' I knew she did really care.
- 'It stands to reason' that you'd see it that way.
- He 'smokes like a house on fire'.
- I went to see a friend and we've decided to 'bury the hatchet'.

Any of the clichés above communicate a great deal about the person using them. We can hide behind clichés to avoid saying something direct or deep. There are some people who believe that it is an impoverished intellect that relies on clichés. What do you think? Is it a lack of imagination? Evidence of a lazy conversationalist?

I prefer to think that there are times when a cliché can be used to good effect. In the not too distant past, husbands were permitted to beat their wives with a stick no thicker than their thumbs and it is from this practice that the term 'rule of thumb' comes. I once used this term in a book and it was only after the book had been published that a friend pointed out its origin. I was appalled. I had believed, in some hazy fashion, that there was a connection with painting, where the painter holds the thumb upwards and looks along the line of the thumb to gain a sense of perspective. Though I would never consider using *that* cliché again, it still worked quite well in the context of what I was writing about.

Notes

1   *Writer's News* is a monthly magazine containing information about competitions and openings for material. It also includes articles on different aspects of writing. Subscriptions can be sent to Stonehart Subscription Services, Hainault Road, Little Heath, Romford, England, RM6 5NP.
2   Antonyms are words with opposite meanings. Homonyms are words that sound alike, but that are spelled differently and have different meanings.

Sources

Baldwin, Monica, *I Leap Over the Wall*, Hamish Hamilton, London, 1987.

Lawrence, Jeremy, *Mix Me A Metaphor*, Gentry Books, London, 1972.

McFadyean, Melanie & Renn, Margaret, *Thatcher's Reign – A Bad Case of the Blues*, The Hogarth Press, Chatto & Windus, 1984.

Rose, Jacqueline, *The Haunting of Sylvia Plath*, Virago, London, 1991.

Further reading

Adam, James S., *Gaelic Wordbook*, W & R Chambers, Edinburgh, 1992.

Bickerton, Anthea, *Australian/English*, Abson Books, Bristol, 1981.

James, Michael, *Yiddish-English Word Book*, Abson Books, Bristol, 1984.

Jones, Jack (ed.), *Rhyming Cockney Slang*, Abson Books, Bristol, 1982.

Kramarae, Cheris & Treichler, Paula, *A Feminist Dictionary*, Pandora Press, London, 1985.

Minard, Brian, *Lern Yourself Scouse* (sic), Scouse Press, Liverpool, 1972.

Reed, A. W., *Aboriginal Place Names*, Reed Books, NSW, Australia, 1988.

Reed, A. W., *Aboriginal Words of Australia*, Reed Books, NSW, Australia, 1987.

Ross, Norman, *What's the Difference? – American/British Dictionary*, Hutchinson, London, 1974.

Ward Lock Educational, *The Old-Fashioned Rules of Punctuation*, *The Old-Fashioned Rules of Grammar Book*, *The Old-Fashioned Rules of Spelling Book*, London.

Webster's Treasury of Synonyms, Antonyms and Homonyms, Avenel Books, New York.

Telling tales: the short story

Telling tales, fables or parables, creating fictional worlds or retelling events that have developed a mythology of their own, is something people have done for thousands of years. In many countries and cultures a strong oral tradition still exists in which stories are passed down from one generation to the next. The concentration span of young children is well suited to the brief telling of a tale, and childhood years can be recalled easily and fondly by adults when they start to talk about fictional stories that were once read to them, or stories that have become family lore. *Tell me what you were like when you were little*, children ask. What was it like in the olden days?

What makes a story short?

'Short story' is a seemingly obvious term for fictional writing that is shorter than a novel. The short story as a specific genre and as we know it today in women's magazines, in collected anthologies, and from the radio, was developed in the nineteenth century. The following word count categories are used as a guideline:

- short story – under 7,500 words
- novelette – 7,500 to 17,500 words
- novella – 17,500 to 40,000 words
- novel – over 40,000 words

Short stories can be as short as the 150-word fables written by Suniti Namjoshi in *The Blue Donkey Fables*, while others are as long as the 22,000-word stories in Isak Dinesen's collection *Seven Gothic Tales* which are defined as 'novellas'. There are no strict rules for how long a piece of writing should be.

Maybe you've assumed that writing a short story will be easier than writing a novel. In one sense this is true. An obvious advantage is in the reworking of material, because the shorter the work the more focused your attention will be. This fact alone makes short stories a good practice area for beginning writers. However, a reader who may tolerate a loose plot or frustrating elements of characterization in a novel (because they might be enjoying the novel for other reasons) may not tolerate such faults in a short story. Short stories are consumed rapidly and are therefore under closer scrutiny than a novel is likely to be. How to instil just the exact measure of plot with precisely the correct amount of tension and timing? Tales of horror, mystery and suspense are quite suited to the short story format because the momentum need only be maintained for a relatively short time. The length of the short story form might seem an advantage but it can also be a test of how to convey many things in a few words. Becoming aware of what is contained in this discipline is part of the process that evolves as we gain greater writing experience. And don't forget that reading other writers' work – in order to see the flexibility of the form – can make that learning process simpler and less like an obstacle course.

In the short story there is room for invention and experimentation. You might not want to 'tell a story' in any literal way, with a 'proper' beginning, middle and end. You might choose instead to write more specifically about a particular moment, or about a recent conversation (one you had, or perhaps one you overheard in a café or on a bus); you might want to capture a sharp truth that is instantly significant to you, or experiment with a tantalizing fragment. Realistic settings might not be appropriate, but that doesn't matter; it's the urge to work with an idea, however small, that will get you started. Perhaps you want to explore different aspects of the same character, trying out different vantage points. Your starting point could result in one or more short stories that could also take you somewhere else, unexpectedly. Short stories can and often do become novels further down the track.

Rules?

Chekhov, along with Edgar Allan Poe, has been credited with the 'founding' of the short story form as we know it today. It was Edgar Allan Poe who pronounced in 1842 that the short story should aim for a 'single effect', a 'unity of impression'. This is probably useful as a general rule and most writers of the genre follow it. There is no space to develop plots of soap opera proportions, with multiple characters, complex interrelationships and in-depth examinations of contemporary issues. What it comes down to is an economic use of words and suggestion.

A second 'rule' of the short story is that it should deal essentially with a 'moment of crisis'. The word 'crisis' here can include a moment of change, or realization. In this extract from Katherine Mansfield's 'The Dill Pickle' a couple are meeting after some years of separation:

> 'Ah, no. You hate the cold ...'
> 'Loathe it.' She shuddered. 'And the worst of it is that the older one grows ...'
> He interrupted her. 'Excuse me,' and tapped on the table for the waitress. 'Please bring some coffee and cream.' To her: 'You are sure you won't eat anything? Some fruit, perhaps. The fruit here is very good.'
> 'No, thanks. Nothing.'
> 'Then that's settled.' And smiling just a hint too broadly he took up the orange again. 'You were saying – the older one grows–'
> 'The colder,' she laughed. But she was thinking how well she remembered that trick of his – the trick of interrupting her – and how it used to exasperate her six years ago. She used to feel then as though he, quite suddenly, in the middle of what she was saying, put his hand over her lips, turned from her, attended to something different, and then took his hand away, and with just the same slightly too broad smile, gave her his attention again ... Now we are ready. That is settled.
>
> (Mansfield, 1981, p. 168)

There is nothing very dramatic about this story, everything is muted, but the woman who initially has ambivalent feelings about this man and their relationship realizes in the course of this conversation what she had not fully grasped before, how utterly selfish he is. Katherine Mansfield is an expert at using seemingly insignificant detail to convey much deeper aspects of human relationships. At the same time, it is possible that the characters in the short story learn nothing, and the 'moment of realization' belongs to the reader – the author colludes with the reader in showing up, through use of irony, the character's lack of understanding or progress.

Ingredients

All aspects of fictional writing – character, plot, dialogue, theme, etc. – can be employed in the short story, and it can be told from a number of points of view. The form and the length will dictate to a certain extent how the story will be constructed. In a novel you could have pages and pages of description on just one character; in a short story a paragraph or even a few sentences might be all you can spare. This does not necessarily mean that the theme, the essence, has to be stated quickly or explicitly. On the contrary, the theme could emerge slowly or be left implied. Remember, too, there are always exceptions to the rule. Isak Dinesen's collection *Seven Gothic Tales*, for example, is made up of long stories constructed like Chinese boxes, stories within stories, where the past lives of the characters gradually emerge and knit together. We meander through a series of life histories.

Settings

A writer may use a particular setting or theme as a framework for a collection. Short story writer Jennifer Gubb, born in Devon, based her collection *The Open Road* on the rural setting with which she was familiar. Some of her stories focus on a specific rural activity, such as a girl's first killing of a hen in 'Blooding', in order to draw wider comparisons: 'Her thirteenth birthday was the day of her initiation into an adult world' (Gubb, 1983, p. 36). We are led to compare the girl's realization of one reality in life – you have to kill if you want to eat meat – with another – her own menstrual blood – an equally necessary physical transition from childhood to adolescence. Jennifer Gubb uses the particular, the rural, to place and explore some of the problems and emotions faced by women in a much wider context. The title story 'The Open Road', for example, uses the car as a literal means of women's emancipation, made more pronounced by the rural isolation. She also takes advantage of the characteristic dialogue of the region to give the stories a firmly realistic quality.

You might want to think about incidents from the past that could be utilized to fit a short story format. Is there a tale to be told about your first experience of menstruation? Are there memories from your adolescent years that you could write about? What age were you when you first felt the pull of sexual attraction? What did that feel like? Were there embarrassing or humorous moments that you chuckle about even now? Can you see ways of making such incidents into a story? What did you learn as you were growing up? If someone mentions schooldays what is it that you immediately think of? Do you remember what it feels like to be fifteen years old? Twelve? Ten? How far back can you go?

Another example of a writer using her strong cultural heritage is Moy McCrory, who was brought up in a working-class Catholic family in Liverpool. Many of the stories in her collection *The Water's Edge* dwell humorously on some of the absurd moments of childhood. She also brings out the difficulties and differences between religion, class and the role of women within this tight-knit community. Maeve Binchy arranged her first two collections (now available in one volume) around the London Underground, calling one book *Central Line* and the other *Victoria Line*. Each story is given the title of a tube station in London and this method works as a means of loosely framing the stories. Think about background and location, and how you can use them. Did you spend your childhood in one place or did you live in a variety of areas? Think about not only the places where you once lived but also about places you've visited. What characteristics can you remember?

The smallest fragment of thought – a left-over question from childhood, a half-remembered song or film, an item of clothing, a familiar object from your grandmother's kitchen – something so small and so faint is all that's needed to begin the journey into the depths of your own imagination. If you have an idea hang on to it as though it were a message in a bottle. Keep your mind open and flexible. Be prepared for the length of time this will take. Keep a notebook handy. Write whatever comes into your head. Don't push too hard for order, and don't think that everything has to make sense. Sometimes the greatest treasures are concealed in boxes that are hard to prise open; or the process might be like a series of Russian dolls, each phase giving way to another, with deeper meaning. Most important of all is to allow yourself sufficient time to think. Time is such a crucial factor, and the gestation period for creative work is likely to vary from one project to another.

Exercises

1   In fifty words characterize the place where you grew up. If you have done the earlier exercise with imagery about the place where you

were brought up (in the 'Making the best of imagery' chapter), use the material you produced there as a starting point.

2 In 500 words write a story about a four-year-old child walking to the park with her mother. Suddenly she finds herself alone. Where has her mother gone? Is this little girl lost? Maybe she isn't, but she might well feel that she is, her world turned upside down from one moment to the next. Is she scared or does she wander off happily?

First-person narrative can be particularly effective in putting you right in the picture, identifying with that little girl, momentarily *being* that child. You will have to think about language and sentence structure relevant to the age group. Monologue can be very powerful, ideal for reading aloud and also for radio.

Experimentation with this theme can mean that you write a succession of drafts. As you grow more confident with the editing aspect of your work (for a fuller discussion of editing see p. 60 in 'Techniques: understanding and practice') you will be able to pick out the word, phrase or sentence that simply does not belong.

Alternatively, you could use third-person narrative but still choose words and a sentence structure in keeping with the child's vocabulary. Often it is the reworking of material, the determination to 'try out' various options, that gives a writer the certain feeling that this way or that is the right approach for her.

3 In 1,000 words write an autobiographical reflection on your adolescence and then turn it into fiction, put it into the third person or tell it from another perspective such as that of a parent, relation or friend. When you've finished ask yourself what has been changed (and what have you learned) as a result of moving the perspective from one narrator to another?

A short story does not have to be written in one sitting. It is better to prepare a group of work sessions with a goal in mind than to strive for a deadline that might simply leave you feeling defeated and unhappy because you didn't achieve more. *Don't write a book, or even a chapter. Write a page, a paragraph, a line, an opening sentence, and make each sentence a brick that goes towards building a structure.*

I had two short stories published in 1985. The first, 'Strange Connie from Two Doors Down', I wrote as a form of therapy when an unresolved situation was hurting me to the point of distraction. I sat at my typewriter late one afternoon gripped by anger and frustration. It felt more like being sick than writing a story. Three hours later I was finished. I felt better immediately. Alice

Monroe once said that 'good writing is the best revenge'. I agree. From that day to this not one word of the story has been changed. It came out whole but I doubted its value when I wrote it because it took such a short time to write.[1]

The second story was my first attempt at writing science fiction. I began with a series of questions about pollution after listening to a radio programme on the environment. What would it be like when all the rivers were unusable, swollen with choking pollution? Would houses have to be modified to protect us from the effects of pollution? Would such measures include having to detoxify each room? How would that be done and how often? I raised my questions with a friend over dinner. We had a riotous evening, each wacky suggestion becoming more fantastic as we egged each other on about the changes we could imagine.

The story took a number of years to develop during which I continued to discuss the project with my friend. Though eventually the subject was dropped from our conversations I would always want to acknowledge how intrinsic a part of the process those discussions were. By this time I had a thick file of notes and was looking for a way into the story. On my way to work one morning, like a bolt from the blue, the opening sentences were right there in my head:

> Lucy could see it from her kitchen window. A huge spawning mass. Engorged with contamination and encrusted here and there with weeping scabs of rotting matter. From time to time another dying tree would succumb: the trunk submerging slowly with a faint, gurgling sound, leaving what remained of the foliage heavily draped with clusters of bubbles, thick with yeasty foam. It looked like some grotesque imitation of a well-decorated Christmas tree.
>
> (McNeill, 1985, p. 150)

What Lucy could see was the Hawkesbury River. I felt so inadequate each time I worked on that story – who did I think I was, attempting to write science fiction? And although I got through the first stages of plotting with some measure of satisfaction, I couldn't work out what the end would be. I struggled with this layered process, the seemingly endless questions, thinking out answers which usually led to further questions. Was the story about pollution? Yes, but more as a setting, a background context, than a theme. If people's lives in this not-too-distant future were to be restricted by the effects of pollution how would any government handle the situation? With limited resources wouldn't population size become a more crucial issue? Would that lead to more state control over women's fertility? Control and secrecy became linked in my mind. Would people be told what was going on? I suspected not. For some time my writing centred on note taking, just getting something down, then feeling stumped, unable to proceed and shoving the file away in a drawer for another month or so. My first ending had Lucy waking from a dream, and though I knew it was a cop-out it was as far as I could go at the time. Later, a writer friend accused me of conning the reader. I felt stung, my fragile confidence abruptly deflated. The doubts increased. Perhaps it was time to forget the whole thing? Oddly, I couldn't get the story out of my mind. What to do? I devised a number of exercises in which I wrote from Lucy's point of view. There was no incredible breakthrough, nothing dramatic happened, but the slow, layered process continued and now I knew I would persist to the very end. It wasn't confidence that pulled me through but tenacity, hanging on in there until the work was done.

No two stories follow the same working pattern. Emotion was the power that drove the first one on to the page, and here I used irony and a sharp biting edge that might not have been detected by readers. Writing the science fiction story was a hard-won achievement, full of frustration and self-doubt, and I would describe that process as very hard work. Later, when the stories were published, I learned about how other people can interpret what you write. Sometimes the reception of work from publishers, readers and critics may bear no relation whatsoever to your experience of creating it – but that's another story.

Ways to do it?

As we have seen already, one approach is to frame your stories by an overall theme or location. On the other hand you might decide to keep the same character in a series of stories. Or you might choose a particular *type* of story or a specific genre that interests you.

A particular kind of story that has been around for many centuries is the fable. Conventionally, fables were devised to convey a moral lesson. In the classic examples, such as *Aesop's Fables*, marvellous or mythical birds or beasts are able to speak and act like humans. Following this tradition to some extent, Suniti Namjoshi's eloquent and knowledgeable Blue Donkey inhabits a world of one-eyed monkeys and talking birds but the fables themselves give ironic comment more than morality lessons.

A popular device recently has been the rewriting of fairy tales with a feminist perspective. In her collection called *The Bloody Chamber* Angela Carter takes those stories from our childhood, 'Beauty and the Beast', 'Snow White', the 'Bluebeard' myth, and so on, and examines the messages about adolescent sexuality that they undoubtedly give. She does this by rewriting the tales from the point of view of the heroine, attempting to redress the sexual imbalance – male as predator, female as victim. She gives women the choice – women may want to be wolves, aggressively sexual, rather than passive victims. Carter's collection is a witty overturning of the sexual mythology of 'simple' fairy stories. In a more lighthearted vein, *Fairytales for Feminists* is a series of books produced by Attic Press in Dublin in which, again, fairy tales have been revised from a feminist perspective, often with ironic endings.

You could try this as an exercise, using fairy stories, old wives' tales, fables or myths. How can you use the basic ingredients to tell the story differently?

Suniti Namjoshi and Angela Carter have moved away from 'realism', in the sense that the worlds they describe are not the world as we know it, but they have their own sense of logic. Joanna Russ's science fiction stories are set in other worlds altogether. In *The Adventures of Alyx*, Alyx appears to be on earth in the first story but subsequent stories are set in different worlds. She is the central character around whom every story revolves, and in each story she is in a different situation and location. We understand her even though the worlds she inhabits are strange. This does not mean to say that her experiences are not relevant to our own. In science fiction you have complete freedom to invent, and as long as the stories have their own internal logic it's OK. You are free to use that invention to comment on the contemporary.

The short story also encompasses the crime fiction genre. You might think that crime is difficult to write in this form – how can you set the scene, the characters, the plot, with its necessary attendant mystery, in a few pages? Yet crime is an excellent genre in which to start thinking about economy of description. A good example is a story called 'Jessie' by Katherine Forrest. Jessie is the head of a police department on the outskirts of Los Angeles and a long standing friend of the author's best-known character,

Kate Delafield. The narrative quickly establishes the scenario: Jessie's close friend, Walt Kennon, is missing. Jessie believes that Walt has been murdered and, for her, the prime suspect is his new wife. Look at how dialogue is used in these opening sentences of the story:

> 'It's a bad time for you to visit, Kate,' Sheriff Jessie Graham offered in quiet apology. 'I'm glad to be here, Jess,' Kate replied with equal quietness. 'I know how close you are to Walt. Right now you need your friends.' Kate Delafield, sipping coffee from a styrofoam cup, sat beside Jessie Graham's desk in one of the plain wooden chairs the county of Alta Vista provided for visitors to its Sheriff's station at Seacliff. She said to Jessie, 'As I recall, he helped you get this job.'
> Jessie nodded. 'I owe it to him.'
> 'You say he disappeared Friday. Any theories about why – or where he might be?'
>
> (Forrest, 1987, pp. 9–10)

In this story Katherine Forrest skips over one of the traditional elements of crime fiction, having a number of suspects, by concentrating on just one suspect. So we are immediately less concerned with *who* did it than *how* she did it. As we follow the two investigators, through their unravelling of how the crime was committed, we switch to the point of view of the perpetrator of the crime, Velma Kennon. This is done not so much to elicit sympathy from us but to examine her motives closely. Meanwhile, there is also the exploration of the past lives of the two friends, Jessie and Kate, so that their characters are deepened. This is a cleverly wrought story that achieves a number of things with great economy of language.

Beginnings and endings

The Russian writer Chekhov advised: 'I think when one has finished writing a short story one should delete the beginning and the end.' In other words, put readers in the middle of the story and let them work out the other parts for themselves. If, like many writers, you labour over beginnings it might seem a bit unfair to suggest that no sooner have you written them then the best thing to do would be to cut them out. However, you need not disregard the opening material altogether, and you may be able to use it elsewhere in the story. An example of a 'deleted' beginning is 'The Organizer's Wife' by Toni Cade Bambara:

> The men from the co-op school were squatting in her garden. Jake, who taught the day students and hassled the town school board, was swiping at the bushy greens with his cap, dislodging slugs, raising dust. The tall gent who ran the graphics workshop was pulling a penknife open with his teeth, scraping rust from the rake she hadn't touched in weeks. Old Man Boone was up and down. Couldn't squat too long on account of the ankle broken in last spring's demonstration when the tobacco weights showed funny. Jack-in-the-box up, Boone snatched at a branch or two and stuffed his pipe – crumblings of dry leaf, bits of twig. Down, he eased string from the seams of his overalls, up again, thrumbling up tobacco from the depths of his pockets.
>
> She couldn't hear them. They were silent. The whole morning stock-still, nothing stirring. The baby quiet too, drowsing his head back in the crook of her arm as she stepped out into the sun already up and blistering. The men began to unbend, shifting weight to one leg then the other, watching her move about the jumbled yard. But no one spoke.
>
> (Bambara, 1982, p. 3)

We have entered the story at a tense moment and the writer is setting the mood, creating tension and mystery before she explains the situation. We are in the middle of the action and we're asking *what is going on here?* The scene is being described in objective terms without explanation. We have to read on to find out why this group of silent men is gathered outside the woman's house, why the atmosphere is hostile and why she seems indifferent to it. Notice how this apparent hostility and indifference is conveyed purely through descriptive action and not by the description of feelings. The story is about a moment of change in a young woman's life. As Virginia moves through the day we travel back into her history. Brought up in a rural town, with few opportunities, Virginia has spent her life wanting to escape. The town is built on granite and is currently under threat from white people who want to buy the land owned by the church in order to extract the granite. When a teacher named Graham comes to town, Virginia hopes he will be her ticket to freedom. But Graham becomes a local activist and is jailed for fighting against the white invasion. The story opens on the day that a decision will be made and Virginia goes to visit the local church leader expecting him to tell her that the church land has been duly sold, that the battle is over. This *is* what he tells her, but she finds herself feeling the opposite of what she expected and reacts angrily. She discovers that she is an inextricable part of this struggle, no matter how hard she has tried to remain indifferent. It is for her an epiphany, a significant moment of realisation.

Another example, this time written from the 'I' point of view, comes from the story 'I Never Eat Crabmeat Now', written by Lisa St Aubin de Teran:

> Looking back, I don't know what is worse to live with; I suppose I just try and forget what I can. There are some things that never go away though, like the smell worming its way back into everything and clinging to the inside of my brain; and then the Daily still missing Fred and asking after him. Then pushchairs, and fish shops just make me feel sick. Last week I saw a budgerigar in a cage picking at a cuttle-fish bone, and that triggered everything off again; now I can't sleep for thinking about Amadeo. What was it? I feel I'll never really sleep well again until I know, but I realize that I might not sleep at all if I really knew the truth.
>
> (St Aubin de Teran, 1989, p. 15)

Here the 'I' point of view, combined with the physical detail and the way the thoughts seem to tumble out as they do in memory, has a very immediate effect. Again, as we're reading this passage we're asking *who is Fred, who is Amadeo?* What is the awful memory evoked by such ordinary things as fish shops and budgerigars? And yet these ordinary things have a malevolent, macabre feel to them that is enhanced by the words 'worming' and 'clinging' and by the line '...I realize that I might not sleep at all if I really knew the truth'.

If you have written one or more stories look at them again to see what they are like if you start with the second or third or fourth paragraphs. It's often a good idea to let material sit for a while before you go back to it. After a break you often see things in a different light. Whatever experimentation or editing we do we have to engage the reader, get her hooked so that she wants to read on and find out why or what happens.

As we saw with the fable, a strong tradition in the short story is the tale with the twist at the end. This can be a strong ironic comment or something more subtle. Consider, for example, this ending from a Katherine Forrest story called 'Benny's Place'. Benny is the nasty and homophobic son of a lesbian who lives with her lover. To torment her he brings as many bugs as he can into her house, knowing that she hates them. He discovers the house contains a secret room built in the days of slavery as part of an escape route for slaves. Later, sought after by the police, Benny hides in this room, unknown to his mother. What he's unaware of is that this is the day his mother has arranged for the pest control people to come and completely disinfect the house with poison gas. You can imagine what happens to him.

Ellipsis

Tail twisters bring stories to a full stop – the punchline – and we are amazed or amused. An elliptical ending is a story that trails off. It doesn't literally have to have the three dots at the end ... but it means leaving open the question of what happens next or what the possible solution to a situation might be. This may seem at first glance unsatisfactory – we like things to be complete – but a story that leaves something enigmatic or obscure makes the reader puzzle out the ramifications for herself.

Experimentation

Consider this extract from a story called 'Girl' by Jamaica Kincaid:

> Wash the white clothes on Monday and put them on the stone heap: wash the color clothes on Tuesday and put them on the clothesline to dry; don't walk barehead in the hot sun; cook pumpkin fritters in very hot sweet oil; soak your little cloths right after you taken them off; when buying cotton to make yourself a nice blouse, be sure that it doesn't have gum on it, because that way it won't hold up well after a wash; soak salt fish overnight before you cook it; is it true that you benna in Sunday school?; always eat your food in such a way that it won't turn someone else's stomach; on Sunday try to walk like a lady and not like the slut you are so bent on becoming ...
>
> (Kincaid, 1984, p. 3)

This litany of instructions goes on for another page, covering such subjects as domestic work, manners, personal hygiene, cooking, nursing, appropriate feminine behaviour, and relationships with men: '... this is how to bully a man; this is how a man bullies you; this how to love a man, if this doesn't work there other ways, and if they don't work don't feel too bad about giving up ...' (Kincaid, 1984, p. 5) It is a very short but ironic summary of what it feels like to be girl. The unrelenting instructions capture exactly that feeling of nagging and censure, with the additional threat of possibly turning into something socially unacceptable.

The short story can be used as a loose starting point for working out ideas in any shape or form. You can even experiment with plays. 'Labour' by Helen Simpson is a five-act Greek play with chorus (albeit in sixteen pages), and it's a very funny account of childbirth. Here's how she introduces it:

> Act 1
> Scene A hospital room, with a discreetly glittering and flashing battery of equipment. On a high bed lies the woman, a metal belt monitor girdling her thirty-nine-inch forty-week globe. Beside the bed is a carpet bag from which spills: a plant spray; a Japanese fan; a large stop watch; a thermos of ice cubes, a wooden back roller. The midwives are checking the monitor's screen, making entries on a partogram chart at the bottom of the bed. A cassette-player by the bed plays Edith Piaf's 'Non, Je Ne Regrette Rein'. The wall clock shows 8 p.m.
> Chorus
> The baby's heartbeat's strong. Unstrap her now. Let's check her notes again. Ah yes. We guessed.
> Another fan of Nature's ancient wisdom,
> Not wanting pain relief nor intervention,
> No forceps, see, nor oxytocin drips
> To speed things up. OK, that's fine by us.
> Whether she thinks the same in six hours' time
> Need not concern us since that's not our shift.
> (Simpson, 1991, p. 81)

The characters consist of the midwives as the chorus, the delivering mother, and Lucina the goddess of childbirth who has a little epilogue.

Novel ideas?

The origins of many a novel lie in short stories that are later expanded. You could decide to rework aspects of the story to make it suitable as a first chapter; or you could develop the characters introduced in the story; or you could use the material as an outline or general resource for the plot.

Exercise

Perhaps you have a short story whose potential can be explored for further development. Alternatively, you could look at a short story written by someone else. Prepare a few questions and notes before you look at the story, to work out ways in which this could be done. The following suggestions will give you some ideas. Add further questions as you read through the story you've selected.

Divide the story into a list of scenes – what happens when – as though planning a film or a play. Transfer each scene in your list to an index card or to a piece of thin cardboard cut into sections. Shuffle the list like a pack of cards and then take the top card. Think about how the story-line would work with this new beginning. If the first shuffle doesn't work too well, have another go. Now ask yourself how each scene could be reworked to give more depth to the narrative. Which aspects of the story do you like the most? Could the narrative style be changed? Are there aspects of the tale that you would want to emphasize? How many characters are there? Would you need more if this story were to become a novel? Is there dialogue that could be developed to provide extra material?

Anthologies

If you have not read many short stories then now is the time to do so. And reading isn't the only thing to do. Set yourself the task of finding out more about the ways in which short stories are marketed. Libraries are a good place to start, or perhaps you know someone who buys a magazine with regular short story features. Ask people you know for their views on short stories. You might want to devise a list of questions to ask. Make notes, and work to broaden your understanding about where short stories are published, by whom, and what appeal they have for women readers. How many variations can there be for a short story collection? Some publishers, like Onlywomen Press in London, bring out a volume of short stories every year by lesbian authors using a different editor each time. Another publisher might choose a specific genre as a theme. In 1985 The Women's Press of London decided to include science fiction as a separate fiction subject area. One of the first books to appear in that list was a short story collection, *Despatches from the Frontiers of the Female Mind*.

In 1989 they published a crime fiction collection, *Reader, I Murdered Him*. Rosemary Jackson takes therapy as the theme running through each of the seven stories in her collection *The Eye of the Buddha*. Erotic stories by women, for women, have been published in anthologies recently, such as those by Sheba Feminist Press, *Serious Pleasure* and *Serious Pleasure 2*. Writing groups can provide the inspiration for an anthology. Five writers, Zoe Fairbairns, Sara Maitland, Michele Roberts, Valerie Miner and Michelene Wandor, formed such a group in London in the 1970s, discussing a different theme at regular intervals and with each writer agreeing to write a short story addressing that theme. Their book *Tales I Tell My Mother* was the result of this joint effort. The more you know about the function and promotion of short stories the better you will feel when phoning publishers and editors to enquire what they might be looking for. You'll also gain a greater sense of what you are doing and why.

Notes

1   McNeill, Pearlie, 'Strange Connie from Two Doors Down' in Mary Hemmings & Jan Bradshaw (eds.), *Girls Next Door*, The Women's Press, London, 1985.

Sources

Cade Bambara, Toni, 'The Organizer's Wife', *The Sea Birds Are Still Alive*, The Women's Press, London, 1982.

Forrest, Katherine, 'Jessie', *Dreams and Swords*, The Naiad Press, Tallahassee, Florida, 1987.

Gubb, Jennifer, 'Blooding', *The Open Road*, Onlywomen Press, London, 1983.

Kincaid, Jamaica, 'Girl', *At the Bottom of the River*, Picador, London, 1984.

Mansfield, Katherine, 'The Dill Pickle', *The Collected Stories of Katherine Mansfield*, Penguin, London, 1981.

McNeill, Pearlie, 'The Awakening', *Despatches from the Frontiers of the Female Mind*, Jen Green & Sarah Lefanu (eds.), The Women's Press, London, 1985.

St Aubin de Teran, Lisa, 'I Never Eat Crabmeat Now', *The Marble Mountain and Other Stories*, Pan, London, 1989.

Simpson, Helen, 'Labour', *Four Bare Legs in a Bed*, Minerva, London, 1991.

Further reading

Binchy, Maeve, *Victoria Line, Central Line*, Coronet, London, 1987.

Carter, Angela (ed.), *The Virago Book of Fairy Tales*, Virago, London, 1990.

Carter, Angela (ed.), *Wayward Girls and Wicked Women*, Virago, London, 1986.

Carter, Angela, *The Bloody Chamber*, Penguin, London, 1981.

Dinesen, Isak (also known as Karen Blixen), *Seven Gothic Tales*, Penguin, London, 1988.

Duncker, Patricia (ed.), *In and Out of Time*, Lesbian Feminist Fiction, Onlywomen Press, London, 1990.

Fairbairns, Zoe, Maitland, Sara, Miner, Valerie, Roberts, Michele, Wandor, Michelene, *Tales I Tell My Mother*, The Journeyman Press, London, 1978.

Fairytales for Feminists, several volumes, Attic Press, Dublin.

Fell, Alison (ed.), *The Seven Deadly Sins*, Serpent's Tail, London, 1988.

Green, Jen, *Reader, I Murdered Him*, The Women's Press, London, 1989.

Jackson, Rosemary, *The Eye of the Buddha*, The Women's Press, London, 1991.

Namjoshi, Suniti, *The Blue Donkey Fables*, The Women's Press, London, 1988.

McCrory, Moy, *The Water's Edge*, Sheba, London, 1985.

Russ, Joanna, *The Adventures of Alyx*, The Women's Press, London, 1985.

Sheba Collective, *Serious Pleasures 1*, Sheba, London, 1989 and *Serious Pleasures 2*, Sheba, London, 1990.

Tuttle, Lisa (ed.), *Skin of the Soul*, The Women's Press, London, 1990.

Wallace, Marilyn, *Sisters in Crime*, Berkley, New York, 1989.

Researching the past:
the historical novel

Maria Edgeworth is credited with writing the first 'historical' novel, *Castle Rackrent*, published in 1800. The historical novel, and particularly the 'family saga', remains one of the most popular forms of fiction. Indeed, history as a subject and setting is used in a variety of ways in different fictional genres. The use of the mythical Arthurian period as a background setting is widespread in science fiction, for example. Many contemporary feminist writers are re-examining the past with a view to providing a revision of the version we have received and to place women back in history.

So, how would you set about writing a historical novel? How much historical knowledge do you need? And what can you do with the genre in terms of ways of telling the story? This chapter is concerned with how you carry out historical research and how you incorporate that information into a novel. Perhaps first of all you should ask yourself to what extent this is a *historical* novel that you are writing. Do you want to provide a comprehensive sense of the past or do you want to write a story that is more about character and plot than about the actual historical location? In either case, whether you want to convey the flavour or the precise detail, you will inevitably have to do some research if you are not already familiar with the period.

The kinds of questions that you'll want to ask stem from a basic curiosity about how people lived then. Next, you'll want to find out what sort of people they were. Where they rich or poor? City or country folk? These are not either/or options – characters could move from one environment to another in the course of a story. The details – of housing, furniture, clothing and food – will have to be adjusted according to where the character(s) are located. With language you will have to decide how much of the original expression, the way things were said and the different vocabulary used, you want to include. What other senses, sounds or smells can be utilized to convey a different era? What were the customs, manners, attitudes, morals, prevailing at the time, and would your characters have agreed with them?

Sources of information

Where will you find the answers? There are numerous sources for both the general and the particular. For a start, other works of fiction might provide some information; there are also biographies and autobiographies, diaries and letters. Historical records of various sorts are kept in libraries and there are specialist libraries for particular subject areas. The local Public Record Office keeps records of all the changes that happen within a particular area with respect to the land, its development and local authority decisions. Newspapers are also a valuable source and individual newspaper offices keep a copy of every edition they print. Museums and art galleries will provide information on how people, houses, landscapes, etc. looked in different periods. Oral history can be found in self-published material or material published by historical and special interest groups. You should not discount your own first-hand experience nor that of older friends or relations who can tell us about the past. There are also various historical societies that will have specialized information on particular people, events or periods. For details about women's history networks and libraries, see the list at the end of the chapter.

Marge Piercy's novel *Gone To Soldiers* is a good example of 'rewriting history'. She deliberately sets out to write the history of the Second World War not from the point of view of the fighting soldiers but from the position of the women who were involved in other ways: in intelligence work; delivering planes for the air force in the US (but not allowed to go to the front); and in the resistance. She takes a number of characters and tells their different stories, offering an alternative view of the war and how it affected these women's lives. In the book's 'After Words', Marge Piercy summarizes her research material:

> I read so many memoirs, biographies and histories of government officials, of OSS and SOE personnel, of camp survivors, of American generals and would-be generals, of marines and those who covered their war, of the French

> Resistance, of the race riots in Detroit, of the decoding
> operations in Washington, Hawaii and England ...'
>
> (Piercy, 1988, p. 772)

She goes on to list books that gave details of women flyers,
women in the resistance, military histories from all services, code
breaking, the holocaust and material from the Holocaust Library.
Not surprisingly, it took her seven years to write the book.

Similarly, Erica Jong, who wrote *Fanny* in the style of an
eighteenth century novel, pays homage to librarians – 'A novel
like this could never have been written without the patience and
forbearance of many librarians' – whom she then goes on to list
(Jong, 1980, p. 554). If you are unfamiliar with but interested in
a particular historical period, the library would be the first place
to start. Librarians are generally helpful people who often take
pleasure in seeking out obscure bibliographical references and
helping with the search process. If your own library doesn't have
the book you want, then its cataloguing data should be able to
give you information about where you could get hold of it.

Sources of inspiration

Material for a historical novel may also come from unexpected
sources. Margaret Forster, for example, wrote a biography of
Elizabeth Barrett Browning and became so involved with the
story of the Browning's maid, Elizabeth Wilson, that she then
wrote a book, *Lady's Maid*, telling the story from the maid's point
of view. Interviewed on radio in 1988 about her biography of
Barrett Browning, Margaret Forster spoke of the complex relationship that had existed between mistress and maid. She
explained that Elizabeth Barrett Browning, despite her strongly
expressed feminist views, had unreasonable expectations of her
maid. For example, she thought nothing of suggesting that
Elizabeth Wilson (who became pregnant by the chauffeur) should
leave her small child behind in England in order to accompany
the Browning family abroad. She expected Elizabeth Wilson to give
a greater priority to her service to the family than to her feelings
towards her own child. It was this that had prompted Margaret
Forster to write Elizabeth Wilson's story in fictional form. She
skilfully interweaves fact, fiction, insight and empathy to develop
the story in a way that sticking strictly to the facts might not have
allowed. In the afterword to *Lady's Maid*, she explains that all the

information she gleaned about Elizabeth Wilson came from Elizabeth Barrett Browning's letters. In concluding the book she writes:

> Wilson was remembered as recently as the 1950s by people in Asolo who had seen her wandering over the country-side, talking to herself. What she talked about – presumably all that had happened to her since 1861 – might some day be the subject matter for a sequel to this book.
>
> (Forster, 1991, p. 536)

It is important to approach your research with an idea of how much licence you will take with the historical detail. Again, this will depend on the kind of historical novel you will want to write. You could concentrate on relationships between people and/or on a theme such as crime and so avoid giving much historical information. With an emphasis on plot and characters, and using history only as a time-zone, the reader will not be encouraged to think about the minute detail of the period setting. However, anachronisms will be picked up by the reader and will mar the effect you are trying to achieve. No area of history should be thought of as the reserve of a type of writer or writing, though it is worth bearing in mind that certain periods of history have been well covered. An obvious example is the Elizabethan period which has been used extensively as a backdrop for romances. The tricky thing about planning to write a historical novel is that you may not know if anyone else is researching the same material. If there is someone else covering the same ground bear in mind that they may be using a different angle on the research and have a different type of book planned. If your aim is to try to have your novel published take heart from the fact that a successful earlier treatment of 'your' period may increase the likelihood of a publisher's interest. Unfortunately this is not necessarily the case with a particular character or event, unless they are so well-known and popular as a subject that the market can bear several versions or treatments. For example Elizabeth I has been the subject of numerous fiction and non-fiction books.

In 1977 I became intensely interested in the story of a female convict, Mary Broad (also listed in documents as Mary Braund). She was transported to Australia (then known as New Holland) on the transport ship *Charlotte* with the first fleet of convict ships that left Portsmouth harbour in May 1787. During the eight-month voyage Mary met another convict, William Bryant, whom she later married. Their first child was named Charlotte after the ship that brought them to Port Jackson, New South Wales. William was a fisherman by trade and the first governor of this new settlement provided him with a boat and equipment so that he could help to provide food. The Bryants' second child, Emmanuel, was a few months old when the family, along with a crew of seven men (all convicts), escaped in William's boat to Timor. The Dutch governor at Coupang in Timor accepted their story that they were shipwrecked mariners and gave them food and clothing.

Things might have gone well for the escapees if their flight had not coincided with the ongoing events of the mutiny aboard Captain Billy Bligh's ship, *Bounty*. Captain Edwards, sent from Britain to arrest mutineer Fletcher Christian and his men, had arrived on the island of Otaheite and captured all those mutineers who had not fled with Christian. Edwards had taken them aboard *HMAS Pandora* as prisoners and set a course for the east coast of Australia. When the ship hit a coral reef and limped into Coupang, Edwards recognized the escapees from Port Jackson as convicts and re-arrested them, throwing them in the hold with the mutineers. Emmanuel, Charlotte and William did not survive the voyage back to England. Mary and the other four convicts who remained were imprisoned in Newgate on their return. Mary was eventually pardoned, her freedom due in part to the efforts of the historian James Boswell. It was a fascinating story and I spent a great deal of my time collecting fragments of information, but my research was still a long way from complete when I learned in 1980 of Anthony Scott Veitch's book *Spindrift*, which tells the story of Mary Bryant. He had been researching the material for several years, incorporating the parallel tale of the Bounty mutineers into a Mary Bryant radio serial, 'The Seafarer', that was broadcast by the Australian Broadcasting Commission in 1978. You could say I missed the boat on that one!

Jean M. Auel might have felt fairly secure that the area she was researching would not have much competition. Ayla is a character from the dawn of time created by Auel for her book *The Clan of the Cave Bear*. Two later novels, *The Valley of Horses* and *The Mammoth Hunters*, continue Ayla's story. Set in prehistoric Europe during the Ice Age, the detail woven into the narrative, especially in the first book, is impressive. In the acknowledgement section of *The Valley of Horses* the author expresses her appreciation to those who helped her with the research, among them a man named Jim Riggs:

> He taught, among other things, how a fire is made, how a spear-thrower is used, how bulrushes make sleeping mats, how to pressure flake a stone tool, and how to squish deer brains – who would have thought that could turn deer hide into velvety soft leather?
>
> (Auel, 1981, p. 6)

Ayla's story includes extensive detail of survival strategy, hunting, ritual ceremonies and food preparation. She is a lone, small child taken in by a tribe, and the narrative is told from her point of view with the immediacy of childhood – on one level things are simple, and on the other they are fraught with the complexity of the dynamics of the group and their constant need to be alert in order to survive.

There are sweeping novels covering historical events of major import and there are other moments, fragments of history, that women writers have picked up on and used to great effect. If there is a legendary figure down your way who could be used as the main character for a book, you might follow the example of Jill Paton Walsh who has written about Grace Darling. Grace was born in Bamburgh, on 24 November 1815. She was the daughter of a lighthouse keeper and brought up first on one and then on another of the Farne islands situated off the Northumberland coast of north-east England. The events that took place in the early hours of 7 September 1838 made Grace Darling famous. That night she helped her father rescue people from a wrecked steam-boat, the *Forfarshire*, that had been on its way from Hull to Dundee. In a strong gale and thick fog the vessel struck rock and forty-three people were drowned. When the tide dropped around 7 a.m. Grace thought she saw four men still alive, and she and her father launched their small boat to rescue them. They found nine survivors (including one woman) huddled on the rocks, and because of the bad weather they had to make two trips to get all nine people to safety.

Paton Walsh uses Grace as the narrator of the novel, beginning the story on the night before the rescue effort. In an author's note she explains that the first half is dealt with 'as exactly and truthfully as I can' (Paton Walsh, 1991, p. 254). The second half deals with the aftermath of fame – Grace became a national symbol of virtue but her renown was very much resented by the local people. Evidence of her status is illustrated by letters pleading for a lock of her hair or a line of her writing. A constant stream of attention came from all sorts of people who wanted to boast that they knew something of this national heroine, but precise details of this part of Grace's life are lacking. Paton Walsh uses her imagination to give her own version of this half of the story. What sources of information did she have? She lists two earlier books: an encyclopaedic biography, *Grace Darling and Her Times* by Constance Smedley, and *Grace Darling, Maid and Myth* by Richard Armstrong, who provides a theory about why local people perversely resented rather than admired Grace after the event. She also used material in the Archives of Crewe Trustees (deposited in the County Library at Newcastle) and the Grace Darling Museum in Bamburgh.

Jane Rogers did not invent the character John Wroe for her novel *Mr. Wroe's Virgins*. He did indeed exist, and was born in Bradford, England, in 1782. During an illness in 1819 Wroe had visions that instructed him to join the Jewish faith. Instead he joined the Bradford Southcottian Church, originally founded by a Devon woman, Joanna Southcott. Wroe sought to reconcile the Jewish and Roman Catholic churches and was accepted as a prophet by the congregation of Ashton-under-Lyme near Manchester in the county of Lancashire. In 1830 he asked for seven virgins and these seven women were provided by church members. Jane Rogers writes, in the 'Historical Note' section in her book:

> Although I have used the outer circumstances of Wroe's life as a framework, I have invented his character. I intend no disrespect, either to the memory of the real man or to his present-day followers.
>
> Of the seven virgins given to Mr. Wroe, there is no record at all – which made it possible for me to write about them.
>
> (Rogers, 1992, p. 276)

She goes on to say, 'Because I didn't know what material I was looking for until I found it, I have meandered through a lot of books about the early nineteenth century' (Rogers, 1992, p. 276). Clearly she made good use of this reading, for there is excellent and specific detail in the narrative about the endless daily drudgery done by the seven women. She tells the story as if from first-hand accounts of four of the female characters she invented: Joanna, pious and full of anguish, who the prophet put in charge of the household; Leah, beautiful and extremely capable, who has her

mind hell-bent on getting the best out of the situation and who
also has a baby who must be hidden from public view if she is to
be accepted as a virgin; Martha, a strong woman who worked as
a farm hand and who is unable at the beginning to talk, though
as her character develops she is increasingly able to to articulate
her experience; and Hannah, given to Wroe by her aunt and
uncle after her father's death. Hannah bides her time, intent on
future escape. Her later involvement with adult education, helping
mill-workers to learn how to read and write, provides an opportunity to highlight important working-class issues in Lancashire
at that time.

These are just a few examples in which you can see how writers
have taken a small historical fact or event and used it imaginatively to retell the story from the woman's point of view.

Sagas

The word 'saga' comes from the Old Norse and refers to narrative
compositions in prose that were written in Iceland or Norway
during the Middle Ages. There are three main sources of saga
tradition: family sagas, dealing with the first settlers of Iceland and
their descendants; kings' sagas, historical works about the kings
of Norway; and legendary or heroic sagas, fantastic adventure
stories about legendary heroes. The definition of a saga in modern
English is a long detailed story or account that deals with a
particular family or a group of characters who are connected in
some way. The saga will begin with one generation and can then
stretch into the future, tracking the consequences and effects of
history on later generations. Alternatively, the passing years may
reveal the impact of history on the same set of characters, using
a well-documented life-span to give the novel its length. The
saga could be thought of as a kind of literary soap opera. If you
have been watching *Coronation Street* for the past twenty-five
years you will have seen the passing of generations. Obviously soap
operas move more slowly and, if they are as well liked as *Coronation
Street*, might never come to an end.

Historical novels are nearly as well loved as romances and the
family saga in its many different forms is the most popular type
of historical novel. 'Blockbuster' sagas such as *A Woman of
Substance* by Barbara Taylor Bradford have been enormously
successful. This novel made Taylor Bradford's first fortune and was
subsequently transformed into a television series. It relies on the

old rags-to-riches 'Cinderella' story: Emma Harte, a poor young maid working in a rich household, is seduced, made pregnant and abandoned by the aristocratic son; determined to seek revenge, she starts a small business to free her from domestic work and ends up the queen of a multimillion dollar empire. Emma proves to have all the qualities that make the successful millionaire: ambition, imagination, determination, intelligence and a certain ruthlessness. She is also, of course, beautiful, sexy and endowed with an innate sense of good taste. The story begins at the turn of the century and we follow three generations of Emma's family through to the granddaughter, who prepares herself to receive Emma's mantle (the author leaves open the possibility of continuing the story of Harte Enterprises Inc.). Such stories, common in blockbuster novels written by women about women getting to the top of the pile, sell very well. Whatever we think of the realistic chances of these plots, or about whether or not the aim in life should be wealth and success, women obviously enjoy reading about female fictional characters who become enormously successful, independent and powerful.

Stand We At Last by Zoe Fairbairns, also a family saga, has a completely different tack. Zoe Fairbairns is not out to write a rags-to-riches novel but one that charts in realistic fashion five generations of women. Beginning in the middle of the nineteenth century and moving through the generations to the present day, it shows how the lives of these women are connected to and affected by the wider movement of history.

Lynda La Plante is better known for writing the highly successful television series *Widows* and the award-winning, two-part television play *Prime Suspect*. Both have strong female characters set in the underworld of crime, which she researches by interviewing prostitutes, pimps, robbers, villains and police officers. She has also published three books, the last of which – *Bella Mafia*, published in 1990 – is a family saga. This novel is about a Sicilian family headed by Don Roberto Luciano. The story begins with a prologue that relates how Don Roberto comes forward unexpectedly as an important witness to help the prosecution win the case against a gangster after earlier witnesses have been murdered. The story then moves slowly back in time to a much earlier period, explaining how Don Roberto became involved with the mafia, how he met his wife Graziella and how he managed to legitimize his business interests. Lynda La Plante is undaunted by the difficulties involved in writing about violence in terms of both the actual description of brutal murder and its effects on people's lives. The violence in this book is sickening and shocking, yet how could any writer ignore this well-known truth that operates inside and between mafia families? She does not flinch from a realistic, credible representation of this unpalatable slice of human life.

How to tell the story – narrative stances

Bella Mafia illustrates one way in which you can tell a story. You can start in the present and then move back to the past, either in first- or third-person narration. A common device used in historical novels is to have 'the tale within the tale'. An example is *Keepers of the House* by Lisa St Aubin de Teran. This, her first novel, was based on her own experience. The story is related by the young Lydia Synclair who has travelled with her new husband from England to his estate high in the Andes of Venezuela. The estate, which has been in the hands of her husband's family since the eighteenth century, has fallen slowly into ruin. With a husband who completely withdraws into himself and an estate that has collapsed because of disease, drought and despair, the young Lydia finds solace through listening to the family history as told by the old family retainer, Benito. This history includes stories of tragic love, cruelty, and failed ambition, which Lydia relates to us in her own words.

You might think about the effects achieved by different narrative stances. You may choose the first person, which could be used in either the present or the past tense. Either way this says 'I was there/am here' and 'it was/is like this'. As we saw, Jane Rogers tells the story from each individual woman's point of view.

Alternatively, the narrative can be told in third person, as Toni Morrison does in *Beloved*. Although Morrison has written a number of novels, *Beloved* – which won the Pulitzer Prize for fiction in 1988 – has received the most attention to date. It is one of the most powerful evocations yet penned of slavery and its consequences in terms of human suffering. Set in the US in the 1870s, just after the Civil War, its main protagonist is Sethe, an escaped slave haunted by the ghost of her dead daughter, Beloved. The narrative slowly unravels the story of the death of Beloved, and takes us back through Sethe's experience of slavery and her escape. But this narrative is not told in a linear fashion – the past and its consequences on the present are related in fragments. For Sethe the pain of the past and of the present, and her reconciliation with the death of her daughter, is a slow process. You get the sense in reading it that the past is almost too much to bear and can be examined only in this fragmentary way. The nub of the story is that when the slave owners track Sethe down, intending to take her and her children back into slavery, she decides to kill the children rather than let them suffer this experience. It is a tragic and beautifully evoked story – the reader can empathize with Sethe's position and understand how someone could contemplate and carry out such a drastic act.

How to convey the historical details

As in any form of fictional writing, if you are introducing a different world you want to avoid the explanatory lump at the beginning that tells everything. Details have to be woven into the text in such a way that the reader picks them up without their intrusion on the narrative itself. *Beloved*, for example, is not written with dense historical detail but with small details here and there to remind you that this is a different era:

> Rainwater held on to pine needles for dear life and Beloved could not take her eyes off Sethe. Stooping to shake the damper, or snapping sticks for kindling, Sethe was licked, tasted, eaten by Beloved's eyes ... She rose early in the dark to be there, waiting, in the kitchen when Sethe came down to make fast bread before she left for work ...
>
> (Morrison, 1988, p. 57)

In contrast you can, if you wish, fill the pages with historical detail. Here's an example from *The Silent Duchess* by Dacia Maraini:

> The feast at which Felice took the veil could not have been more splendid, with the entire aristocratic throng dressed with great elegance: the women swinging their trains, their hooped skirts, their dresses from Paris, their muslins light as a butterfly's wings, their heads arrayed in gold and silver nets, wearing ribbons of velveteen, and lace and silk that floated down from painted girdles. Amidst feathers, dress swords, gloves, muffs, bonnets, artificial flowers, slippers with pearl-studded buckles, tricorns covered with plush, tricorns gleaming in the light, suppers of thirty courses were served. And between one course and the next, crystal goblets were filled with lemon sorbets perfumed with bergamot ...
>
> (Maraini, 1992, p. 110)

The writing throughout *The Silent Duchess* is a deliberate assault on the senses. Set in eighteenth-century Sicily, the novel charts the history of three generations of the Ucria family through the eyes of Marianna who is deaf and mute as a result of being sexually abused as a child. Most of what she experiences is described through sight, taste and most particularly smell. The wealth of historical detail in this novel is almost overwhelming, rich and dense – what kinds of food they ate, the clothes they wore but most of all the smells. Here, for example, is a description of Marianna's mother:

> The child stops for a moment, overcome by the honey-sweet scent of the snuff mingled with all the other odours that accompany her mother's awakening: attar of roses, coagulated sweat, stale urine and lozenges flavoured with orris root.
>
> (Maraini, 1992, p. 10)

Looking at the history of this period from Marianna's point of view shows us the narrowness of women's lives, destined either for motherhood or for the church. It is also a novel that charts Marianna's intellectual and emotional growth. Married at thirteen to her uncle and bound for the next twenty years to a life circumscribed by family duty, Marianna finally achieves freedom.

Sources

Auel, J. M., *Clan of the Cave Bear*, Coronet, London, 1981.
Fairbairns, Zoe, *Stand We At Last*, Pan, London, 1984.
Forster, Margaret, *Lady's Maid*, Penguin, London, 1991.
Jong, Erica, *Fanny*, Granada, London, 1980.
La Plante, Lynda, *Bella Mafia*, Pan Books, London, 1991.
Maraini, Dacia, *The Silent Duchess*, Peter Owen, London, 1992.
Morrison, Toni, *Beloved*, Plume, New York, 1988.
Paton Walsh, Jill, *Grace*, Penguin, London, 1991.
Piercy, Marge, *Gone to Soldiers*, Ballantine Books, New York, 1988.
Rogers, Jane, *Mr. Wroe's Virgins*, Faber & Faber, London, 1992.
St Aubin de Teran, Lisa, *Keepers of the House*, Penguin, London, 1983.
Taylor Bradford, Barbara, *A Woman of Substance*, Grafton, London, 1981.

Further reading

Hoffman, Ann, *Research for Writers*, A & C Black, London, 1986.
Wibberley, Mary, *On Writing Romantic Novels*, Buchan & Enright, London, 1987.

Further information

CWIRES (Christian Women's Information & Resources), Blackfriars, St Giles, Oxford, OX1 3LY.

Fawcett Library, City of London Polytechnic, Old Castle Street, London, E1 7NT. (Historical and contemporary women's studies archive.)

Feminist Archive, Trinity Road, St Philips, Bristol, Avon, BS2 0NW.

Feminist Library, 5 Westminster Bridge Road, London, SE1 7XW.

Lesbian Archive and Information Centre, BM 7005, London, WC1N 3XX.

Women's Audio Archive, 45A Redchurch Street, London, E2 7DJ.

Women's Library, 30 Chaucer Street, Nottingham, NG1 5LP.

Piecing the puzzle together: murder she writes

Women have been prominent among crime fiction writers throughout this century, and their innovative ideas have had a huge impact on other writers as well as readers. Agatha Christie, Dorothy L. Sayers, Ruth Rendell, Patricia Highsmith, P. D. James and, more recently, Sara Paretsky, have all played a part in making crime writing a genre in which women lead the way. More and more women are writing 'whodunnits' and publishers, such as Pandora Press in Britain, have reprinted novels of lesser known women writers from earlier times.

There's nothing new about having a woman as the central problem-solving character. Agatha Christie's Miss Marple has been around since the early 1930s, but there were already existing role models. Establishing who the first woman detective was and who created her remains a matter of some dispute but Mrs Paschal, a character who narrates her adventures as a 'lady detective' in a book thought to have been published in 1861, is a strong contender for the title. The cheap book editions produced at this time were known as 'yellowbacks' because they were usually bound with yellow paper or cloth. As they were often undated, and in this case the name of the author given as 'Anonyma', Mrs Paschal's appearance cannot be pinpointed with complete accuracy. Crime writer and historian of the subject Ellery Queen[1] disputed the reliability of the evidence supporting Mrs Paschal's book and put forth Andrew Forrester Jnr's anonymous heroine, referred to as 'the female detective' in a book of the same name, as the best candidate.[2] It would seem that Mrs Paschal's creator(s) didn't want to claim her and Andrew Forrester Jnr didn't want to name her, so no matter which came first, the woman detective had a shaky beginning.

From the early 1860s to the beginning of this century there were at least twenty fictional women detectives and the term 'lady detective' cropped up in book titles several times. Many of these women were motivated by a desire to clear the sullied name of a husband or sweetheart. Others made use of the skills and experience required by their everyday work to help them. Hagar Stanley was a pawnbroker and combined what she knew of that trade with a bit of detective work on the side. Hilda Wade, a nurse, was blessed with a photographic memory, a great help when sifting through clues, remembering faces, and recalling who said what, and so on.[3]

In 1897 author Anna Catherine Green created Miss Amelia Butterworth.[4] Like the later Miss Marple, Amelia was elderly, had a keen nose for following the trail of the criminal and possessed the sort of curiosity that had her easily labelled a 'busybody'. Sometimes described as a 'meddlesome old maid', she made discoveries which proved unsettling for those who had something to hide. Later, Green created a second female detective who contrasted with Amelia Butterworth in every possible way – Violet Strange was young and oh so feminine. Two characters who worked in collaboration with their husbands were Clarice Dyke (now there's an interesting name for a female sleuth) and Dora Myrl, who took her work home with her when she married another detective, Paul Beck.[5] A later book entitled *Young Beck: A Chip off the Old Block* tells how Dora and Paul's son, Paul Beck Jnr, becomes a detective, following in the footsteps of his clever, talented parents.

The use of a woman in crime fiction as the central mystery-solving character can boast a long history, and in the last two decades particularly it has been women writers who have been the most innovative within the crime genre. Women writers have changed many of the traditional elements, from the crime, the investigative process, the examination of motives, to the breaking down of stereotypes of women as saints or sinners and the provision of new settings and new background information. They have illuminated matters of concern to women in ways that make the lives of women and their experience in the world more visible.

Chicken or egg?

Are crime fiction writers born or made? Was that first successful novel written quickly in a flurry of excitement, the words tumbling from a great waterfall in the imagination, or was there a slow process of self-taught learning? There can be an immediate attraction to crime fiction writing – 'having the right sort of mind for it' as a workshop participant once suggested – and there can also be a layered approach, building up an understanding of what's involved, allowing time for confidence and skill to develop.

How would you describe your attitude? Do you sometimes finish reading a crime novel and feel dissatisfied, wondering whether you could have done a better job of it yourself? Are you good at anticipating what direction the author will take next? Do you find yourself tut-tutting at the plot weaknesses and thinking of alternatives that could have been introduced? Do you think of plots but then drop the whole idea? Do you feel drawn to this kind of writing but worry about where to begin? Do you read a lot of crime fiction? If you do, would you say you have a strong sense of what you like and dislike?

Now's the time to answer some of those questions. Select a thick notebook that you can use as a workbook while reading through this chapter. Make the book large enough to be divided into sections yet small enough to be carried about easily. Keep one section at the front for use as a diary of exploration and label about another ten sections according to what you think are the important elements to look at in crime fiction. Make sure you have enough pages in each section so that when the flow of ideas come you will not be distracted by lack of space. In the first section, the one you are using as a diary, answer some or all of the questions raised in the previous paragraph about your responses to the crime fiction you have read so far. The intention here is to assess your level of understanding and analysis (as you would honestly describe it at the moment) of the different elements of crime fiction. How much have you thought through the questions raised by your reading, and how do you think you could utilize your criticism in your own work? Later on you can update your assessment. You might wish to write in the form of a letter to yourself or some other person – a character perhaps. Remember that what *you* think is as worthy of serious attention as any other person's point of view. Don't skim over the questions, for that could mean you don't take your own exploration seriously enough.

You will have a distinct advantage if you are a crime fiction reader already, for you will have gained some knowledge of how the structure works even if you don't feel able to express with any certainty what you know or have learned as a reader. What have you found interesting in the crime fiction stories you've read recently? Was there anything about the characterization, the way the writer dealt with some aspect of the story, that appealed to you? We do absorb more than we realize, so trust in your own opinion and your ability to appraise other writers' work. If you haven't read crime fiction very much, ask yourself why. It is never too late to start reading but it is important to know if you are truly interested in crime fiction writing. Ask your friends what books they've read recently. Visit your local library or bookshop. Jumble sales and markets are often good places to find cheap books and you can add to your library of useful books without too much expense.

Allow the idea of writing a crime fiction short story or novel to take hold of you. Use time alone to think about ideas. If you have no time alone, or if you have no 'free' time, use a few minutes several times a day while you're doing something that doesn't require intense concentration – washing up, making a cup of coffee, travelling to work on the train or bus ... If you have friends with whom you can discuss books then so much the better – if not, use your workbook diary section to record your responses to material you've read as well as suggestions for further research. Soon, you'll notice there is greater clarity in the way you look at crime fiction. Don't be concerned if your reading enjoyment drops away for a while. After an initial period that may last weeks or months, according to how much time you have to devote to the task, you'll find that it's possible to read with two different levels of perception. If you decide to attempt a story without first having read a few crime fiction novels you'll have less insight and understanding about what's already been tried, and the challenge, though not impossible by any means, will certainly be more difficult. This is particularly true of genre writing and does not apply to other areas of creative writing.

When a writer begins to toss around ideas for a novel she may not know for quite some time what direction the plot will take or where each chapter/stage is leading her. As outlined in the 'Techniques: understanding and practice' chapter, a book may be written from start to finish with well-planned chapter headings worked out in advance and a carefully constructed layering of detail and information. This model is often what new writers have in mind when they imagine how a book is written. It is possible and not unusual to have only the idea for an ending, or maybe a few pages about a character, or an issue around which a plot can be built. A story in the news might have a haunting quality for a writer and she may 'give herself over' to a process of exploration. The

outcome might not be clear at all, and she could live with that
story for several months or years before using it. Such a book will
develop organically. It isn't necessary to choose a particular
method or structure at the start but it *is* of value to understand
what components have been identified already in crime fiction
writing.

Within the boundaries of crime fiction there are a smaller
number of categories, and these may overlap at times. The
detection of crime by a central character, espionage plots and
thrillers form the major areas by which crime fiction is defined,
but these are not categories that can be pinned down firmly. The
spy story or espionage plot is likely to have a broader geographical spread than the more usual kind of crime fiction story where
the scene of the crime and the list of suspects may be located in
the same city, village or even the same house. Thrillers are written
with a heightened level of suspense built into the plot, intended
to create fear in at least one of the central characters, and the reader
is encouraged to empathize with those feelings of fear. To scrutinize
in more detail what goes into crime fiction writing and finally to
be able to piece it together we must first dissect the whole into
separate parts.

The plot and the narrative

Broadly speaking there are two types of crime fiction novel. In one
the priority remains always with the puzzle – solving the mystery
of the murder(s). In the other the focus is shared between the
puzzle and the storyline. The first I'll call the *puzzle priority plot*
and the second the *shared priority plot*.

The puzzle priority plot

With this type of plot the writer is offering the reader a challenge.
Can the reader solve the puzzle before the end of the book when
all will be revealed? Some writers make it extremely difficult for
any reader to work out the puzzle. Intricate and overly complex
plots with clues too well hidden can mean that the end result will
be confusion rather than intrigue. Working out who did what to
whom, and why, becomes a matter of guesswork, not reasoning.
Stories with clues dropped in subtly, and in such a way that it is
at least possible for a reader to work out the puzzle and follow the

investigation with interest and involvement, offer good entertainment value.

It is important to make the story hang together, to keep the crime-solving context apparent and credible. A plausible ending is vital, for readers will judge a writer's skill particularly in connection with the resolution. If you are a crime fiction reader you will have some idea of how satisfying or frustrating endings can be. If the reader continues to mull over the related events for some time afterwards this may be evidence of the writer's skill; but if there is reader resistance to the plausibility of motive, the way in which the crime was committed, by whom, and so on, it might mean that the writer has paid too little attention to detail and has not layered sufficient information into the plot.

Devising a list of questions to pin down exactly what you thought about the puzzle can be extremely helpful. Sometimes we have a hazy sense of something niggling at us about a book we have just read, but all too often we leave it at that. Asking questions will sharpen our perceptions and increase confidence. Here are some questions to begin with. You may reject some or all of these once you start compiling your own list. It's as well to remember, too, that these questions are less specific than your own list will be because you will have a particular book in mind:

- How useful were the explanations given in the wind-up of the story? Was there too much haste in getting the story over and done with?
- How well did the build up, including clues and information about suspects, fit with the way things worked out?
- Were there any minor characters or scenes that, in retrospect, had no bearing on the build-up of the plot?
- How plausible was the method by which the crime was committed?

Let's take this last question and imagine a scenario where we are asked to accept that a female murderer killed her male victim and then made it appear that he had hung himself from a roof beam. We'll want to know *how* she did it. It won't be a simple matter of suggesting she put the rope around his neck, slung it over the beam and heaved the body into the air by pulling hard on the rope. The woman might have had help, she could have been a wrestler or a weightlifter, her job might have made her quite strong, or she may always have been physically strong, but having readers believe that this character could *do such a thing* in the first place

– murder this man and then leave his body dangling – would take some thoughtful character planning. This is an extreme example, of course, but the challenge of any fictional murder is to bridge any possible credibility gap. Skimming over certain details might work once, maybe twice, but if the weaknesses of plausibility are not addressed, it is likely that such a writer will lose her audience. There might be other features in the story that encourage us, as readers, to overlook these weaknesses and this is more likely when a shared priority plot is used.

The shared priority plot

Agatha Christie's books, ever popular and outsold only by the Bible and Shakespeare, featured elaborate detail. Her characters were drawn from the upper crust of society and the settings suggested wealth, power and comfort in varying degrees. Like an archer with bow and arrow poised for action, Agatha Christie fixed her attention firmly on the bull's-eye target, and this target was the puzzle. Likewise, from the first page to the last, the reader's attention is fixed on the puzzle of who did it and how.

Ruth Rendell swings the pendulum in the opposite direction and her writing style cannot be categorized simply. She is unpredictable from one book to the next. Some of her stories, particularly those of earlier vintage, do follow a more traditional formula but her formidable skill lies in her ability to cross over into areas previously unexplored and to expand the narrative scope, sometimes beyond recognition. Her book *Going Wrong* is a character study of a man unwilling to let go of a former girlfriend. Conveniently convinced that her family was to blame for the break-up, and seeing them now as actively working to prevent a happy reconciliation, he injects a self-serving rationality into his perceptions. The narrative dispenses with the notion of a puzzle in the usual sense and concentrates instead on what this single character is thinking, telling the story from his point of view. Macabre and unsettling, particularly for women readers, it produces the kind of fascinated repugnance we feel when staring at something horrible. Although we have that 'I'd-rather-not' feeling, still we read on. Why? Do we want to understand? Or is it that we want justice or some kind of vengeful satisfaction? Skilled in the art of creating suspense with timing and pace, she has used this male perspective with frightening accuracy but there is no shared weighting between the plot puzzle and the narrative. The narrative has the focus and the plot exists like backdrop scenery in a theatrical performance.

If Agatha Christie's books can be placed firmly within a puzzle plot context, and if we agree that Ruth Rendell is moving more and more into uncharted waters, establishing a greater narrative strength in her more recent work, then who are the writers we can turn to when looking for examples of the shared priority plot? An obvious name to mention would be P. D. James. *Innocent Blood*, for example, is the story of a woman recently released from prison for serving a murder sentence. Someone connected with her victim is seeking revenge. We learn about the murderer and her motives and as this gains our sympathy the tension builds when the avenger draws closer to her. There is a push-pull tug between the crime (who did it and how) and the story behind the crime, often with careful attention to description of setting, motives and the characters involved.

Jennifer Rowe, better known as a crime fiction writer in Australia than elsewhere, recently published a book entitled *Grim Pickings*. The story centres around a traditional family gathering at the home of an elderly aunt. The whole family comes each year to pick apples from an orchard behind the house. The first page tells us of the day the family arrives at the house. Beds have to be made and rooms prepared, although everyone knows where they'll be sleeping because the pecking order has been established a long time ago. Married folk get priority and a room to call their own, whereas the couple who only 'live together' are provided with two single camp beds placed end to end along the back verandah – privacy is limited, but then that's the price you pay for not playing by the rules. At the heart of these values is the aunt's niece. This woman, possessed by a passion for order and control, causes emotional havoc in one room after another and her power, seldom challenged, waxes and wanes according to how she feels about the people she's talking to. The family, so 'normal' yet so awful, is completely engrossing, and you fail to notice how the chapters are passing without anyone being bumped off. The narrative is well developed long before the puzzle comes into being; then, once the murder has been committed and the list of suspects compiled, narrative and puzzle draw neck and neck. Finally, with a momentum that runs full throttle towards the conclusion, the puzzle pulls well out in front, creating suspense, clamour and compulsive reading for the last seventy or so pages. Therefore you can see that it's possible to juggle the emphasis between the plot and the story in different ways to suit your material.

The Crime

Does murder have to be the central feature of crime fiction writing? Would kidnapping work instead, or maybe a clever burglary? One of Dorothy L. Sayer's best-known short stories, 'The Necklace of Pearls', has not even the whiff of a dead body to distract from the search for those missing pearls. The writers who have stretched the definitions of crime fiction, such as Ruth Rendell, initially write within the conventions of the genre and then, as their confidence and skill grow, advance their story-lines across new territories. They illustrate that murder does not necessarily have to be the central issue. Nevertheless, murder remains the ultimate crime.

It's difficult to discuss the crime without also mentioning the victim(s) and the perpetrators. I prefer to think of the three as a triangle, constantly in motion, with the spotlight of attention moving from one point to another in rapid rotation. Let's begin with a murder victim. Male or female? If it's a woman, how gory will a woman writer want to make the death? If it's a man, will a woman writer want to think of a woman as the murderer or simply as a suspect?

Imagine that there's a group of women aboard a moored houseboat somewhere along a river. Where is that river? Who are these women? There's a party going on with about twenty women present. Two friends have come on to the deck at one end of the houseboat. There could be some tension between them. Maybe they've been looking all night for an opportunity to talk to each other? One of the women leans over the rail and sees a large branch floating by. Then, looking closer, she sees something else. There's a body entangled with the branch. The woman draws back from the rail. She cries out. Her friend hurries over and together they stare, transfixed, as the body thumps against the side of the hull. What happens next? Is the body male or female? What if one of the women aboard knows the victim? Will some personal circumstance link one or more of the women with the victim, in a way that is not obvious right away? Could these two friends become involved in the investigation?

Discovery of a body is a usual starting point. Creating different scenes, such as the houseboat setting, serves as a springboard, making it possible for you to move in a number of different directions. New ideas will occur as you delve deeper. Once your imagination is ticking away and you have a plot basis to work with, you can decide if this is the opening you want to begin telling the story.

In a speech given at the Australian National Word Festival, in Canberra, March 1991, P. D. James talked about crime and morality.

> In my own books I have very explicit descriptions of murdered bodies. It seems to me that the moment when the body is discovered is a moment of great importance in the novel and I like to describe the scene through the eyes of the person who actually finds the corpse. In some books this person is particularly vulnerable, is either young or very innocent and therefore it is a moment of extraordinary horror.
>
> I like, in fact, to describe that horror, but I don't think I ever want to describe in detail acts of torture by one human being against another. That is not perhaps because I have moral objection to it, although, of course, I have, but because I would find it extremely distressful and frightening to write. But has a writer an obligation to exclude that kind of appalling violence by one human being against another? Has he an obligation to exclude it from his writing as he does from his life?

P. D. James did not attempt to answer these questions but she did go on to speak about intention:

> What is my intention? If I am including violence because I feel this book wants pepping up a bit, it is going to sell better if I have some sexual scenes and some violent scenes, then I am violating my own artistic integrity.
>
> (James, 1991)

What do you think? How explicit would you want the discovery of a dead body to be? There are recorded instances of people needing months, even years, of therapy to help them overcome the horror of having found a murder victim. If you've seen police officers interviewed on TV at the start of a grisly murder investigation you will no doubt have heard them describe the murder as 'the worst I've ever seen'. In real life the person who finds the body is often overlooked. Media attention will probably be centred on the state of the corpse, where it was found, how the crime was committed, the character of the victim and the victim's family. If the killer is found, the court case is often a much vaunted event. Artistic integrity is an individual matter and emphasis is likely to differ according to the individual. Feeling squeamish and uncertain about these complicated issues is an understandable early part of the crime-writing process.

The villain(s) of the piece

If the murderer is a man and his victim is female then having this man brought to justice is a satisfactory conclusion, not only for the story-line but for women readers who can feel that there are times when violent men are forced to take responsibility. Believing that men who act violently towards women will be caught and made to account for their actions can help us to feel more optimistic about our lives. If the person who catches the criminal *is a woman* then there might be a measure of gleeful satisfaction for the woman reader. But what if the murderer is a woman? Statistics prove that women have good cause to fear male violence, so to think of women as the perpetrators of violent crime, or as murderers, requires a shift in perception. The woman murderer that *can* be imagined easily by new writers is the woman who acts in self-defence. It can be seen as justifiable that a woman acts in her own interests, to defend her life, her children, and/or her sanity.

When women face prosecution for killing to protect themselves the legal profession's perception of self-defence makes it clear that men devised the law for men. Here's how Ann Jones, in her book *Women Who Kill*, describes how the law of self-defence works:

> When one man attacks another with his fists, the court assumes that they are more or less evenly matched and generally does not allow the man attacked to counter with a weapon. To acknowledge that a 110 pound woman might need a weapon against her 225 pound husband, or that she might try to catch him off-guard is not special pleading but facing facts. To a small woman untrained in physical combat, a man's fists and feet may appear to be deadly weapons, and in fact they are: many women miscarry after a beating, and most women killed by their husbands are not shot or stabbed but simply beaten and kicked to death. The woman who counters her husband's fists with a gun may *in fact* be doing no more than meeting deadly force with deadly force.
>
> (Jones, 1980 pp. 299–300)

Let's look at a real life case. Inez Garcia was tried for murder in California following an attack made on her by two men. The much publicized story raises the question of whether a woman who is raped has the right to kill the rapist after the rape. Jim Wood, reporter for the San Francisco *Examiner*, wrote a book about the trial, *The Rape of Inez Garcia*.

This is how Inez Garcia's nightmare began on the evening of 19 March 1974 in Soledad, California:

> Louis Castillo and Miguel Jiminez came to Inez's house at 8 pm, allegedly to talk to Fred Madrano, who was also renting the house. While waiting for him, the two men started drinking and taunting Inez. When Fred arrived home, he was harassed and threatened and beaten up in the fight that followed. Inez, frightened, told Louis and Miguel to leave, and stepped outside to make sure they left. They forced her to come behind the house with them where trapped, she was beaten, her clothes torn, and she was raped.
>
> In a state of shock and hysterical from the attack, Inez went back inside and loaded her .22 calibre rifle. At this time she received a phone call from the two men who had just attacked her. They threatened to make it worse for her if she did not leave town. About one half hour later she found her attackers five blocks away, beating up Fred for a second time. She saw Jiminez draw a knife and called out. Jiminez turned and threw the knife in her direction. Inez fired, killing Jiminez and missing Castillo completely.
>
> (Wood, 1976, p. 12)

Inez was thirty years old at the time of the attack. Of Cuban and Puerto Rican descent, she had come to Soledad with her eleven-year-old son to be near her husband who was then in Soledad prison. Inez was charged with first-degree murder for killing Miguel Jiminez. Trying the case was Judge Stanley Lawson, conservative Republican and a man about to retire from the bench. In the end, Inez was found guilty of second-degree murder. In his book Jim Wood makes the following point:

> If Inez's husband had learned of the rape after it occurred, taken a rifle, hunted down the men who did it, and shot them, do you suppose for a minute that he would have been convicted of second-degree murder?
>
> (Wood, 1976, p. 217)

The final paragraph includes a conversation between Inez Garcia and Jim Wood. Inez is about to begin her sentence, and no one knows how long she will be imprisoned:

> 'I'm going to have to stay a long time,' she repeats slowly, 'but I don't know. If I had to do it over again, I would, even if it meant' – she hesitates – 'you know, the death.'
>
> (Wood, 1976, p. 221)

It was not until March 1977 that Inez Garcia was finally exonerated of the murder charge and freed from prison. If I were to compile a list of areas in crime fiction neglected by women writers, the subject of self-defence cases would be high on that list.

Methods

Can you imagine a woman using a knife, a gun, or maybe poison? Why do you think a woman might kill? And who would she kill?

Poison as a means of killing has had a long history of use by both women and men, people who knew about herbs and plants and what to use for what purpose. Tofania di Adamo, a Sicilian woman born about 1640, marketed a brand of poison based mainly on arsenic. Arsenic was known to be good for the complexion and Tofania's services as a consultant for those interested in using it for poisoning remained secret for a while. When her growing reputation, and a number of suspicious deaths, brought her to the attention of the police in Naples around 1660 Tofania begged the help of nuns and was given a safe haven in a convent. To flush her out the police spread a rumour that Tofania had poisoned the city's water supply and the panicked nuns handed her over. Tortured, Tofania was said to have confessed to poisoning 600 people, including two popes. After this the facts become vague. Much later, in 1709, she was strangled to death and her body tossed over the wall of the same convent in which she had sought shelter.[6]

It was Mathieu Joseph Orfila, a Spaniard born in 1787 on the east coast of Minorca, who made an early contribution to the detection of organic poisons in the organs of the body. Orfila was a remarkable self-taught man who won a scholarship to the University of Barcelona and became a doctor. Later he went to Paris, and it was here that he began to give lectures on chemistry to large groups of students. One day in class something went wrong. Orfila was embarrassed in front of his students when a planned experiment turned out differently from the expected result. The experience caused him to repeat his experiments, concentrating on a number of poisons, mixing them with different substances and discovering, to his amazement, that frequently these poisons could not be detected. Respected as a scientist, Orfila soon became a detective as well. The impact of his work, his methods of analysing samples of substances to detect whether poison was present, meant that he was asked to appear in court, sometimes for the prosecution, sometimes for the defence, and his opinion was so respected that his evidence was all that was needed to acquit or condemn a suspected prisoner.[7]

There was no shortage of poisons in Orfila's lifetime. He was first consulted about a suspected poisoning case in 1824. Mercury, opium, phosphorus, quinine and chloroform were all available in the nineteenth century and more were becoming known in a remarkably short span of time. Morphine was discovered in 1803, strychnine in 1818, aconite and belladonna (both extracts from deadly nightshade) in 1833. Metallic poisons were simple to detect but the vegetable poisons were a different matter altogether.

Fictional stories about women using poison as a means of ensuring death are fewer than might be expected if we compare them with the statistical evidence of female poisoners, of which there have been a number, including serial killers. Why might this be so? Does it have something to do with 'active' and 'passive' methods of murder? Would we rather think of a fictional character with a smoking gun in her hand than imagining her mixing up a deadly cocktail in the blender? For a woman the distinct advantage of poison is obvious. You don't need physical strength to use it and, for those women desperate enough to plan a murder, poison might well seem a simple and effective way of getting the job done. Australian writer Claire McNab had her fictional female killer in *Lessons in Murder* use a Black and Decker drill to bore into the skull of her victim. Emma Lathen (the pen name of two women who co-write Emma Lathen novels) in *Banking on Death* had Mr Robert Schneider killed by means of a marble book-end. What method would you choose? Why?

Exercise

Take a large sheet of paper (a few pages from an exercise book stapled or glued together would do) and draw a horizontal line across the middle. Label one end of the line *Passive* and the other end

Active. Write down all the weapons and methods you can think of that could be considered suitable for a murder. Decide at which end each method should go. There are bound to be obvious means that you can write in straightaway; others will occur to you gradually. Don't expect to finish this exercise for some time. You may find that pondering on the complexities of a method raises interesting and useful questions about exactly how it could be used. You could also number each method – this will allow you to write up corresponding questions in your notebook, with the option of working back and forth between your notebook and the diagram.

The scene of the crime

Deciding where the murder takes place will be an integral part of the planning, though it need not be the first thing you work on. One of the classic detective puzzles – the 'locked room' mystery – was first written about by Edgar Allan Poe in *The Murder in the Rue Morgue*.[8] No forced entry is evident and the puzzle is mystifying. In real life the locked room mystery can be traced as far back as the early part of the sixteenth century in a case concerning the murder of Lady Mazel. She lived in a big Paris mansion and slept by herself each night in a room where the door was fitted with a special type of spring lock. It was assumed that the door could not be opened from the outside. One morning Lady Mazel did not emerge. The servants called in a locksmith who broke into the room and discovered her dead body covered in multiple stab wounds. The murder weapon was in the room and money had been taken, plus a gold watch. Searching for clues, the police found the following items in Lady Mazel's room: a lace cravat (a cheap variety), and a napkin bearing the family crest that had been twisted into the shape of a nightcap. In the attic they found a blood-stained nightshirt.

The improvised nightcap fitted the household's valet. His story of being asleep in the kitchen the night before only made things look worse. He said he'd woken up to find the back door open. Thinking one of the other servants had been careless, he'd simply locked up and gone to bed. The blood-stained nightshirt did not fit the valet, but another servant identified the cravat as belonging to a former footman. When it was discovered that the valet had in his possession a skeleton key that fitted various locks throughout the mansion, including Lady Mazel's bedroom, the police were convinced they'd found the culprit and did not extend their enquiries further. The valet died as a result of being tortured, without confessing to the murder.

The story didn't end there. A few weeks later, the former footman was arrested. Working now as a horse trader, he'd been picked up on some minor charge and when searched had been found to have in his possession the missing gold watch. Predictably, the man was tortured and confessed the whole story. He'd been dismissed by Lady Mazel and was determined to have his revenge. He'd slipped unnoticed into the house on the Friday morning previous to the murder. Hiding in the attic for the next two nights, he'd lived on bread and apples that he'd brought with him. Sunday morning had come and everyone had gone to church. Now was his chance. He'd slipped into Lady Mazel's room, crawled under her bed and stayed there until the household had settled down for the night. He'd then woken Lady Mazel and demanded money. She'd tried to call for help and he'd killed her. Taking the money and the watch, and leaving behind those telltale clues, he'd returned to the attic to dump the bloodied nightshirt and had slipped out of the building via the kitchen door, leaving it open in case he disturbed the sleeping valet who was seated there with his head on the table.[9]

Though the mystery is in one sense flawed by the fact that there was, after all, a key to Lady Mazel's bedroom, it's ironic that this was unknown to the killer who went to elaborate lengths to get into the room. To gain access to the mansion it was necessary to know the comings and goings of the people who lived and worked there. Routine in such a place would have been regular to the point of monotony and for this reason it was almost certain that the dead woman would have known the murderer. We can also see how circumstantial evidence can fix attention on one suspect to the exclusion of others. If we were to update this story and change its geographical location what might we end up with?

To keep the plot contained we could create a different world – the mansion might be the setting for a holiday, or it could be the focal point of a community or village. The aim would be to contain the plot, to establish boundaries that would limit the number of characters and outside influences. Agatha Christie used the contained setting a number of times with the murders taking place on a boat or a train. With a limited number of suspects in this locked-in setting, they usually all had some motive for murder.

If, on the other hand, we abandoned the containment idea entirely and worked with a killer who attacked randomly and who was unknown to any of the victims, the clues, the suspects and the investigation itself would operate in such an open way that anything would be possible and no easy conclusions could be drawn. The containment setting offers familiarity as a feature to be worked with, whereas the wide-open scenario uses the unknown as a no-holds-barred factor, demanding that the investigators look at what is common about the attacks as a construct upon which the story can be shaped.

To make that clearer, let me take you back to the cravat identified as belonging to the dismissed footman. This clue is a definite link, placing the footman at the murder scene. If we were working with a wide-open plot, clues found at the scene of the crime could lead anywhere or nowhere, at least for a time. Imagine a body has been found in a lane behind a busy shopping area. Two office cleaners find a glove, a cuff-link or maybe a blood-stained handkerchief. They may be able to say that these items belong to a building superintendent who works in the same building as themselves but it's more likely that they won't know who the items belong to at all. The contained plot will give us a suspect list quite quickly but the open plot will make it harder to grab hold of any suspects for a time.

Background

The background setting for a crime novel presents an opportunity for us to use what we know of a particular subject and to weave it into a story for greater interest. Barbara Paul's book *The Fourth Wall* is set in the theatre. The opening sentence is aptly dramatic, with the promise of more gruesome excitement to come: 'Sylvia Markey was holding her cat's head in her hands. Just the head.' The short sentence structure and the shocking thought of what has happened to the cat instantly pull the reader into the story. This setting is tightly contained, neither the characters nor the plot move outside it, and the novel is very informative about the theatre.

Winner of the Mystery Readers of America Macavity Award for Best First Novel, *The Ritual Bath* by Faye Kellerman is set in a Jewish community – a *yeshiva*, located somewhere on the outskirts of Los Angeles. The first crime, a rape, happens after a woman leaves the *mikvah* – a bath-house where the women regularly bathe. This ritual bathing is important to the women of the *yeshiva*, a form of '... spiritual cleansing. A renewal of the soul.' Not only does Faye Kellerman inform readers about the traditions, beliefs and customs of this closed community, she also writes openly about anti-semitism and uses the issue to stand as a possible motive for the crimes. The two central characters are Rina and Moshe, and Moshe is suspected by the police of committing the attacks. He is vindicated in the end when he and Rina tackle the rapist head on. The officer in charge of the investigation arrives in the nick of time but it is Rina and Moshe, both suffering injuries as a result of their encounter with the rapist, who rightfully get the credit for his capture.

Using third-person narration, Faye Kellerman tells about one night when Rina, well aware that an attacker is on the loose, is alone in the *mikvah*:

> Tonight the sounds seemed closer. The crackling of twigs, dull noises that could have been footsteps. It had been going on for the last ten minutes, but there was still a half hour's worth of work to do. She was sick of being frightened of shadows, terrorized by a phantom that lacked the courage to show its monstrous face in the day-light. She wanted this ogre captured and felt her fear turn to rage.
>
> (Kellerman, 1986, p. 69)

Later in the story Rina is attacked by a man wearing a ski mask:

> She saw a figure appear. It was Moshe. 'Help me!' she screamed at the wisp of a man. The attacker was taller and heavier, but Moshe was armed with an oversized volume of the Talmud. Raising it, he blinked several times and brought it crashing down on the man's head. The impact stunned him for a moment. Rina ran over and struck out at his face, trying to pull off the ski mask. He kicked her in the abdomen, she doubled over, and the man broke free.
>
> (Kellerman, 1986, p. 266)

The account of this attack, and Rina and Moshe's successful efforts in bringing the assailant to ground, takes four pages in the telling. It is an excellent example of economical writing, with each sentence pruned back to the minimum. Nothing is overstated and the reader is gripped by the pace.

Faye Kellerman does stretch the credibility gap when it comes to characterization, and this has to do with the growing relationship between Rina and Decker, the police officer in charge of the investigation. Despite the initial attraction between Rina and Decker, Rina insists that she could only marry again within the boundaries of her religious convictions. It transpires that Decker was born to Jewish parents but adopted as a small baby by a Baptist couple. Decker has insights about his own internalized anti-semitism and has a growing need for more understanding of what it means to him to be Jew. Decker's search for his Jewish identity dovetails neatly with Rina's desire to marry a Jewish man and raises a question about making coincidence work too hard for a happy ending.

The second character that stretches credibility is the rapist. Throughout the story this man is portrayed as trustworthy and capable because he teaches at the *yeshiva* every day. Once uncovered as the brute he really is, his sanity instantly dissolves and we see him as a man in need of psychiatric help, or to use a word taken from the book, a 'wacko'. Accepting that it is possible for a deeply disturbed man to pass as competent in the day to day while underneath great turbulence is undermining aspects of his personality, it is nonetheless too much to suggest that the slide from one state of being to another can be so rapidly accomplished once public exposure takes place. The resolution phase of the book is weakened considerably by the treatment of this character.

The Fourth Wall and *The Ritual Bath* are examples of the puzzle priority plot. Settings and/or background information have been used to provide an extra something to make the puzzle more interesting, fascinating even, but not to distract from it.

What would you say you know a lot about? Music? Education? Food and drink? Using what you know, and expanding on it, is only common sense. What you don't know today, you could learn tomorrow.

What settings can you think of? Jot down any ideas you have. Information that has been recorded, even if only scribbled notes on scraps of paper, is always there to come back to, but thoughts slip away never to be found again. You might want to create sections in your workbook for the plot and the story, or you might prefer to use your diary section for note taking and move the ideas across at a later date. Do what feels right for you.

Watching the detectives

There can be a single character or several characters involved in solving the murder(s). Usually this person, or persons, will fall into one of four categories:

1   The police officer, usually a detective
2   The private eye
3   The amateur sleuth or person brought into the situation by personal or professional circumstances
4   The narrating sidekick.

The police officer

This person is intended to work as part of a team. In real life, teams of detectives are assigned to a murder case immediately after a body has been discovered in suspicious circumstances. It is uncommon within police murder investigations to have one detective working alone. In fiction, however, state-employed detectives are often a rum lot, possessed by a strong, individualistic streak that has them using strong-arm tactics and heavy-handed persuasion as they go about making their enquiries. Often at odds with the police force structure, they adopt methods and tactics that go against the grain of usual police procedure. The tension created by this approach might well provide dramatic interest if another police officer, upstanding and correct, finds out what's going on. To date it has been male characters who have been portrayed in this macho fashion. These police types have a lot in common with the less respectable private eyes who act as a law unto themselves, the only difference between them being that one has the law on his side and the other does not. P. D. James broke new ground with the creation of her male detective Adam Dalgleish. He's a dapper man, a poet who knows a thing or two about the arts and wears better fitting clothes than his stereotyped counterpart, the 'flatfoot', who appears to have more brawn than brain. As previously mentioned James often gives greater emphasis to who commits the murder and why than to who follows the clues and how. Incidentally, P. D. James also has a female private investigator, Cordelia Grey.

And what about female detectives? American television gave us *Cagney and Lacey*, the only two women detectives to receive wide acclaim for their efforts in bringing criminals to justice, week after week. The characters themselves were quite aware of their position and their difficulties – these were obvious in the story-lines, and sexism was always an item on the agenda in their working environment. This was the first female buddy series. Unlike the majority of TV cop series featuring men, *Cagney and Lacey* divided its interest between the characters' public and private lives, often exploring the tensions between the two. Do you remember the scenes in the loo? This was their inner sanctum, a place in which to discuss problems and worries away from the watchful eyes of male colleagues. It was clever to have made such good use of the loo, and symbolic as well. We're often told that it is not possible to have women working in a male environment because of the shortage of loo space. How fitting, then, to have given it prominence in this way.

Detective Kate Delafield, the creation of author Katherine V. Forrest, is a well-respected member of the Los Angeles police force. In *Murder at the Nightwood Bar* she and her partner, Detective Ed Taylor, are called in when a woman's body is found in a car park shared by a motel, a café and the Nightwood Bar. Delafield is a lesbian but no, she's not 'out' at work and the dilemma bothers her constantly. She knows that the women in the Nightwood Bar are lesbians and worries about Taylor's reaction if he asks the wrong sort of question and gets an unexpected answer:

> *Where does my integrity begin and end? she asks herself. What if someone asks pointblank if I'm a lesbian?*

The reply occurs to her immediately

> *They won't ask.* She was looking into the faces of the women at the bar. *They won't need to.*
>
> (Forrest, 1987, p. 11)

Kate has to ask the bar occupants some necessary questions and she knows that will be difficult:

> The woman glared at Kate. 'Enjoy being one of the boys? Kicking your own sisters around?'
>
> Kate said evenly, 'I don't kick anyone around.' She knew she must use diversionary tactics, break up this group, separate them before they solidified in their hostility.
>
> (Forrest, 1987, p. 13)

But help comes from an unexpected source:

> 'Patton,' Magda Schaeffer said, walking towards the woman, her hands on her hips, 'you cool it. You lay off all your political shit for just these few hours out of your life so these people can do their jobs and get out of here. The sooner they finish the sooner they'll be gone.'
>
> (Forrest, 1987, p. 13)

The confrontation between Kate's job and her unspoken identity as a lesbian works as a subplot to the murder investigation and, as in *Cagney and Lacey*, this woman is principled and conscientious. Katherine V. Forrest does include romantic interest in her stories but Delafield never has an easy time of it.

How do you feel about a police officer as the problem-solving character, central to the plot? To outline the challenges you think relevant for either a female or a male character is a necessary part of characterization. What would your character be like? Principled and straight down the line on all points? Likely to kick over the traces if the need arises? What examples of fictional police officers can you think of? You may want to finish this section about investigators before making further notes, but if you've already begun to think about a police detective character write down whatever thoughts and ideas you have now. Even a few comments can make a starting point and you can add or develop ideas later.

The private eye

The private eye operates as a self-employed individual, and finances will dictate what hired help she or he has. The stereotype of the male private eye is that he is rather shabby, works out of seedy premises in a run-down part of town, is able to 'mix it' with the best and worst of villains, is 'smart with the ladies' and tough with men and women alike when 'the chips are down'.

American writers Dashiell Hammett and Raymond Chandler, writing in the late 1920s and 1930s, were among the first to use the fictional private eye, and it is no coincidence that the characters they created could be easily imagined by American readers. We know that carrying guns is accepted as a right in the United States. There is also a strong cultural emphasis on the individual, and it is more likely that personal fears for safety could be resolved by employing your very own private eye. Despite the shady kinds of operations engaged in by these male private eyes there was always a degree of integrity evident in their personalities. The way that integrity was acted out could differ from one private eye to another but, like the head on a good glass of beer, their finer points would always rise to the surface.

In the 1930s few publishers outside the US could hope to compete with the low cost of publication the Americans achieved with large print runs, so the popularity of their private investigators extended to many countries. These cheap books saturated the market. Even now there is a strong American emphasis in crime fiction writing, although the genre has had an 'up-market' swing and hardbacks are bought more frequently than would ever have been the case before the 1980s. The recent increase in fictional female private eyes may not reflect reality but oh, what a welcome relief they are. You may already be familiar with Sara Paretsky's character, V. I. Warshawski, but there are others worth a mention.

With a BA from St Louis University and an MA from Southern Illinois University, Clio Browne was qualified to be the history teacher her mother had always wanted her to be. However, her father, Caspar Browne, had been the first black private investigator in St Louis and, in the tradition handed down from father to daughter, the fine reputation of the Browne Bureau of Investigation (BBI) continues. Clio knew from the time she'd walked into her father's new office, the year she was eleven, that she would one day sit in the same swivel chair, puzzling over other people's troubles. *Clio Browne, Private Investigator* is the name of the novel written by Dolores Komo. In Clio she has created a strong, older woman who is well able to handle the intricacies of a tricky investigation. Notable aspects of the character are her resilience and her implicit recognition that frustration and hassles are inevitably a part of a private investigator's job description. Clio takes us inside her thinking process as she is on her way to talk to a well-known gambler:

> Listening to the sound of her heels clicking along the polished deck, Clio wondered what approach she should take with Artie Dowling. He had a reputation for being vocal but not violent. He'd never been convicted of anything more serious than failure to post his registration sticker to his windshield, although every gambler in the city knew where to find one of his high-stakes poker games when they wanted to play.
> (Komo, 1988, p. 78)

Note how the focus of attention is moved from Clio's clicking heels to the layering of information about Artie Dowling. One of her first assignments had been for a company where a member of staff was suspected of passing stolen products to an accomplice during working hours:

> Clio wanted to get close to the action without being observed and exchanged clothes with a bag lady behind a nearby trash hopper. The lady agreed to throw in a rickety old

> shopping cart full of dumpster-gleaned treasures along with
> the clothes for a deposit of fifty dollars.
>
> (Komo, 1988, p. 56)

A good arrangement all round, and Clio's disguise works well. She
sees what is going on and the case is wrapped up in no time at
all. But:

> When she went to return the cart and get her own clothes
> back, the lady was gone, along with the fifty, her best
> business suit and a brand new pair of I. Millers.
>
> (Komo, 1988, p. 56)

The greatest skill in this kind of characterization is in allowing the
reader to identify with Clio's way of looking at things and with
the way she initiates and responds to what's happening. We can
easily imagine doing what Clio does, and her very human qualities
add credibility to the story.

Linda Barnes had written four crime fiction novels about a
male private eye, Michael Spraggue, before introducing the
character Carlotta Carlyle in a short story entitled 'Lucky Penny'.
In the novel *A Trouble of Fools*, Carlotta is on the job again.
Brought up on a rich diet of Jewish stories featuring gutsy women
galore (some of whom are in her own family), Carlotta is six
foot, one inch tall, wears size 11 shoes and drives around in an
old red Toyota. Unexpectedly, a client catches Carlotta at home
doing housework:

> Now I admit I have looked better. My sweats had seen their
> heyday long ago, and most of my right knee was visible
> through a tear. My shirt was slightly more reputable, an
> oversized bright red pullover. I don't wear it much because,
> to tell you the truth, it doesn't go well with my coloring. I've
> got red hair, really red hair, the kind that beggars adjectives
> like 'flaming' and Mom always told me to wear blues and
> greens, but every once in a while I break loose.
>
> (Barnes, 1989, p. 4)

Speaking with her client, Miss Devens, Carlotta is reminded of her
Aunt Bea who also could: '... see clear to the back of your soul and
plumb the depths of unworthiness lurking there ...'. Carlotta
realizes something:

> No. I didn't know her from some other time or place, not
> personally. But I have known women her age, women of steel

who grew up in an era when feathers and fans and batted eyelashes were the name of the game. The smart ladies learned the score, played along.

(Barnes, 1989, p. 10)

How much to charge Miss Devens will depend on how much Carlotta thinks she can afford:

'How much do you charge?' she asked.
I glanced down at her shoes. My full-price clients are mainly divorce lawyers with buffed cordovan Gucci loafers. Margaret Devens wore orthopaedic wedgies with run-down heels, much worn, much polished, shabbily genteel. My pay scales started a downward slide.

(Barnes, 1989, p. 11)

So now we know: next time you're wondering how to calculate the cost of your services, check the shoes of the person who's paying the bill.

Many women writers appear to be working with the intention of having their female private eye characters come across as ordinary people doing a not-so-ordinary job. Why? Do they add a dimension of human frailty in order to give an endearing quality to their female characters? Or is the aim to demystify the investigation process? What do you think?

I was unfamiliar with the character Sam Marlowe until a young person very close to me pointed out that she was a favourite of hers. Tony Bradman created Sam Marlowe, the girl detective, and he has written three books of her adventures so far. She's a very believable character and very observant of the things she sees around her, of the people she meets and of her family. She is not too concerned about telling us when she's feeling very scared either:

I panicked. I know I've said before that's not what a detective should do, but I couldn't help it. I ran. I dashed towards the doorway, but just before I reached it, my knees seemed to give way, and I fell. I turned round and looked up. The nightmare figure loomed over me ... This is it, I thought. My whole life flashed before me. It didn't take long. I'm only eleven, after all.

(Bradman, 1990, p. 121)

The importance of characters like Sam Marlowe as role models for girls cannot be underestimated. Do you know of any others?

All of these private investigators are brave but they admit their fears along the way. Via such fictional characters we, the readers, can gain a sense of strength and confidence, a sort of *if they can do it then I can do what I have to do too*. These women work with a code of ethics recognizable to today's women readers but there is nothing saintly about them. If a method of gaining information requires a little bending of the rules about trespassing or getting into an office or building in an unorthodox manner, then so be it.

What sort of private eye would you wish to create? Will she tell the story herself or would you use a third-person narrative to relate events as they happen? Learning to identify how a story is being told is a very useful skill. Keeping your notebook beside you when you read means you can jot down any different writing methods you come across. Providing your private eye with a background of family, friends, a place to live, an office and a car is like creating jigsaw pieces that make up a composite picture. Fitness is often stressed, and it's not unusual to find our female private eyes putting themselves through a jogging session every morning or working out in the gym so that they can keep their minds and bodies alert and ready for anything. Another thing to think about is relationships. Private eyes are notorious for having problematic love affairs. Most finish up on their own or have no romantic attachments whatsoever. If there's a fascinating plot unfolding then perhaps a love interest gets in the way.

The individual or amateur sleuth

The individual or amateur sleuth has to be given an angle, a connection – something that involves her personally with the murder victim, the victim's family, the investigation or some other aspect of the story. The variety of options is seemingly endless. Has the sleuth been charged with the murder and somehow escaped police custody in order to find the killer herself? Was it her dearest friend or lover who was murdered, and does she feel that she just has to do something about it, knowing that the police will charge the wrong person? The difference between this category of fictional problem-solving character and any other is that personal reasons alone link this individual to the murder investigation. The challenge is to make the circumstantial link convincing. Having achieved this, the character can act in a freer way than either the police or the private eye. Without a proscribed police procedure to follow or a paying client to satisfy, the amateur sleuth can make up her own rules as she goes along. This factor alone can provide the writer with a fresh approach to the plot. The amateur sleuth will initially be responding to events, one thing will lead to another and the reader will be able to imagine that she could have acted in the same way if placed in the same position. Another advantage for the writer is the potential to develop the character. This amateur could be introduced to us as a bumbling fool in the first chapter. She might make mistakes and promptly learn from them, and she could become more aware of relevant issues, world affairs, or simply have a greater understanding of human nature as a direct result of the investigative process. One outcome (with an eye to future stories) would be to have the character become a private investigator after this initial experience of crime solving. Who knows, she might even join the police force, although more often the movement tends to be the other way.

One Tuesday evening Emma Victor is answering the phone at the Women's Hotline office in Boston when she receives a call from a woman in trouble. The woman knows Emma's name and begs her to go to the north end of Lexington Street the following night at nine o'clock. She says she will be recognizable by her beige raincoat, and hangs up the phone before Emma can protest. Reluctantly, Emma shows up as arranged, only to find nearby the dead body of a woman in a beige raincoat. Looking down on the dead woman's face, Emma describes what she sees:

> Two long thin welts, puffy and red, were blazing across her cheek. There was snot running out of her nose. But even with the panic and red welts it was a pleasant face. A face that had a conversation with me in a French restaurant, just two weeks ago. The night came back to me, like a bolt shooting into a lock.
>
> (Wings, 1986, p. 12)

With this link established between the victim and Emma Victor, Mary Wings sets the scene for her novel *She Came Too Late*. Emma is hooked into the mystery and is left with the feeling: '… that someone had needed me and had gotten dead' (Wings, 1986, p. 21).

The use of characters who are involved in related professions is also common – professionals such as lawyers and journalists, not specifically trained for detective work but easily connected to crime. This is the link that Marion Foster (a pseudonym for Shirley Shea) uses in *The Monarchs are Flying*. The story is set in Spruce Falls, a hard-rock mining town in Canada. Leslie Taylor is accused of murdering her former lover, Marcie Denton, and Harriet Fordham Croft is engaged by the victim's husband to prosecute. We take up the narrative at a point when Leslie is objecting to her own lawyer, Haberdash Poulis, because he is disobeying her explicit instructions not to put her mother on the stand:

> Eyes fastened on Leslie's back, Harriet saw the rigidity of the straight shoulders, the defiant tilt of the dark head. She'd learned more from that single outburst than from any of the facts Clarence had dug up. She loved her family and wanted to spare them the indignity of malicious public scrutiny. She knew the trouble she was in and she was determined to face it alone. She was also proud and stubborn and strangely vulnerable for someone of her maturity and obvious ability.
>
> (Foster, 1987, p. 70)

Harriet feels reluctant about acting for the victim's husband, something doesn't feel right, and she is very impressed by the way Leslie has behaved in court. It isn't long before Leslie dismisses her male lawyer and appoints Harriet to defend her in the forth-coming trial. Although the glamorous Harriet Fordham Croft is a brilliant lawyer, with 'the memory of a computer', she would not have the success she enjoys were it not for her paid assistant, Clarence Crossley:

> It was thanks to him that so many of her cases ended in acquittal. With a network of contacts and the nose of a bloodhound, Clarence Crossley could find out anything, anytime, anywhere.
>
> (Foster, 1987, pp. 33–34)

Having Clarence do the leg work while Harriet scores her triumphs in court gives us a role reversal situation in this working rela-tionship. Those of us who remember court scenes where Perry Mason, the distinguished American lawyer, unmasked one killer after another would have little difficulty recognising the similarity between Clarence Crossley and Perry's right-hand man Paul Drake.

Gillian Slovo was once a journalist herself, which must have been of some value in providing background information for her character Kate Baeier, a freelance, sax-playing journalist, unemployed when the novel *Morbid Symptoms* opens. Kate is in the Carelton Foundation building on her way to the office of the *African Economic Reports* (a small organization producing a monthly business magazine and a political newsletter) when she is stopped by two police officers. What is she doing there? Bob, the building caretaker, comes along and tells her that Tim Nicholson, who worked for *African Economic Reports*, is dead. After more questions, some of them irrelevant and objectionable, Kate is allowed to leave. The following day she is asked to attend a meeting organized by the different organizations in the building at which she is requested by them to look into the matter:

> Because you know us all, you knew Tim, and your work shows you can carry out efficient research.
>
> (Slovo, 1984, p. 12)

There are a couple of other reasons too. Kate understands the confidentiality issue and, well, she is out of work isn't she? Her small fee and expenses will be paid by contributions from all the organizations in the building but *African Economic Reports* will bear the brunt of the cost. The reader gets the impression that Kate's investigation is more to do with journalism than a murder investigation. No one, not even Kate, realizes how dangerous this investigation will prove to be, or that her life will be threatened as she begins to delve deeper.

The narrating sidekick

Earlier, in talking about the 'locked room' puzzle, I referred to a book by Edgar Allan Poe, *The Murders in the Rue Morgue*, that contains the first fictional detective. Poe's narrator was a character who listened with rapt attention as Auguste Dupin, the classic armchair detective, sifted through the clues. From his position as admirer of a brilliant theorist, the narrator unfolds the story. In 1886 Sherlock Holmes came along with his friend Dr Watson, and the tales of these two, recorded in books, heard on the radio, and much later seen in TV productions, emphasizes Watson's admiration and respect for the superior skills and deductive powers of Sherlock Holmes. These characters tell the story from the observer's point of view and act as a foil to their much more perceptive friends. It is hard to imagine any woman writer creating a 'Watson' character to narrate with similar admiration the tale of a female problem-solving character, but this kind of narration could be used effectively.

The clues

What exactly is a clue? The answer is simple: a clue can be anything. Creating categories for the assembly of clues is easier than pinning down how important any individual clue might be. A clue can be something tangible, or something said, or an action or deed that seems at odds with the character or with the situation. A tiny button, or scrap of material left behind at the murder scene, a few hairs clinging to the victim's clothing, traces of blood and scrapings of skin found beneath the dead person's fingernails – all of these might be called clues. By itself a clue might not have great value, and it might only be with an accumulation of evidence that a charge of murder can be made. Such evidence can indicate the presence of a person at the murder scene but might not be proof that this same person killed the victim. There could have been a struggle, and that button, that scrap of material, those few stray hairs and the traces of blood and skin, might all relate to events that happened *before* the murder took place and even before the killer arrived.

Alternatively, the clue could be verbal. When questioned, any of the suspects, or even a person unconnected to the crime, might make a remark or convey information that will later uncover the identity of the murderer. A suspect might have said she or he caught a train at a certain time from a certain station, but if a porter working at either station on the day in question is able to give irrefutable evidence that the times mentioned do not fit, this information will shake or shatter that suspect's story. Confronted with the lie, our suspect could crumble and confess all or, equally possible, she could give a second account of her whereabouts – this time the truth. Faced with the prospect of a murder rap, will she promptly supply good reasons for giving a false alibi in the first place? Did she protect someone? Was she worried the boss would find out that she was not doing her job that day? Perhaps she was concerned she would be found out, not as a murderer but as a two-timer conducting an illicit affair that no one knows about?

What if a suspect returned to the scene of the crime to retrieve incriminating evidence? The plot might involve a hidden waiting observer. This observer may have found the incriminating evidence and have set up a trap, waiting each night outside the victim's house in the hope that the suspect would return to the scene of the crime. Ah, here they come now, right on cue. Is the suspect acting like an innocent person fearful of being wrongly accused? Is it the murderer acting like a criminal eager to escape detection? If it is the murderer this outcome may conclude the investigation and the story could be almost over. If not, we might yet be reading of a further twist in the plot. Any small piece of evidence can appear incriminating on the face of it, but there could also be a harmless explanation – an explanation that diverts the relevance of the clue away from the guilty culprit.

Sleight of hand

There's a teasing game adults play with children where the aim is to have the child look away from what is happening in front of her by diverting her attention with some pretext. Look over there, can you see that spider on the window? While the child tries to find the spider, something belonging to her – a toy, biscuit, maybe a piece of cake – is whisked away. Some children may not notice anything amiss, others will respond immediately in protest. When it comes to clues, the same sort of game is being acted out between writer and reader. Seeking to drop in a given number of clues, the writer hastens to divert the reader's attention elsewhere. Here's how it's done. Imagine this: you are reading a 'whodunnit' and have learned that a letter has been found, written to the murder victim by one of the chief suspects. One tiny, important detail is included but its significance is played down by what happens next. The mood changes abruptly. The investigator's phone rings. She picks up the receiver, says impatiently 'Yes, no, I'll be right there', then hangs up. Racing towards the door with a gleeful whoop, our heroine is so full of excitement and energetic movement that she hardly has time to grab a coat or her car keys. Action impels the reader to follow, caught up in the momentum. And what about that letter? Will you remember the contents? Or that tiny, important clue, dropped out of sight while your attention was deliberately distracted?

Alternatively, the clue may be perceived as insignificant or irrelevant because it contradicts what we've been told in the story so far. If a suspect has an unshakable alibi for the time at which the murder was committed it may not occur to a reader to rethink the alibi. This suspect may have got from A to B with outside assistance. Another possible explanation would involve an accomplice who changed things at the scene of the crime, after the murder had taken place. Do you remember the time recorded on the victim's watch? And do you remember that the detective who arrived at the murder scene first noted the time recorded on that watch and said it probably indicated the time of death? And what about the electric fan that was kept in the room where the body was found? That fan was on and working when the housekeeper arrived that morning. She automatically turned it off before noticing the body alongside the bed. Either or both of these actions – altering a watch or using an electric fan near the body – could affect, or at least confuse, any conclusion about the actual time of death. The murderer might also become agitated, realizing that these actions had been performed without his or her knowledge.

False trails

Another way of embedding clues, unnoticed, into a plot is to have an early chapter containing a number of facts and small details listed as part of the original setting up of the plot. This will usually be the 'scene of the crime' chapter, though other variations would apply as well. The information is then linked, incorrectly, to a possible theory about who the killer is or how the murder has been committed. The placing of such emphasis on a wrong-footed theory, promptly followed by action developing from that line of thought, allows certain crucial clues to lie forgotten, or hidden. They may not be referred to again until the final pages when a peripheral character who has escaped suspicion throughout the book is suddenly confronted and exposed as the killer.

Traditionally it is assumed that real clues are buried in the plot like needles in a haystack. Because of this assumption a crucial piece of information made to loom conspicuously large in the plot can have much the same effect as the hidden clue method. Frequently, this kind of 'prominent distraction' strategy is used with characters rather than with information. Someone discovered near the murder scene and questioned the day the body was found may seem like a suspicious character to the police, but because there is some doubt, or because it's understood a charge of murder won't stick, no arrest is made. For many readers this first suspect is perceived as a decoy, and they decide immediately to look elsewhere for clues. This is not the killer, they think – he or she is much too obvious. But if this character really is the murderer then it could come as a shock. It is almost certain that you have come across this tactic yourself on more than one occasion. If the reader's attention is gently but firmly directed away from information about clues, then the plot puzzle exists as unseen background that will only come into focus when the end of the story is in sight. It is both a challenge and an acquired reading skill to slip past the obstacles a good author uses to keep the mystery intact.

When the story is being told by the problem-solving character her thinking process will often be revealed to the reader at various stages throughout the book. There might be a major reshuffling at some point, a sifting through of the evidence (particularly after a series of dead ends), where the narrating character lists or arranges all that she has gleaned so far. The factual and circumstantial information is sifted and suddenly, as though a magic word had been spoken, something becomes clear. Like a last jigsaw piece slotted into place, all will be understood by the investigating character and it is then up to the reader to calculate or guess, from what has been read, who the guilty party is.

Suspects

Few of us can ever really know what passion someone else feels. The spark, the trigger, that mobilizes irreversible change may not appear to be significant but it could prove to be the last straw. How many times have you been shocked by the depth of feeling you suddenly perceive in someone, perhaps during an argument? 'I never knew you felt so strongly about this ...' you might say. That depth of emotion, hidden for days, weeks, months, years, is a good place to begin when thinking about suspects. Consider situations and people you are familiar with. Try to recall something in the past that has stirred up a cauldron of feeling. What about the last argument you had with someone? Here are two exercises you can use.

Exercises

1 Using only 'she' or 'he' for the person you are in conflict with, write down what you remember of the facial expressions, gestures and movements you observed. For example:

Her mouth tightened. Was she about to cry? I tried to think of something to say, something comforting, but my mind went blank. 'Ida,' I whispered, 'Ida, please listen.'

Her eyes flashed in anger. 'Get out' she screamed, 'Get out.'

He threw himself forward, his arms reaching across the table, palms stretched towards me in a pleading fashion. But, when I looked at this face, the cold eyes, the set mouth, the grim expression of hate, I knew he meant me harm.

Both of these examples are first-person accounts. Now try the same exercises using the third person. You may feel awkward and self-conscious but accepting these feelings as part of the process is the best way of overcoming them. The longer you persevere, the easier it will get.

2   Now that you have worked with the practical, observable nature of your experience, it is time to think about the causes of the conflict(s) you remember. What exactly is conflict, and how is it created? We all have feelings, but do we all feel the same way? Inevitably, what we feel will be influenced by our past experience and the cultural and family values we grew up with. Misunderstandings occur every day and sometimes wrong interpretations are loaded with imagined insult. The giving of misinformation could be a deliberate tactic meant to deceive, or it could be an innocent error. We can feel abandoned, isolated, offended, outraged by other people. Statistically, the possibility of murder as a result of such feelings is remote. It is not the feelings but what we do with those feelings that matters. Have you ever wished someone dead? Have you ever voiced such a wish? Innocent remarks can take on a new and sinister meaning once a murder has been committed. Make some notes about the conflicts you remember and what you thought they were about. Is there an underlying theme you can see? If you do find yourself rekindling angry responses, channel those feelings into your work. You may well be surprised at what comes out.

From these notes take specific situations and experiment by telling the story from different points of view. Try to be the other person telling her side of the story. Once you have explored familiar conflicts, think about some of the values you grew up with. What were you taught about honour, pride, respectability, modesty, envy, jealousy? Explore possible motives – jealousy, revenge, greed, envy – for committing any sort of crime, not just for murder.

Remembering that your suspects are simply suspects, and the fact that the greater number will be proved innocent in the end will help you to decide how plausible the possible accusations made against them ought to be. Will the charge of murder seem a travesty of justice? Will the personality of a suspected character be so awful that he or she becomes an easy target in a sloppy investigation? People can find themselves in bizarre situations, interrogated by the police and unable to account for their whereabouts on the night in question, perhaps because of fear and perhaps because their memory fails them. Murder happens to ordinary people. Murder inquiries involve people who never expected to find themselves in such a distressing predicament.

So you've got a blank page in front of you or in the typewriter and you look at it, hoping for inspiration. Nothing happens, except that you're telling yourself this is probably a waste of valuable time and you ought to be doing something really worthwhile. What now? If you have the opportunity, grab your coat, pen, notebook and whatever else you need, and take yourself out for a few hours, maybe a whole day. Explore the streets of your local area. Perhaps you have the means to go further afield, a town or city not too far away. Don't make your outing plans too elaborate or you could find yourself caught in a procrastination trap.

Public transport has always been a great source of inspiration to writers. The conversations overhead on a bus or train can spark off a thinking process that could get you started right away. Whatever you can make use of, write down; don't let an idea that excites you drift way. Be warned, too, of the danger of frittering your attention down too many paths. Observe the people around you. Imagine a murder scene – near that restaurant over by the canal, what about that ghastly car park late at night, or will the body be found behind that park bench? When you do find two or more people engrossed in conversation and you can listen without appearing nosy and rude, try not to look but imagine what these people look like. What background setting would you want them to have? Can you come up with brief potted histories of their lives? Cemeteries are worth visiting. Not only are they quiet places where you can think, but there are all those names on the headstones and other information sure to arouse your curiosity.

Stories may need to be carried around in your head for a time before the clarified structure becomes apparent. Continuous note taking can help that process. The more note taking you do the more you'll feel a need to keep everything to hand. It can be very annoying when you cannot find that vital scrap of paper, or that page on which you wrote a good opening paragraph. A few minutes arranging your notes for easy reference will save time when you're in full flow and don't want to be distracted by unnecessary interruptions.

3 A source of inspiration can come from tiny news reports in newspapers. Television news is not quite so helpful as the facts can slip past too quickly. In this final exercise I'm using information gleaned from an actual story and giving the barest details to allow you to use the information as a springboard into an imagined plot. The headline reads: 'Man's body found in shallow grave' followed by only eight lines of information. We're told that new owners of a house were digging out a small area for a goldfish pond when they came across a corpse. The only other information conveyed is that a previous owner, a woman, is helping the police with enquiries. We can probably guess that the grave has been dug sometime in the past six months or so, but is the plot really as simple as it looks? What do you think has happened here?

Notes

1 Ellery Queen was the pseudonym used by two cousins, Frederic Dannay and Manfred Bennington Lee. After three successful books written as Ellery Queen they wrote four books under another pseudonym, Drury Lane.
2 Michelle B. Slung (ed.), *Crime on Her Mind*, Penguin, London, 1984, p. 14.
3 Ibid, p. 18.
4 Ibid, p. 19.
5 Ibid, p. 18.
6 Colin Wilson, *Written in Blood*, Grafton Books, 1990, p. 55.
7 Ibid, pp. 67–69.
8 Ibid, p. 31 and Julian Symons, *Crime and Detection Quiz*, Weidenfeld & Nicholson, London, 1983.
9 Colin Wilson, op. cit., pp. 31–32.

Sources

Barnes, Linda, *A Trouble of Fools*, Coronet, London, 1989.
Bradman, Tony, *Sam, The Girl Detective: The Case of the Missing Mummy*, Yearling Books, London, 1990.
Forrest, Katherine V., *Murder at the Nightwood Bar*, Pandora, London, 1987.

Foster, Marion (pseudonym for Shirley Shea), *The Monarchs Are Flying* , Pandora, London, 1987.

James, P. D., *The Australian Author*, vol. 23, no. 2, Winter 1991.

James, P. D., *Innocent Blood*, Sphere, London, 1981.

Jones, Ann, *Women Who Kill*, Victor Gollancz, London, 1991.

Kellerman, Faye, *The Ritual Bath*, Fawcett Crest, New York, 1986.

Komo, Dolores, *Clio Browne, Private Investigator*, The Crossing Press, California, 1988.

Lathen, Emma, *Banking on Death*, Penguin, London, 1983.

McNab, Claire, *Lessons in Murder*, Silver Moon Books, London, 1990.

Paul, Barbara, *The Fourth Wall*, The Women's Press, London, 1979.

Rendell, Ruth, *Going Wrong*, Arrow, London, 1991.

Rowe, Jennifer, *Grim Pickings*, Allen & Unwin, Australia, 1988.

Slovo, Gillian, *Morbid Symptoms*, Pluto Press, London, 1984.

Wilson, Colin, *Written in Blood*, Grafton Books, London, 1990.

Wings, Mary, *She Came Too Late*, The Women's Press, London, 1986.

Wood, Jim, *The Rape of Inez Garcia*, G. P. Putnam's Sons, New York, 1976.

Further reading

Autobiographies by retired police officers, books about trials and investigations, biographies/autobiographies about individual cases.

Cameron, Deborah & Frazer, Elizabeth, *The Lust to Kill*, Polity Press, Cambridge, 1987.

Carlen, P., Hicks, J., O'Dwyer, J., Christian, D., Tchaikovsky, C. (eds.), *Criminal Women*, Polity Press, Cambridge, 1985.

Dunhill, Christina, *The Boys in Blue: Women's Challenge to the Police*, Virago, London, 1989.

Edwards, Susan, *Women on Trial* (a study of the female suspect, defendant and offender in the criminal law and justice system), Manchester University Press, Manchester, 1984.

Hartman, Mary S., *Victorian Murderesses*, Robson Books, London, 1985.

Marks, Laurence & Van Den Bergh, Tony, *Ruth Ellis* (executed in 1955 for killing her lover), Penguin, London, 1990.

Mukherjee, S. K. & Scutt, Joycelynne A. (eds.), *Women and Crime*, Allen & Unwin, Australia, 1981.

Padel, Una & Stevenson, Prue, *Insiders: Women's Experience of Prison*, Virago, London, 1988.

Peckham, Audrey, *A Woman In Custody* (a personal account of one nightmare journey through the English penal system), Fontana, London, 1985.

Rhodes, Dusty & McNeill, Sandra, *Women Against Violence Against Women*, Onlywomen Press, London, 1985.

Sayers, D. L., 'The Necklace of Pearls' in Carol-Lynn Rossel-Waugh, Martin Greenberg & Isaac Asimov (eds.), *The Twelve Crimes of Christmas*, Avon, New York, 1981.

Stanko, Elizabeth A., *Intimate Intrusions*, Routledge & Kegan Paul, London, 1985.

Stern, Vivien, *Bricks of Shame* (Britain's prisons), Penguin, London, 1989.

Weis, Rene, *Criminal Justice* (the story of Edith Thompson who was executed in England in 1923), Hamish Hamilton, London, 1988.

Wilson, Colin, *The Mammoth Book of True Crime*, Robinson Publishing, London, vol. 1, 1988, vol. 2, 1990.

What if? Science fiction and fantasy

Science fiction, and the variety of novels and stories loosely gathered under its umbrella, is premised on the notion *what if?* What if the world were ordered like this? What if other worlds do things differently? What if we could travel in space and/or time and/or other dimensions? What if science developed in such a way as to alter social organization radically? What if the world expired through natural or human-made disaster? What if sexual reproduction were no longer fixed? What if sexuality could be experienced in different forms by different individuals?

Writing science fiction or fantasy novels is technically not much different from writing any other kind of novel. Character, plot, setting and theme are all aspects that you will have to think about. Science fiction/fantasy is a genre where you can explore the world of ideas, and invent alternative realities or different worlds. The challenge is how to present these different worlds or ideas to the reader. To keep readers involved the narrative should have an internal coherence that will make these ideas or scenarios seem imaginatively possible. This chapter is largely concerned with the wealth of ideas generated by women writing science fiction/fantasy in order to show you how writers make their imagined worlds believable.

The imagined world of Medena

What if your grandmother had been a noted scientist, one of a team who explored the planet of Medena and helped to design modifying technology so that humans could adapt to life on this new planet? What if the last spacecraft that brought people from Earth had been destroyed in a bad dust storm? What then?

For a lot of people born on Medena, Earth is now simply a place they've heard about from older folk. Humans have lived on Medena for seventy-five years at the time of our story but *how* they live is very different from the old ways. One factor has changed the whole fabric of day-to-day life – the kind of air they breathe. Humidicribs keep newborn babies safe and breathing well until a *quad* is ready for them. A quad is a unit designed for four: two oxygen breathers and two carbon-dioxide breathers. Some people's way of breathing has been altered irreversibly as a result of the early technology used on the newly inhabited planet. Two babies of each breathing type are needed in each quad in case one gets ill or has breathing difficulties. All illness is somehow related to breathing difficulties and so it remains a constant concern. Putting two breathers of each type together means there will be some useful compatibility. Just as flowers and humans have compatibility (we know that flowers draw in what we breath out, particularly during daylight hours), so the principle on Medena works in much the same way.

What do you think is the main point behind this scenario? Are we really concerned with Medena or with something much closer to home?

These babies living in quads do not bond with adults, as is more often the case on Earth, but will bond instead with each other. The setting of the scene on Medena allows us to ponder on what it might be like to experiment with the questions of child-rearing methods, of how we form social units, offering alternatives to 'the family' as we know it and examining the implications for society as a whole. Our story could begin with your grandmother's adventures in space, the arrival on Medena of the last spacecraft, or at any other point that conveys information about what has gone before.

The Medena scenario runs through this chapter for you to use as a basic idea for experimenting with various science fiction themes. Many women express distaste and even revulsion when I first broach the subject of science fiction as part of a creative writing course. They explain that science fiction and its past links with violence, war and aggression, using technology as the means of exhibiting power and control, are so 'fixed' in the majority of books written by male writers that there is a need for them, as women readers, to reject what they see as male obsessions. This can mean that readers have rejected the genre totally, convinced that all science fiction is the same. If your response to science fiction is overlaid by negativity, from whatever source, then reading this chapter through before beginning any of the exercises is advisable. Assessing or reassessing your viewpoint could be a necessary first stage before contemplating any serious plotting.

The first science fiction novels were written in the nineteenth century and the genre has since subdivided like an amoeba into numerous 'subgenres'. It is a genre that now encompasses many different kinds of writing and it is still expanding. What exactly defines *science* fiction? Where do the Arthurian myth fantasies and the subgenre known as 'sword and sorcery' fit? Where would we place surrealist writing, magic realism and other kinds of writing that rely on myth and fantasy? The difficulty with regard to naming the genre is aptly described by Josephine Saxton, a writer whose own work is an example of 'not fitting':

> The whole question of science fiction, even without the added problem of gender, is vexed. Science fiction is not only all things to all women (and men), but is now merely a label stuck upon a jar filled to breaking with all kinds of things. The kind of jar I mean is the one on the mantelpiece into which are put pins, hairgrips, rubber bands, receipts, old lipsticks, plastic gewgaws out of the cornflakes and anything else which does not properly quite belong elsewhere. It may also harbour valuable jewellery and large notes, but it is not the jar containing the pot pourri, because some of it stinks.
>
> (Saxton, 1991, p. 205)

None of this fiction fits into what we would call 'realism' (fiction that seems to mirror reality) and it's more useful to think of this kind of writing as the *representation of alternative realities*.

Origins

Science fiction and the present-day fantasy novel are linked to the Gothic novel tradition which began in the eighteenth century.[1] As previously noted, the Gothic continues to play an important part generally in contemporary imagination – think about how many horror novels and films are produced every year. Elements of the Gothic are manifested in science fiction through the fear of the unknown, the bizarre, the weird – something nasty at the bottom of the spaceship, heroines thrown into hostile and alien landscapes full of hidden terrors.

A classic part of the Gothic tradition is the vampire myth. The Dracula story[2] has become an archetype, and its themes of immortality, transformation and sexuality prove very popular in science fiction/fantasy. It has been used a number of ways – comically, as in Jody Scott's novel *I, Vampire*, and sadly in short stories such as 'The loves of Lady Purple' by Angela Carter and 'O Captain, My Captain' by Katherine Forrest. The latter is a love story within the context of a mystery science fiction and illustrates that there's no restriction on how you can use ideas.

When people think about the origins of contemporary science fiction, writers such as H. G. Wells and Jules Verne come to mind, but it was a woman, Mary Shelley (the daughter of Mary Wollstonecraft), who wrote the first science fiction novel – *Frankenstein*, subtitled *A Modern Prometheus*. She initially wrote a short story and then, encouraged by her husband (the poet Shelley), developed this into a novel. The book was first published in 1818.

Prometheus (the name means foresight) provides an example of voluntary sacrifice for a greater good. He defied the law of Zeus and stole the fire of the gods in order to pass it on to humankind. For thirty years he was punished, held in chains on a high cliff in the Caucasus mountains. Each day an eagle flew down and devoured his liver and each night the liver was restored. Like Prometheus, Frankenstein was punished too, not only because he'd dared to create human life but also because he had failed to assume due responsibility for it. Deprived by its hideous appearance of positive contact with humans, Frankenstein's creation becomes an evil force, killing Frankenstein's wife, brother and best friend. The analogy between Prometheus and Frankenstein does not prove for me a credible comparison but there's no doubt that Mary Shelley wrote with great foresight (could this be a more appropriate link with Prometheus?) and the ongoing fascination with the creation of life has been popularized since in a number of different forms.

The wider question of what it is that makes us human is also a theme that continues to attract science fiction writers. By questioning our ability to replicate ourselves by machine, or by inventing alien comparisons, we are really asking questions about our own psychological or emotional make-up. The character of the android Data in *Star Trek* repeatedly addresses this issue, and androids in other fictions yearn to have that 'missing link' between the machine and the human. This was the central theme, for example, in Philip K. Dick's novel *Do Androids Dream of Electric Sheep?* adapted in the film *Bladerunner*.

Science fiction stories in the style of Wells and Verne constituted much of the magazine fiction at the beginning of this century but it wasn't until the late 1920s that magazines specifically devoted to the genre, such as *Amazing Stories* and *Astounding Fiction*, were developed.[3] These magazines were edited by Hugo Gernsback, who coined the term 'scientification' in 1926. Needless to say, women rarely featured in a positive light, although there were women writers around during the 1930s and 1940s, such as Leigh Brackett and C. L. Moore.

Overt feminist ideas did not gain much attention until Alice Sheldon (who wrote under the pseudonym James Tiptree Jr), Joanna Russ and Ursula Le Guin took up the challenge from the 1960s onwards.

Technological magic?

What is the difference between fantasy and science fiction? We could say that what distinguishes science fiction from fantasy is its use of technology and/or science as a central theme. But if we say that the use of science makes the story rational and logical, and that magic makes it fantasy, where do we place those stories that make the magic appear rational by the use of paranormal powers? And what about stories in which writers invent their own science? Isn't that equally a form of magic?

The Mists of Avalon by Marion Zimmer Bradley is a good example of a novel that falls into the fantasy category. The matriarchal society of Avalon and the paranormal powers possessed by the women – telepathy and the ability to foretell the future – declined and ceased when Christianity was introduced and people changed their faith. The idea that something can only exist through faith is not so far-fetched – it is, after all, what supports the Christian church and many other religions. Nor are past matriarchies so unlikely. Anthropologists have strong evidence that matriarchal societies existed in the pre-Christian era, and many myths, such as the Celtic myths and the Greek myth of the Amazons, have strong independent women warriors.[4]

Mary Shelley's *Frankenstein* and *The Mists of Avalon* represent the two extremes of the elastic science fiction/fantasy genre. And the boundaries between science fiction/fantasy/fairy story can be happily blurred, as in Josephine Saxton's 'The Travails of Jane Saint'

– a futuristic quest story in the vein of *Alice in Wonderland*. Josephine Saxton observes that publishers thought her writing was 'so odd it had to be SF' (Saxton, 1991, p. 208).

Hard or soft?

Recently science fiction has been divided between 'hard' science fiction and 'soft' science fiction, but this is a false division. Many women writers would be placed in the 'soft' science mode in the sense that they are analysing social relations or cultural politics in their novels. Making this distinction reinforces the cultural division of hard equals male equals rational and soft equals female equals emotive and intuitive. While it may be true to say that male science fiction writers favour action over character development, is there any real evidence that they are more 'scientific' than women writers? Science fiction is frequently promoted as the ultimate 'active' adventure story chock full of goodies and baddies, along the lines of *Star Wars*. The technology may be futuristic but the plot is simply an updated version of Hollywood's interpretation of the history of the colonization of America by the white settlers – the taming of the 'wild west'. The projection of colonial wars into outer space is given greater credibility by making 'the enemy' grotesque. No need for Native American war paint here, just invent a body shape that will shock or threaten. Now no one will mind if the 'goodies' use their ray guns to zap those 'baddies' into submission.

Thematically, women writers have concentrated on ecology, psychology, anthropology, sociology, and politics. The most popular theme is the redistribution of power and social organization. Women writers have often created non-hierarchical worlds, matriarchies, utopias and the opposite of utopias, dystopias (worlds where the worst is imagined). This is not to say that women do not use science – they do, and in very inventive ways. Pamela Zoline, for example, in her short story 'The Heat Death of the Universe', takes the second law of thermodynamics, the theory of entropy, which measures the 'order' of a system (which is paradoxically at a maximum state of order when it is at the maximum state of randomness) and applies the theory with great effect to the daily frustrations of a Californian housewife, who is living in an ordered kind of chaos.

Working with those two simple words *what if* can be the first necessary spark that gets us going. Once ideas are flowing we can use our ideas and creative processes to cast comment on *what is*. What aspects of day to day life would you wish to look at more closely? Using Medena as set out in the beginning of the chapter, you can turn your attention in any direction.

Themes

This is a genre in which you can experiment to your heart's content. You may be interested in the use of science and technology; or you may be more generally interested in looking at the different ways in which society can be organized; or you may be interested in creating entirely new worlds. Perhaps you simply want to have fun with the ideas and the implications involved. If you approach the work with fun in mind, you might not be so deterred by the inevitable thorny questions that will arise. As with any type of writing, you can do no better than to read as much as you can of the genre in which you are interested. If you want to avoid repeating ideas it would be useful to read Joanna Russ's short, funny article 'The Clichés from Outer Space' which includes The Weird-Ways-of-Getting-Pregnant Story and The Noble Separatist Story so you can see what has already been well covered.[5] In the following section we'll look at some of the themes that have been explored.

The past, present and future

Time travel is an ever popular theme in science fiction that has been used in a number of ways. Octavia Butler's *Kindred* has a heroine who is drawn literally into the past, into early nineteenth century America, where as a black woman she is automatically treated as a slave. If it were not for the physical hurt she suffers while in this time zone (and she carries bodily evidence of that hurt with her when returning to the present) she would believe she was going mad. She realizes increasingly how her fate is tied to that of a white man, the son of a plantation owner. He is one of her forebears, and when his life is threatened (and this happens more than once) she is dragged back into the past to help him. She has hopes of influencing him, perhaps making him more enlightened with regard to slavery, but as he gets older he becomes more like his cruel father and her desire to save him is weakened. The relationship between the heroine and the man she is destined to help is complex and the reader becomes intensely involved with the heroine's perceptions and experience. Time here has become a fifth dimension. What can seem ridiculously implausible as a plot or theme when talked about can become incredibly believable when read in a book. If the reader is going to suspend disbelief, something in the writing has to be convincing enough to convey that the story, the setting, the theme, are somehow possible. *Kindred* achieves this as both science fiction and as history and illustrates how very often science fiction novels can combine different categories such as romance, mystery, or even crime.

Old ideas in a new bottle

The New Gulliver by Esme Dodderidge is a new variation on an old theme, as the title implies. The novel also employs the 'outsider as observer' technique. Lemuel Gulliver crash-lands into a land called Capovolta and discovers a complete reversal of the social order of our world – women are dominant and men subservient. His initial incomprehension develops into a modified acceptance of being treated as little more than a sex object, until finally he rebels at what he sees as the injustice of the situation, not only for himself but for all men. The novel explores all the difficulties that men face in this far-flung society: inequalities at work; lack of recognition for ability; little or no support for childcare and housework; being treated as a sex object; sexual double standards, etc. Sound familiar? In Capovolta the 'natural' order has been reversed and the 'logical' explanation of the social order follows from this. Lemuel reflects on the organization of his own society and recognizes it as being equally unjust. The outsider as observer is a common and often a useful ploy in science fiction scenarios. In this way the customs, habits, morals or philosophy of the society you have imagined can be explained to the newcomer as a necessary part of the narrative and thereby explained to the reader as well.

Utopias/dystopias

The word 'utopia' literally means 'no place'. Feminist utopias are often worlds without men, a no-man's land. The creation of utopias for women is one of the most popular science fiction themes, followed closely by dystopias. In perhaps the first example, *The Book of the City of Ladies* (first published in 1405), Christine de Pizan, a French writer and scholar, wanted to rewrite women's history from a woman's point of view and suggested that the only effective way to do so was to build a women-only city where they could live safe from the bias of men. Christine de Pizan's book is written, as stories very often were in those times, as an allegory rather than as a realistic suggestion that women could separate themselves from men in this way. Yet it is an illustration that the idea of separate societies for men and women is not new.

A more straightforward effort to construct a utopian community of women came later in *Millenium Hall* (1762) by Sarah Scott. The hall is populated by a group of women who have for various reasons rejected marriage and wish to spend their life in this all-female community. The women carry out charitable works for the less advantaged in their surrounding neighbourhood and enrich their own lives through learning and culture. Their communal living offers an alternative way of life to the outside world dominated by wealth and greed. The motives of these women, influenced as they are by Christian virtues, are similar to those of women dedicated to a religious order. Readers today might find the pious tone off-putting but this is the first realistic attempt to suggest that the world could be ordered differently if 'feminine' values were promoted.

Charlotte Perkins Gilman's *Herland*, written in 1915, is the best known of her three utopian novels where she creates a utopia without men – a society of mothers. The women of Herland have a history dating back two thousand years. Once there had been men but through war, earthquakes, volcanic outbursts and revolts by slaves against their masters they had all perished. Only young girls and some older slave women remained. Nature had further isolated them. Natural disaster had, literally, walled them in. This society of women comes about by a sort of miracle – one young woman gives birth to a child. Mystified, the other women wonder if there could be a man around somewhere but none is found. The woman goes on to have four more children, all girls. Convinced now of the woman's virgin state, these dramatic events are viewed as gifts from the gods. As the five daughters reach their mid-twenties, they too begin to bear children, each one also having five, again all girls. Gilman avoids any discussion of sex between women (we have to place the book in the era in which it was written), allowing the women's religious beliefs to cover any problematic areas she may have felt were too challenging to deal with.

Marge Piercy's utopia *Woman on the Edge of Time* broke new ground when it was published in 1976. The science fiction writer J. G. Ballard coined the phrase 'inner space' for those stories that take place 'in the head'. What this means is that the imagined world in the head of a character is real in the context of the novel. *Woman on the Edge of Time* is such a novel. It opens painfully. Dolly is pregnant and Geraldo has just beaten her up. She comes to her aunt, Connie Ramos, for help. Enraged at Geraldo's brutality in wanting to have the baby aborted, Connie flies at him with a wine bottle but it is she who winds up in a hospital bed. However, this is no ordinary hospital, it's a mental hospital. Here she meets the character of Luciente, who comes from another time. She lives in the village of Mattapoiset, Massachusetts, where it is now the year 2137. She understands that Connie is a 'receiver', making it possible for Luciente to move back in time to the twentieth century and get to know Connie. At first it is Luciente who does the time travelling; later on Connie can do it too. She discovers many differences between the two time zones. Take, for example, the yellow building Connie asks Luciente about: '... like a lemon mushroom pushing out of the ground. Decorated with sculpted tree shapes, it was windowless and faintly hummed' (Piercy, 1984, p.101). This is known as the 'brooder'; genetic material is stored and embryos nurtured there until they are ready for birth. As the 'brooder' has freed women from their biology, alternative methods of parenting are opened up – men can lactate, and children have three parents instead of the usual two. The novel juggles the present with two possible futures. On one occasion Connie finds herself not in Mattapoiset but somewhere else. This is the harsh world of a future New York (a dystopia) and that Connie is able to see this world suggests that there are two possible outcomes for humankind. We can learn something crucial from the comparisons made here. Marge Piercy tackles issues of race as well as gender. Ethical choices have had to be made in this future world, such as whether the quality of life is more important than the prolonging of life, and there is a true sense of morality. Addressing these sorts of issues makes for a thought-provoking book. The best science fiction written by women, such as *Woman on the Edge of Time*, challenges readers to think about the choices we make, *now*, *today*, and how those choices can lead us towards dystopian/utopian values.

In *Walk to the End of the World* Suzy McKee Charnas first gives a dystopian view of society with the community of the Holdfast, where female subjugation is taken to the extreme. Women are completely repressed and treated as slaves. In *Motherlines*, which follows (both books are now sold in one volume), she presents an alternative utopian possibility. In *Motherlines* we follow the fortunes of a woman, Alldera, who manages to escape from the Holdfast. She discovers two groups of women in this new environment: other escaped women called the 'free fems', and the 'horsewomen' who have long been independent of men. These two groups are antagonistic and suspicious of each other. Alldera initially spends time with the horsewomen and then joins the free fems. She finds the horsewomen's ways and customs ultimately more congenial, despite her reservations about their solution for procreation – mating with horses. An elaborate scaffolding is erected for use at a special mating ceremony in order to make the occasion as uncomplicated and pleasant for the young women as possible. The problem of the reader having difficulties with the concept of women mating with horses is circumvented by having the free fems feel the revulsion for us. As we learn and understand more about the riding women's society, and because the free fems are not sympathetically portrayed, this disturbing idea becomes acceptable. It's one of those science fiction ideas that explained out of context sounds very strange but works well within the novel.

Margaret O'Donnell's less well-known book, *The Beehive*, is another fine example of a dystopia. It is set in an unnamed country where dictatorship has been the norm for the past thirty years, bolstered by propaganda, wholesale indoctrination and a tyrannical, unspeakably terrifying secret police. Women are in one of two groups, either wives, forced to become child-bearers, or grey ones, who are treated as an underclass. Their hair must be grey, their clothes shapeless, and their lives asexual. Given the Orwellian vision in which the story is played out, the women learn how to take the situation tightly under control and the book posits the question: can the grey ones bring off a non-violent revolution? The moral of the story could be a motto for elderly women everywhere – never underestimate the wit and wisdom of the grey ones.

There is nothing narrowly 'scientific' about the ideas used in any of these novels. They are all about different, alternative forms of social organization and indirectly reflect, for better or for worse, on our own situation as women in contemporary society.

I think my stepmother's an alien

In the realm of science fiction and fantasy all varieties of human and non-human forms exist. There are altered humans, for example horsewomen in *Motherlines* who are the product of women and horses, and artificial humans, as in Josephine Saxton's short story 'Gordon's Women', which is a witty reversal of the *Stepford Wives*. In Jane Palmer's *The Planet Dweller*, a planet is a female character who actively moves and communicates. Beings can transform themselves, as in *Carmen Dog* by Carol Emshwiller, where women turn into animals and vice versa with resulting chaos. There are all sorts of beasts, robots, androids, cyborgs, hybrids and, last but not least, men as aliens. As mentioned earlier, the question of how *human* artificial life forms can be and the implications of this is a popular theme. It even stretches to computers, that may now provide the greatest source of menace to us socially and individually.

Machines are central to Elisabeth Vonarberg's novel *The Silent City*. This is how the story begins:

> She didn't know he could die. He had dark, weather beaten skin, a mane of tangled white hair, and hazel eyes that were always smiling from a network of wrinkles. Perhaps it was the wrinkles that were always smiling. You couldn't tell just by looking at his mouth – his moustache was too thick. She didn't know he was a machine.
>
> (Vonarberg, 1981, p. 3)

This man/machine is Elisa's grandfather and they live in the 'City', the final storehouse of knowledge and science. Beyond the City lies the vast unknown. Elisabeth Vonarberg is another example of a woman writer concerned with issues of social order, gender and genetic science. Like so much of science fiction, *The Silent City* can also be read as a comment on today: Elisa rebels, rejects the City (home? tradition? patriarchy?) and finds her own way outside before returning to be part of the changes that make the City more useful and accessible to a greater number of people. If we accept that science fiction can cast a reflection on how things are here on Earth, then what does it mean if the fiction we write perpetuates the attitudes around us? How ought we to think about and create aliens? Do we befriend, tame, patronize 'others' in ways that colonize? Are the people or beasts encountered really alien or are they part of ourselves? Is it inevitable that we view 'others' as the enemy – something/someone to be afraid of unless we can gain control somehow? If the alien is a computer will your attitude towards it be different from the attitude you would take if it were a plant or an animal, or a life form close to our own? Are we seeking to embrace this 'foreigner' or emphasize the differences between us? Are the labels 'other', 'enemy', and 'foreigner' interchangeable?

Anne McCaffrey's collection of stories *The Ship Who Sang* was first published in 1971. The story that gives the collection its title has a moving account of Helva:

> She was born a thing and as such would be condemned if she failed to pass the encephalograph test required of all new-born babies. There was always the possibility that though the limbs were twisted, the mind was not, though the ears would hear only dimly, the eyes see vaguely, the mind behind them was receptive and alert.
>
> (McCaffrey, 1972, p. 7)

Helva's parents have a tough decision to make. Will they decide on euthanasia or will they give their permission for Helva to become an encapsulated 'brain'? Helva becomes the 'guiding mechanism' or 'brain' of a scout ship, partnered by either a man or a woman (the choice is hers) as the mobile half. The information Anne McCaffrey gives about Helva's situation is very detailed and the choice between death and becoming the thinking part of a spaceship could be interpreted as a comment on how our world responds to people born with disabilities.

Exercise

Alien woman

You suspect your next-door neighbour, a woman about your own age, of being an alien. This is not a sudden or hasty suspicion. You've seen and heard things that at first you ignored. Later you felt puzzled, mystified, and now, all these months later, you know for sure that all is not what it seems next door.

You could think of this exercise as an opportunity for humour. In group work you might work with one or two others to create an identikit picture and to list the number of things that convince you that this woman is an alien.

What sort of people populate Medena?

Already we have people there – some breathing air, others breathing carbon dioxide. What will these people be like now that they are no longer Earth-bound? Will they all be able-bodied? How thoughtfully planned will the settlements they establish be? And transport? Will all who wish to use it be taken into consideration? What about other life forms and other ways of looking at human-ness? If there are issues you feel strongly about, can you find ways of expressing your views through a science fiction scenario?

Disaster scenarios

This is well-trodden ground as a theme for science fiction. Earth has expired. Why? Who was to blame? Was it some trigger-happy, finger-twitching fool, accidentally or deliberately releasing the biggest nuclear bomb ever invented? Might it have been an ecological disaster? Some outside force? What about unavoidable consequences beyond our control? Might there have been a huge explosion, a collision between our planet and another? An invasion?

Disaster scenarios could be thought of as 'off with the old and on with the new', a popular way for writers to begin to tackle science fiction concepts. It might be the heroine's job to save the world ... she might be part of group that escapes ... What if she is a well-meaning alien, misunderstood and treated badly when she tries to warn people on Earth that danger lies ahead?

What other changes can you think of that might affect our world? What if our supply of oil were to be entirely used up? What if there were some catastrophe of world shattering proportions?

Our lives are at present built around the car, even if we don't own one. It would be hard to imagine a world where abandoned metal carcasses were strewn along useless roads and highways. What might be the reason for such a change? Pollution? What other changes would this bring about? Would people sleep in cars? Would we find weird sculptures in parks and gardens, constructed of twisted metal and chrome? What other suggestions would you make for their use?

Medena could be used as a disaster scenario. The first chapters might explain the reasons for exploring other planets. Will Earth have been destroyed wholly or might it survive, the damage bad but still capable of being repaired? Has Medena been cut off for some years due to damaged spaceships and few resources left for repairing them? Might people from Earth arrive on Medena one hundred years hence and thereby act as a narrative device for the reader's understanding of the comparison between *what was* and *what is* now?

Where to find material?

Whatever happened to the whelks?

This material was taken from a newspaper story and is included here to illustrate how you can make use of news items to set you thinking. The opening sentence reads: 'All around Britain's polluted coastline a strange tragedy is unfolding – as the whelks change sex.'

The article informs readers that female whelks are growing penises and developing sperm ducts, and that scientists (unnamed) are '100 per cent certain that pollution is to blame'. These seaside creatures are among the most common found on British beaches. Their shells are about one inch long, usually white, yellow or orange, with black bands. The journalist explains that this bizarre transformation stops the whelks breeding and threatens their future. He points out that they have disappeared altogether from some coastal areas. What exactly can the problem be? Researchers put forward the theory that anti-fouling paint (used on boat hulls) was to blame; sure enough, when they painted the shells of unfortunate female whelks, penises sprouted '...and grew to alarming lengths'.

What can we make of all this? When I read this article I had visions of walking along a beach somewhere in Britain and stumbling over enormous penises protruding from tiny shells. If paint can have such devastating effects on whelks, what other creatures might be similarly transformed? Perhaps you'll create a future fishing village where environmental issues such as the adverse effect of pollution on female whelks provides the basis of a story. Not wanting to influence your thinking by expanding on the article too much, I leave you to ponder on the fate of the female whelk.

I'd recommend keeping a file, cutting out newsworthy items that are of interest or that stir your imagination. You could view this as a long-term project but that doesn't mean you file items away and never look at them again. Sort through your cuttings periodically, write lists of questions or notes, discuss the news item with others. In short, allow yourself to wonder about possible scenarios.

Learning how to speak

An important part of the alternative realities created by women
is the use of language – both the invention of new vocabularies
by which to describe things, and an analysis of the ways in which
language structures our reality. As the chapter 'Finding the right
words: women and language' illustrates, we live with a language
that represents a culture stacked against us; we lack positive
words to describe ourselves and we are often completely omitted
from general terms referring to the human race. 'He' stands for
'she' we're told, because 'he' includes us all. *Native Tongue* by
Suzette Haden Elgin recognizes the power of language – the fact
that we invent 'reality' through language, and that by inventing
and using a women's language women can therefore change
reality. In this novel women who 'belong' to a house of interpreters
know that if they can form their own language, with a completely
different linguistic structure, they can alter the perception of
reality. They believe that in doing so they will be able to gain power
and independence from their oppressors. The basis for this new
grammar is provided by the author at the back of the book.

It is not unusual to find that an author has included a glossary
of the new language invented in her novel, as for example Mary
Gentle in her novel *Golden Witchbreed*. No other genre offers
quite the same freedom for experimentation. Here are some of the
words Mary Gentle put into use:

becamil: the webweaver beetle, giving its name to the tough
multi-coloured waterproof fabric spun from its web.
Hives are kept commercially all over the Southland.

hura: species of hard-shelled water clam found in rivers
throughout the Southland.

kazza: carnivorous reptilian quadruped, often trained in the
Southland as a hunting animal. Short white pelt with
blue-grey markings.

ke, kir: neutral pronoun used for the young of the Orthean
species, and sometimes for the Goddess.

Exercises

1   This applies to both science fiction and fantasy. Science fiction
and language make a happy combination and the following exercise,
using made-up words, can be a lot of fun. The more you play around

with the ideas, the more you will want to expand your grasp of the possibilities. Here is a list of made-up words. You could make up your own if you'd prefer, or start with this list and expand your vocabulary of made-up words as you get the hang of using them.

huzza	couci-couci	biblacious
pardella	risp	rodell
burdace	nossa	secoive
tilibut	risha	deralpa
faddence	inpa	gostoon
vella-vella	ontice	goigned
butoony	pamparoo	gillytucked
mintazup	jassle	parmiello

The following passage was written by three women, Irene, Trish and Sheena, as part of a group exercise describing an alien woman (as in the exercise on p. 176) and was read out to much hilarity. The words in the list above are different from the made-up words used here so as not to detract from your experience of the exercise. Once you have used the word list you could try the alien woman exercise again, incorporating your word list.

Iriesha

Iriesha was a remarkable woman. She wore her wosten hanni in a cousper and her gledage was considered a trifle jiddy for Walthamstow. From the start, the way that she moved in her kibert was thought too urtal for a tutor of Adoic studies at the Tech. And this was only the tubic Iriesha.

Alone in her room she entered an inner vadissio landscape. Letting down her hanni, sorethally leaning back on her silmy sativa, she dorzingly stroked her feo with her hi-tech spandula. Seconds away from the palthyest relna of her yat there was a blost on the door.

'Oh thrip, bet it's that metchip Crut-Crut.'

Fade out, music and commercial break (the radio pushing the latest in hi-tech spandulas and other enterprising appliances).

Now, it's your turn. You'll discover that using the words can be tricky at first. Do we use the made-up words as adjectives, nouns, verbs and so on, which could change much of the meaning, or do we write out a paragraph or two and then insert the words randomly? Experiment with both of these methods and compare the effect.

This exercise helps us to free up our language and made-up words can provide a safety cover when attempting to write on subject areas that may be difficult for a writer to contemplate – eroticism for example. You may want to explore this further with the following exercise.

2   In a land far away the people have decided that sexual relationships with others is out. Instead they have pleasure cabinets on
many street corners. Using the word list describe your experience when
you step into one these booths.
3   This exercise is designed for using the new word list. Our narrating
character is at an airport. She has returned from a holiday abroad on
her own. As she's walking across the tarmac from the plane she
cannot shake the feeling that there's something different about this
place. It seems more like years she's been away than just a week. Once
inside the terminal building she can hear people using a language that
is not her own, but oddly enough it's also strangely familiar as
though she has heard or spoken it in a recent dream. The words she's
hearing are words she knows. How could she have forgotten? They've
been somewhere in her mind all this time, as though waiting for her
to remember. She looks around. Will her friend be here to meet her?
Has the week away changed her so dramatically that her friend
won't recognize her? Surely not.

Describe what this character sees and hears. Take whatever direction
you wish. It could be a dialogue with the friend, or continued thinking
by the character or a description of the woman in the third person,
or a piece written from her point of view.

Making up new words can be exciting and adventurous, though
there might be some obstacles to overcome too. The main aim
behind this kind of work, particularly in combination with a
science fiction plot or outline, is to learn how we can have impact
'out there', far beyond the confines of the printed word.

It's worth saying here that invented language should be used
with some caution, particularly at the start of a short story or novel.
The reader does not want to be bombarded with a whole new
vocabulary. Too much of anything can confuse, and without
context and consistency you can risk lack of clarity. You do,
presumably, want to be understood. There has also been a build-
up over the years of science fiction language: hyperspace, matter
transmission, suspended animation, androids, cyborgs, 'terra' for
Earth, etc. The more you read science fiction the greater your
awareness of these terms will become.

Fantasy

The term 'fantasy' is often overlaid with negative connotations
and/or dismissed as escapism. The vampire myth is fantasy but
it obviously attracts writers and readers and goes on appealing to

something in the human psyche. As I have said throughout this chapter, science fiction is a very loose term for all novels designated as such. Fantasies, or perhaps it is only male fantasies, have often achieved cult status, for examples Tolkein's *The Lord of the Rings*, Mervyn Peake's Gothic *Gormanghast* trilogy, and Richard Adams's *Watership Down*.

Recently there has been revived interest in the medieval period of history, this time centred on the Arthurian myth. There was a fabled Celtic warrior in the sixth century called Arthur whose feats were referred to in early Celtic writing. It was not until the beginning of the twelfth century, however, that the legends were fully narrated.[6] By the fifteenth century Arthur's legend had developed an extensive literature which was woven together by Sir Thomas Malory in his *Morte d'Arthur*, printed in 1485. Arthur the folk hero has always been more fiction than fact, but the myth of Arthur has been an important part of the English culture. It's worth looking into why it seems to offer such fertile ground for writers. The myth of Arthur was popularized in the Victorian period by writers and artists, particularly those of the Pre-Raphaelite Brotherhood, and embodied a romanticized, nostalgic yearning for a previous time in history characterized by the values of chivalry. Embellished over the years, it offers up a number of scenarios that appeal to writers of fiction: magic, noble quests, love triangles, politics, intrigue. For women there is an opportunity to rewrite the story in a Celtic rather than a Christian setting or, as mentioned earlier, to place it in a transitional period as in Marion Zimmer Bradley's *The Mists of Avalon*.

Women in Celtic society had more power and freedom of movement than those in the subsequent Christian era. Maeve, for example, is a woman in Irish mythology renowned for her intelligence, beauty and prowess as a warrior.[7] Some novels use specific mythical figures, while others simply have a medieval flavour. Those with a medieval flavour are often set in a different time on another planet. Such novels have earned the epithet 'Sword and Sorcery' – novels like Tanith Lee's and Anne McCaffrey's that feature dragons, demons, magic and so on. The advantage of this kind of setting is that it is both familiar and strange to the reader. The author can rely on certain associations and at the same time confound expectations. Female characters no longer have to be passive and virtuous Christian queens but can be scholars, warriors, lovers. A typical example is the work of Patricia Kennealy who writes novels based on the idea that the Celtic people were originally space travellers who inhabited Earth for many thousands of years and were part of the mythical Atlantis. Again, it was when Christianity was introduced and their use of 'magic' questioned that they decided it was time to leave, in the year 453 AD. *The Copper Crown* features a young warrior queen, Aeron, with mind-reading abilities, who finds her Keltan empire threatened by age-old enemies and who seeks to make an alliance with Earth – the first contact since the fifth century. Patricia Kennealy mixes Celtic myth (Arthur features again), space technology and magic.

Moyra Caldecott's trilogy *The Tall Stones, The Temple of the Sun* and *Shadows on the Stones* (now available in one volume) is a story of love and discovery. The 'Lords of the Sun', guardians of the mighty stone circles of ancient times, are able to travel astrally across the world, making contact with fellow adepts from China to Minoan Crete to Egypt. The novel suggests that we are neither limited by our physical bodies nor bound by the usual perceptions of time and space.

The use of paranormal powers such as telepathy, prescience, telekinesis and teleportation can become something of an expectation in the minds of readers of science fiction/fantasy. If you are attracted by the idea of a character who is able to tune in on other people's thoughts or who can move herself around with the help of instruments, concentrated thought or some other means, do bear in mind the need for *context* and *consistency*. It is inadvisable, for example, to introduce special powers at a convenient moment (say when a crisis occurs) without conveying relevant information prior to this point. Give careful planning to your opening paragraphs/chapters. Understandably your character(s) could use their powers to resolve problems unexpectedly and/or to get out of tricky situations but *too much of anything* may weaken the strength of your characterization. You want to avoid the 'it was all a dream' scenario, though dreams have been used effectively. In Lisa Tuttle's *A Spaceship Built of Stone*, for example, colonizing aliens first of all implant the idea in people's minds through dreams that they are a rediscovered long-lost civilization.

The writings of Patricia Kennealy and Moyra Caldecott illustrate how the division between science fiction and fantasy is blurred. Another example is Marion Zimmer Bradley's 'Darkover' series. Darkover is a planet that Bradley has explored from many angles and there are at least nine Darkover titles.

Other boundaries?

There are some writers whose work is difficult to label. Josephine Saxton has already been mentioned. Angela Carter and Jeanette Winterson are writers that have produced novels in the realm of the fantastic, macabre and fairy tale – novels that have affinities with the Gothic. The term 'magic realism', which is sometimes applied to writers such as these, was first coined by Franz Roh to describe the work of German artists in the 1920s who portrayed the fantastic in a realistic manner. More recently the term has been adopted to describe the work of Latin American writers such as Isabel Allende and Garcia Marquez, who combine elements of dream, fairy story and mythology in their writings.

Another example of a writer whose work uses fantasy and has a dream-like quality is Leonora Carrington. In *The Hearing Trumpet* the heroine, Marion Leatherby, is a deaf, but certainly not senile, ninety-two-year-old who proudly sports a short grey beard. When she is placed in a nursing home by her vindictive daughter-in-law and ineffectual son, ironically named Galahad, she finds herself not only in a very strange environment (the dwellings are constructed in a variety of shapes to resemble toadstools, Swiss chalets, railway carriages, a boot, an Egyptian mummy) but with a motley collection of women with curious habits. The regime imposed by the resident psychiatrist is repressive and Marion wonders '... if it were not possible to organize a small mutiny?' (Carrington, 1991, p. 50). Marion dreams of going to Lapland but becomes embroiled in an apocalyptic moment in history that involves a wicked abbess, the holy grail, witchcraft and the inversion of the natural climatic order. She happily discovers that Lapland comes to her. Bizarre? Yes. The key is that Marion Weatherby is a very sensible woman and as we see things from her point of view we accept that these very odd things *can* happen. It has that internal consistency that makes us, as readers, accept it. It's also a very funny book.

Writing for children

Another way to think about fantasy is to remember the fantasies created for children. *Lord of the Rings* and *Watership Down* have already been mentioned and there are the classics, *Alice in Wonderland*, C. S. Lewis's 'Narnia' stories and the tales of Beatrix Potter. In children's books weird and wonderful things happen – we have entered into the world of the imagination. Writing for children, whether it's pure fantasy or science fiction, requires the same planning, plotting and flexibility of approach as writing for adults. Don't be misled by the simpler vocabulary and shorter length of children's books. It can be a hefty challenge to pitch your story with the right angle, allowing younger readers to feel involved with the tale you tell. Think of this form of writing as specialized, demanding skill and insight (developed through experience and commitment).

Although it is often suggested that a writer should have a particular age group in mind before beginning to write, I'd suggest instead that you create a reader to whom you will tell your story. Think of this reader as a character even if she/he is modelled on a real child you know.

Unless you intend to work on something like a picture book, with few words on each page, the question of readership age need not arise. The division of children into age-reading groups may be a part of the marketing strategy a publisher has to adopt, but it need not be your problem. Many young children have stories read to them by adults and might therefore become familiar with books beyond their reading age. If there is a subject I do not understand I look out for a book written for older children. The explanations are usually more understandable, the illustrations clearer and overall much effort has gone into the material to make the meaning truly accessible. In books intended for adults there's an identifiable difference between what is explained and what is assumed the reader already knows. It is advisable to look at a number of children's books, on a broad range of subject matter, and decide for yourself how well the writer has understood who she is writing for. What matters is that you communicate effectively, talking *to* the reader and not *at* her/him, avoiding too simple a language or the voice that talks down from a lofty height. It may take practice but, with a young reader in your head to talk to, you can strive for an appropriate style that is right for you. Ursula Le Guin's *Earthsea Trilogy* is referred to as a book for teenagers, but to categorize it within that one age group is to overlook the vast number of adult readers who have enjoyed it too. Herein lies the skill of writing science fiction.

Writing Points

If creating entirely new worlds or realities seems daunting, remember simple ideas can work – in fact, there could be a danger in overrating novelty of ideas and themes. Margaret Atwood's book

The Handmaid's Tale shows how a novel premised on something very simple – the taking away of women's power by removing their access to money (a reality for many women anyhow in today's world) and maintaining repression by forbidding communication – can make a compelling story. More important than novelty is being able to use the narrative to carry the reader along the journey. Instead of striving for total originality allow yourself to be pulled forward by an initial impulse and build around that.

If you or I read a novel set in today's world we accept, without much thought or argument, a certain number of assumptions – assumptions that rest on our prior knowledge of how things work in our world, how life is lived, and so on. The writer can rely on these assumptions to a degree. But what if we read about another world, a different time-zone or a fantastical plot that challenges our imagination to take on a completely new viewpoint? Immediately, those everyday assumptions begin to slip away and we have to rely largely on the writer's narrative and descriptions, with particular emphasis on the early part of the telling. This means that more specific description is called for. How do you impart that information without creating a bewildering lump of explanation in the beginning, slowing down the narrative and probably boring the reader? One option is to use dialogue, another is to open with action.

Dialogue can set the scene, tossing the weight of explanation back and forth between two or more characters, and yet it can also maintain the narrative pace. Action can be dramatic, life threatening or confusing, throwing the reader in at the deep end. It can establish empathy for the character that will draw the reader's attention. As the characters resolve that first situation/problem the reader can be told *how*, *who* and *why*, and in this way follow the characters as they move against the backdrop of the larger world around them. You might find it easier to work with one character initially and introduce more as your experimentation becomes more focused. And don't forget to make use of the five senses which can help to convey a new or strange environment to the reader.

Back to Medena

In concluding this chapter we return to the Medena scenario. Can you now see ways in which this could be used?

Can you describe the breathing apparatus needed by the four children in a quad? Will the equipment need to be changed as children grow older? Who will look after their needs (and how) while they are small? Could the quads be mobile units moving in and around a basic structure designed to take care of them? You might choose to work with diagrams or maps or you might discuss your ideas with other writers and friends. There is no right way to proceed, only your own way. If the story excites you, great. Write down some notes, or open up a file card system in which you can expand on each different aspect as you develop it.

What I have found most encouraging about this exercise – which I have used for more than three years now in creative writing workshops and with all sorts of groups – is how it has worked to change people's attitudes to science fiction. Not always, of course, but often enough for me to realize that what women (and some men) don't like about the science fiction they've previously read has been its use of war and violence. Seeing the potential of science fiction allows a new perspective to emerge.

We have only to change one thing in our physical environment to provide an opportunity for a science fiction scenario. Any experimentation you decide on could begin with this basic premise. What other simple changes could we make in order to consider far-reaching implications? Changes in the way society works or more fundamental changes in our physical environment? What about housing? Is it likely that after, say, the year 2050, we might all have to live underground?

The last place on Earth?

There is a place in South Australia called Coober Pedy where many of the buildings are underground. Opals are mined here but it is a strange town, more like a war-zone than a place to live in. The rocket and atom bomb testing areas of Woomera and Maralinga are close by and there's still an American base at Woomera. Maralinga is prohibited territory these days. Local aboriginal people, the Koori, were left uninformed of the danger when the atom bomb tests of the 1950s took place. Many British and Australian servicemen were ordered to watch the blasts while wearing only summer uniforms and with nothing to protect their bodies from the radiation emitted with the huge mushroom clouds. Thus many people were killed or have had to deal with shocking physical after-effects.

And Coober Pedy, what is it like? The scenery is desolate and ghostly, but the trucks you see everywhere move at a frantic pace. The word EXPLOSIVES is marked on the side of those trucks, but to see them whizz along the bitumen road you get the feeling it's all just a great joke. There's red desert sand, red rubble, red dust, the odd salt lake, corrugated water tanks, tin sheds, broken-down cars and trucks. The dust settles with persistent glee, attaching itself to everything in sight. The Stuart Highway runs straight through town and if you walk along the main street you'll pass by underground opal caves and gift shops, an underground bookshop, church and motel. The mines and the town are so interlinked you cannot think of one without the other. Could Coober Pedy be a one-off god-forsaken place, or could it be a harbinger of the future as we plumb the depths of the Earth for treasure and conduct life-threatening experiments in the name of national defence?

What do you think? Where and how do you imagine we might be living fifty or one hundred years from now?

Notes

1   For a fuller discussion of the history of the Gothic novel see the appendix on 'History of the novel', p. 214.
2   Bram Stoker, who published *Dracula* in 1897, is generally credited with having written the first Dracula novel but he was influenced by a story called 'Carmilla' in Joseph Sheridan Le Fanu's collection of short stories *In a Glass Darkly*, published in 1872.
3   See Roz Kaveney, 'The Science Fictiveness of Women's Science Fiction' in Helen Carr (ed.), *From My Guy to Sci-Fi: Genre and Women's Writing in the Postmodern World*, Pandora Press, London, 1989, p. 79.
4   See, for example, Riane Eisler, *The Chalice and the The Blade*, Harper & Row, San Francisco, 1988.
5   Joanna Russ 'Clichés from Outer Space', in Jen Green and Sarah Lefanu (eds.), *Despatches from the Frontiers of The Female Mind*, The Women's Press, London, 1985, pp. 27–34.
6   See Nickianne Moody, 'Maeve and Guinevere' in Lucie Armitt, *where no man has gone before – women and science fiction*, Routledge, London, 1991, p. 201, and first narrated in Geoffrey of Monmouth's *Historia* (c.1135), in Margaret Drabble & Jenny Stringer (eds.), *The Concise Oxford Companion to English Literature*, Oxford University Press, Oxford, 1990, p. 24.
7   See Nickianne Moody, op. cit., pp. 194–199.

Sources

Armitt, Lucie (ed.), *where no man has gone before – women and science fiction*, Routledge, London, 1991.

Atwood, Margaret, *The Handmaid's Tale*, Virago Press, London, 1987.

Butler, Octavia, *Kindred*, The Women's Press, London, 1988.

Caldecott, Moyra, *The Tall Stones*, *The Temple of the Sun* and *Shadows on the Stones* (published in one volume), Arrow Books, London, 1986.

Carr, Helen (ed.), *From My Guy to Sci-Fi: Genre and Women's Writing in the Postmodern World*, Pandora Press, London, 1989.

Carrington, Leonora, *The Hearing Trumpet*, Virago Press, London, 1991.

Carter, Angela, 'The Loves of Lady Purple' in *The Bloody Chamber*, Penguin, Harmondsworth, 1981.

Charnas, Suzy McKee, *Walk to the End of the World* and *Motherlines*, The Women's Press, London, 1989.

de Pizan, Christine, *The Book of the City of Ladies*, Pan Books, London, 1983.

Dick, Philip K., *Do Androids Dream of Electric Sheep?*, Rapp & Whiting, London, 1969, republished as *Blade Runner*, London, Panther, 1982.

Dodderidge, Esme, *The New Gulliver*, The Women's Press, London, 1988.

Emshwiller, Carol, *Carmen Dog*, The Women's Press, London, 1988.

Forrest, Katherine, 'O Captain, My Captain' in *Dreams and Swords*, The Naiad Press, Florida, 1987.

Gearheart, Sally Miller, *The Wanderground*, The Women's Press, London, 1985.

Gentle, Mary, *Golden Witchbreed*, Arrow Books, London, 1984.

Haden Elgin, Suzette, *Native Tongue*, The Women's Press, 1985.

Kaveney, Ros, 'The Science Fictiveness of Women's Science Fiction' in Helen Carr (ed.), *From My Guy to Sci-Fi: Genre and Women's Writing in the Postmodern World*, op. cit.

Kennealy, Patricia, *The Copper Crown*, Grafton, London, 1986.

Lefanu, Sarah, *In the Chinks of the World Machine*, The Women's Press, London, 1988.

McCaffrey, Anne, *The Ship Who Sang*, Corgi Books, London, 1972.

O'Donnell, Margaret, *The Beehive*, Magnum Books, London, 1982.

Palmer, Jane, *The Planet Dweller*, The Women's Press, London, 1985.

Perkins Gilman, Charlotte, *Herland*, The Women's Press, London, 1979.

Piercy, Marge, *Woman on the Edge of Time*, The Women's Press, London, 1976.

Saxton, Josephine, 'Gordon's Women' in *The Travails of Jane Saint and Other Stories*, The Women's Press, London, 1986.

Scott, Jody, *I, Vampire*, The Women's Press, London, 1986.

Scott, Sarah, *Millenium Hall*, Virago Press, London, 1986.

Shelley, Mary, *Frankenstein – the Modern Prometheus*, in Fairclough, P. (ed.), *Three Gothic Novels*, Penguin Books, Harmondsworth, 1982.

Tuttle, Lisa, *A Spaceship Built of Stone*, The Women's Press, London, 1987.

Zoline, Pamela, 'The Heat Death of the Universe' in *Busy About the Tree of Life*, The Women's Press, London, 1988.

Vonarburg, Elisabeth, *The Silent City*, The Women's Press, London, 1990.

Zimmer Bradley, Marion, *The Mists of Avalon*, Sphere Books, London, 1984.

Other information

Getting started and keeping going

Is fear the full stop that prevents you from writing the next sentence? Does it follow you like a shadow, insisting that you're wasting your time with this writing business? Does fear appear out of nowhere like a genie from the bottle, unwittingly summoned at moments of doubt?

We cannot hope to eliminate fear altogether; it will always be there, a needle on the graph of our lives, constantly moving in accordance with our changing circumstances. Working positively with fear depends on knowing how it operates. I feel fear when I hear good writing read aloud in a group. This used to be a wagging index finger that told me I was inadequate and unable to express myself on paper as well as this writer could. I still have that fear and it still operates as an indication of good writing but it no longer threatens me in the same way. The feeling is the same but my response is different. I now make the fear work for me in a positive way. I can accept it. I can tell that writer her work is good and see it as separate from myself and my work. Such fear could be *situational* – the type that goes with the complex nature of our work and what we are striving to achieve with that work. There are also fears we nourish unintentionally. We may not have created these fears but we can work to limit their impact. I call this second type *messages from within*.

I cannot stress enough how important it is to your potential as a writer to become aware of what you are telling others *and yourself* about you, your life and your work. A woman can be completely *unaware* of the extent to which her inner dialogue is working against her, defeating or diminishing her aims, hopes and dreams. Raising the issue of self-talk with women writers is not a difficult matter, but attempting to show how central it is to developing our confidence and a fair assessment of our talents and worth is the most awesome challenge for me as a creative writing

tutor. Why? Because so many of us don't listen to what we are
saying when we speak about who we are, as women, as writers.
Once you begin to look at the inner dialogue, observing yourself
and others and noting what is said, you could be amazed at what
you hear. If you have done this work already you'll know what I
mean; if you haven't, now is the time to start.

If asked to read your work aloud, do you begin with a deep
breath and launch right into the opening sentence without
preamble? Or do you preface your reading with a humorous,
self-mocking gesture or a put-down comment that goes something
like this:

> 'I know this isn't very good ...'

> 'I warn you, I'm not as good a writer as ...'
> (the woman who has just read previously)

> 'I dashed this off early this morning but I know
> it's probably not what you want/meant/etc.'

> 'I'll read it if you want me to ...'

Taking ourselves seriously enough to think we have ability, and
not so seriously that we cannot weather the inevitable knocks, is
a tricky balancing act. Becoming aware of how frequently we do
the 'knocking' ourselves is as important as learning how to write
good material.

Time wasting

Have you ever come across Narrow Horizons? She's so overly
concerned with proving that she's *not* a time waster that she
fails to give herself enough time to experiment and learn. Instead
of asking herself questions about point of view, or another place
to begin, or her character's motives, Narrow tends to see her
writing process as linear, heading off in one direction and sticking
to that as though her life depended on it. What to do? What to
say? How to reach her? If you're a good friend, perhaps you
could talk to her. I'm sure she'd listen.

Fear of not being brilliant

Do you suffer from the 'Virginia Woolf' syndrome? You know
you've got it when you feel you can't start writing unless your style

or originality are a stunningly brilliant match to everything Virginia Woolf achieved in one of her novels. Do you really think she wrote any of her books in one draft? I once belonged to a self-help group, set up for people who had been in psychiatric centres. We had a saying: 'If a thing is worth doing, it's worth doing badly at first.' Necessity compelled me to work with this saying all those years ago. Later, applying it to my writing, I gave myself permission to make mistakes. It helped me a great deal – we do learn from our mistakes don't we? What about you? Do you think you will recover from the 'Virginia Woolf' syndrome?

Discipline

I have difficulty beginning new projects. The bigger the project, the longer the procrastination. If it's a book, I know I'm going to have to wade through 2,000 to 8,000 words of useless rubbish before writing a worthwhile, workable beginning. This knowledge feeds the procrastination. Oh no, I say to myself, all that effort ... Yet I accept that this is a part of my writing process, and rarely do I keep those pages and pages of typed notes. You could say there's a tug of war going on between *knowing* and *accepting* the process. Accepting must win if I'm to move on, and I do eventually reach a point where enough is enough. The main difference between the established, published, known writer and the struggling beginner centres around discipline. Think of discipline as a general heading under which come *motivation*, *determination* and *commitment*.

Motivation

This is an integral aspect of discipline but it is not the whole story, nor is it a 'fixed' ingredient. Although we may be motivated to write for a number of reasons the strength of that impulse will depend on various factors. Motivation may be there but how strong is it? Does it exist as a wistful longing, nestling around the heart, adding dreamy notions to your future? What if fear gets in the way – that elusive beast lower down in your body that manages to hold your guts tightly in its grasp?

Virginia Woolf argues the case admirably for a '... room of one's own and £500 a year'. Now, I'll call in an idle fairy godmother, ask her to grant you one wish, and before you can say CRIPES! there you are in a well-equipped room minus any money worries, given all the time you could possibly need, a relaxed and comfortable atmosphere, and even a special someone to bring you coffee and cookies while you sit, leisurely poised on the brink of writing the novel of the century. What then? Would your first words tumble on to the typewriter with gay abandon or is that you, curled up in the corner, laid low by dread and doubt? Writing can prove to be a scary proposition. As one woman said to me recently, 'you can like the lifestyle but be dead scared of the job.'

Determination

Determination comes in here and needs to be thought of as a good friend to motivation. It is determination that says, 'I know it's tough and all that, but I've made up my mind and I won't be deterred.' Although determination is all about persistence and patience and a whole lot more, it can also be fuelled by anger in a positive way. In fact, anger can help determination to survive and grow strong. A rejection slip drops through the letterbox. What will I do? Weep? Worry? Give up? Decide I never could write anyway? Or ...?

I work with rejection and setbacks as a kind of dare. I have a conversation with that publisher that goes something like this: 'So you think that's going to stop me? Well, you wait, you'll be sorry you didn't accept my work, I promise you that.' Publishers are renowned for rejecting manuscripts that later become best-sellers. I may need to look at the material again to be sure that the rejection is a publisher's folly and not a weakness in my manuscript. Then, having satisfied myself on that score, I can choose to bide my time until another opportunity presents itself or I can send the material off to another publisher. Also bear in mind that a rejection from a publisher may not be because of poor writing. It may mean that the publisher wasn't suitable, or was not interested in the subject matter, or that the particular area you are writing in is well covered at the moment. Don't despair; be determined.

Commitment

This acts as a wedge, keeping the door ajar so that I can give further consideration to possible options, such as the reworking of the structure or content, or being more flexible about feedback or harsh criticism that I suspect could be helpful. Without that wedge a limiting sort of single-mindedness might take over, slamming the door shut rather than contemplate another moment's effort.

Commitment reminds me I am a writer with integrity, that I want to produce work of the highest possible standard, and that I'm not just interested in a prompt result I might regret later on.

There are times when motivation is a strong force pushing me on and on, and there are other times when, due to unforeseen setbacks, it will flag without warning. Determination comes along then, handing out recipes for keeping my spirits up, nothing too dramatic or startling (unless anger intervenes), and the steady throb of reliability works wonders to get me moving again. Commitment walks alongside, notebook in hand, reading out my list of principles and self-imposed rules. The list grows, keeping pace with my experience. It is commitment that causes me sleepless nights, wrangling over decisions and challenges, pointing out something I've overlooked or ignored, asking questions I know I'll have to listen to in the end.

Obstacles from outside and within

Family and friends might want to see you earning money before they take you seriously. *You* might want to see you earning money before you take yourself seriously. A conditioned, cultural modesty could prevent you from thinking of yourself as a writer, a *real* writer. I'm not advocating an inflated assessment of your ability but we might agree that:

(a) You need and/or are entitled to a period of time to learn and explore before later – much later – you can ask questions about how much ability/potential you have; or
(b) you could decide now that your writing intentions are not linked to financial reward or validation from a public audience.

In either case, how may we help ourselves to move past the obstacles? How do we get that good idea down on paper before it dissipates? There are times when we reach out to pull the beginnings of a poem, story or plot towards us. If we were asked why it didn't happen, the answer might well have to do with time. As a general rule, it takes longer to write a short story than a poem. For some, the shorter length of a poem is appealing. Reworking a poem is a more portable process, and snatching the odd hour here or there is usually manageable. No need for a typewriter or a word processor (assuming for the moment that you could afford either), just pick up the last draft and take it with you – on the train, to the kitchen table while the baby's asleep, packed in with your holiday gear, or kept on the table by your bed to be looked at before you turn in. Olive Rogers, a working-class poet based in Liverpool, explains that she's become so used to the poetry-writing process that she finds it difficult to contemplate writing prose. For every advantage you can name in your working process there's bound to be a disadvantage, or challenge, following close behind.

If time is short don't set yourself unrealistic standards or deadlines that can only be described as self-defeating. Regular, allotted working sessions each week may prove a better system than trying to grab time from other activities and preoccupations. If you and those around you become used to the idea of one or two nights a week as your 'writing nights' you will find that those evenings can be like an oasis that is easy to reach without argument or constant negotiation. You may need to be firm and determined to start with, but you can make it work, and once the habit has been established those working sessions will become an accepted part of your life.

If you have somewhere to work it can be a real advantage to leave things arranged exactly as you wish to give you a continued sense of work in progress. Maybe you believe this is impossible. Why? A sheet or a cloth thrown over a table or desk may not be as complicated to arrange as you think.

The following suggestions are intended to help you make good use of whatever time you have:

1 Keep a notebook with you at all times. Why not different sized notebooks – a tiny version for your pocket or handbag, larger varieties where space and size are not a problem? Jot down thoughts, ideas, funny sayings, descriptions of people, clothing, feelings, the weather, anything. It will all be there waiting for some future period of your life when you do have the time.

2 Use a diary regularly, in any way you wish. If you are pushed for time, short entries will do. Wry comments about your life and your ongoing situation, your relationships and so on, are all good writing practice. When you get more time you can indulge in longer, more reflective, introspective, entries.

3 Use emotion as a trigger, making use of your notebook or diary if possible before any planned confrontation. You may find that your articulation is acutely honed when you are angry or upset and that the flow of words comes like a raging waterfall.

If you don't feel so comfortable with words when your feelings are raw and painfully apparent, use your writing process to tease out exactly what it is that you are upset or confused about. In this way you will develop your understanding of your own needs and wishes. In short, don't waste that emotion, use it.

4 Keep photocopies of letters you send, and think of each one as an exercise in originality. You never know when a thought or phrase might come in useful.

5 Word association exercises are ideal for keeping your motor ticking over. Allow ten to fifteen minutes for the exercise from start to finish. Choose three words. These three can be taken from anywhere – from out of your head, from a book or a dictionary – but try not to have a hidden agenda in mind. The choice of words makes no difference at all. Simply write as fast as you can whatever comes to mind after you've heard or read that word. If there's someone around ask that person to supply the words, one at a time, with an interval between each word to allow you time to write. Make yourself responsible for saying when you are ready for the next word. Children may enjoy this task and usually respond with involved interest. Encourage them to try it too. The rule is that you must *stop* writing the minute that the pen lifts up from the page. Persistence is your best companion here, so keep at it. If the words come at a cracking speed one day and not the next don't be deterred. After a month's effort you'll find you've developed a rewarding habit. I consider this one of the best exercises I've ever used.

Working in a group

So much teaching and group work is invisible, understood and assessed only by those directly involved. Women's styles and strategies in education remain largely unrecorded. Where do we look for ideas? What models can we refer to? In sharing some of my ways of working I would hope to contribute to the development of a wider dialogue and range of resources. I refer below to a course rather than to groups, though the points covered are likely to be relevant to writing groups, even those organized without a facilitator.

Over the years I've observed five broad strands of motivation that are linked to the reasons why women attend creative writing courses. Making use of these observations, I've been able to develop a deeper understanding of course participants, and to pitch my approach more appropriately to meet their needs/wishes . Here I've invented characters named *A, B, C, D* and *E* to illustrate what I mean.

A describes herself as an avid reader. Although she is a lively participant in discussions about issues and ideas relating to books and women's lives, she is more confident about what she reads than about what she writes. Her feedback to others is warm and encouraging, yet she may constantly apologize 'for not having written anything this week'. She sometimes wonders aloud why she keeps coming, undermining the value of her extensive knowledge and her ongoing contribution to the group. I think of this woman as a *passionate reader*.

B comes to the course raring to go. Previous experience, directly or indirectly related to writing, has given her a measure of confidence in creative expression, and this accumulation of experience is influencing her to get something moving right *now*. Able to zoom in on the course content, *B* is just full of ideas and questions and wants to learn as much as she possibly can. She will be well motivated to complete assignments and is willing to do more than is expected of her. When I think of this woman I think of how *timing* is working for her.

For *C* this might be her first creative writing course so she'll be feeling unsure of what she says in discussion, frequently prefacing her opening remarks with a joke about herself. Her understanding of what her strengths are may not come to the fore for some months, or for even longer than that. When she makes a thought provoking point she cannot easily accept the compliments made about her wisdom, laughing them off with an embarrassed, self-conscious grin. She is usually an older woman and she may relish talking or writing about the past, making sense of it in a therapeutic or diary-keeping way. The word I associate with *C* is *experimental*.

D has been through what I refer to as 'the think tank of education'. She has been taught the *how of it*: how to write essays, how to think of comparisons, how to work to externally imposed deadlines. She may possess an almost inexhaustible fund of references and have firm ideas on what constitutes good writing. When *D* attempts to 'free-up' her writing she feels restricted by these past influences and her struggle may not be expressed as openly in class as she feels it internally. Often highly critical of her own attempts, she is nonetheless full of praise and insights about the work of others in the group. *D* knows that she is struggling for more than a writing flow, and when advised to begin with her own life may find the challenge quite a tall order. When I think of *D* I think of a woman *needing to find different ground*.

E has probably kept a diary for a long time and may have written poems since childhood days. She is familiar with women poets old and new, knows what she likes and yet has rarely shown her work to anyone else. She is drawn to the warmth and welcome of the group like a stranger coming in from the cold and listens intently to all that is said without compromising her own opinions. Others respect her straightforward approach and might wish they knew her better. Because *E* first carefully sifts through what she wants to say it is difficult for her to participate in discussion. Mutual trust is the crucial ingredient if the course is to work well for her, and she knows that the privacy she needs so badly can make it difficult for her and for others to know how to proceed together. *E* reminds me constantly of *the power writing has to heal*.

You might identify with one or more aspects of these five fictional women, or with none at all, but I hope the descriptions can give you an idea of what's involved when designing a creative writing course. *B*, for example, might want to read what she has written after the first class at the earliest possible opportunity. Less confident participants could then feel that a certain standard had been set, a standard they might see as being higher than any they could attain. Other participants, who may be hesitant about reading material too soon, might postpone the moment as a result.

For reasons such as this I find it worthwhile to negotiate a set of guidelines with participants when we first meet as a group. I explain that I have a small list of suggestions as a starting point for these guidelines, and I give information about how and why they've been useful in the past. The list is then gone through carefully and other suggestions from the group are discussed. The agreed set of guidelines is photocopied for each member and there is always the possibility of further additions and/or negotiations at a later stage.

The following two points are foremost in my mind when I discuss guidelines with a group. I prefer the course to be well established (say week six in a ten week course) before participants read material produced as part of the course. I ask that they each aim to put together a portfolio of work, so that when we meet for the sixth time every woman will have a range of pieces to choose from. A greater, stronger trust will have developed in the group by that time, and if there's been enjoyment and laughter from one week to another (and there usually is) reading aloud will be perceived as the sharing process it is, rather than as a threatening ordeal. Perhaps you feel this period of six weeks could be hard on some students. I have found that talking about the issues when compiling a list of guidelines means that everyone can understand the reasoning and accept it. This doesn't mean that there is no reading aloud, as exercises done in a session can be read, but there is no pressure on any woman to do so if she would rather not. Feeling the safety in this choice alleviates anxiety. Working in small groups helps too.

Giving and receiving feedback

Constructive criticism is intended to be helpful and instructive but frequently, all too frequently, it is harmful and off-putting. Take the story of two schoolgirls who saw a poster advertising a poetry group that was looking for new members. The group had been meeting for years and some of the founder members prided themselves on their critical abilities. When the two girls came to the next meeting they were greeted with a great show of warmth and asked if they had any previous experience of writing poetry. Yes, one replied, their English teacher had encouraged them and even published a few of their poems in the school magazine. In response to suggestions that they read something they'd written the two nervously agreed. A strange silence followed the readings, finally broken by one of the members clearing his throat before launching into a lengthy patronising criticism of their poems. He was well into his stride and so preoccupied that he didn't notice the girls were close to tears. They didn't wait to hear him finish, almost falling over each other in their haste to get out of that room. Their critic sat back open-mouthed with astonishment as he watched them leave. Turning back to the group he asked what could he have said to upset them so much? 'Don't they want to know how to write good poetry?' he demanded.

Trust is such a crucial factor when it comes to feedback – giving it or getting it. Why should you trust anyone who isn't caring or sensitive in the way they talk about your work? As we gain experience and confidence we can put some distance between ourselves and what we write. Riding out the impact of reviews (good or bad) is a necessary part of life for anyone who is in the public eye. Expecting not to feel the discomfort of negative criticism is unrealistic. Again and again you'll hear writers compare what they have written with a child they have parented. 'This is my baby' they'll say. So imagine for a moment that you've got a two-year-old daughter. As she toddles down the front path one morning one of your neighbours leans over the fence, looks at the child and says: 'She really is ugly, isn't she?' How would you feel? If your confidence is low and you haven't been writing for very long, then negative feedback can be received as an intense experience of rejection. It's important, therefore, that you feel in control of the way in which you want to have feedback and from whom.

The feedback sandwich

What is positive feedback? I use a method I call the feedback sandwich. To comment on someone else's work you begin by telling them something specific you liked about the material. Maybe it was the opening sentence, the good use of vocabulary, the way humour was used? Having made positive points you can now turn your attention to weaknesses you've noted. You ask a question to clarify a passage near the end. The writer explains further and you continue, expressing your view that the plot seems a bit wobbly in conclusion. Finally, you make a more general comment that is positive and encouraging. Using this approach participants can feel, as writers and listeners, that they are developing a shared understanding of what is involved. Feedback becomes part of the educative process. I talk about feedback right from the start, encouraging each woman to jot down odd words or sentences to assist her when giving feedback. This focuses the concentration and the ability to listen.

There is also feedback by post. I devised this strategy as a means of receiving/giving feedback one to one, but still operating within a group context. It could be used during a course (between participants) for more detailed feedback or by writing groups who meet regularly (say monthly) but who still want a progression of work to continue from one meeting to the next. To explain how it works I'll use one woman's short story as an example.

The writer brings her story to the meeting, having prepared in advance a list of group members' names and dates (spread a few days apart) for the coming four weeks. Her story is given to the woman whose name appears at the top of the list. This reader takes the story home, looks at the material a day or so later, writes down her comments and then addresses two separate envelopes. One will contain the short story which will now be forwarded to the woman whose name appears next on the list. The other envelope containing the written feedback will be posted to the short story writer. The dates on the list can be worked out so that each reader has a set time in which to read the material and pass it on. If members of the group are busy during this period they may not wish to be included in the reading list this time round. If the group is large the writer can ask for volunteers, or select a number of readers whose views and experience she thinks are relevant to what she is working on.

During the next month the writer receives her feedback letters and if there is a consensus of opinion, suggesting for example that the opening paragraph is not working well, she can weigh that collective viewpoint against her own judgement. The group agrees that readers won't discuss material being sent around so the writer can trust what she's being told and be assured of confidentiality as part of the process. Part of the next meeting might be set aside for discussion of the short story and there could well be curiosity among the readers to know what the others have said.

Four readers with one week each to read, comment and pass on material would be ideal. As there would probably be more than the one writer's material circulating at any given time, be prepared for a few hitches to do with timing. It can happen that four weeks have gone by and not all of the readers have seen the short story. If that is the case, the list and dates can be adjusted to fit the next four-week period. The advantage of this method is that if group members are unable to meet as often as they'd like, the work can still be ticking over, providing a sense of continuity.

Forming a group

If you don't want to join a writing class as such but want to form a group it would be a good idea to set some ground rules like the ones discussed above to help every member of the group to feel encouraged and not overawed. Discussing your ideas with other interested readers can sharpen your perceptions and develop your confidence in saying with greater clarity what you think. You may have friends who thoroughly enjoy reading a particular kind of fiction but who would never contemplate writing. Setting up a number of discussions about a particular genre could be an important aspect of your writing process. Once you have established a rapport, either with one person or with a small group (too many might defeat the intended purpose), you could make use of the opportunity to expand your ideas for a book. Using the other person(s) as a sounding board you could gain valuable feedback on the strengths and weaknesses of your work and even get suggestions on how to develop it. Participation in the plotting process of a novel could prove a worthwhile experience for your friends, and may lead to further possibilities.

Another way of finding interested persons would be to pin a note on a noticeboard at the local library or some other place where you can be sure it will be seen. Pen-friends are a useful alternative if you live too far from a city or town, and having a written response or an ongoing dialogue in a series of letters could serve as useful notes to refer back to.

It's true that many writers don't like discussing the humble beginnings of a story, fearing perhaps that those tender, wispy fragments might blow away or disappear once exposed to scrutiny. You may feel nervous at the thought of such exposure. Yet if we don't try to build a structure for the outpourings of our imagination we might find that all we ever have are wispy bits that go unseen forever. Concentration on the craft of writing, exploring ideas, plots, characters, storylines – nurturing what we have thought, discussed and written in note form and further reading and/or research we have done – will increase our interest and output. For most new writers, getting that momentum with which to begin is the hardest task of all.

As a strategy, sharing ideas with others might be something you need only to get you started. For others it might become a great source of inspiration, challenge, comfort and support. Next time you read a book take a look at the acknowledgements section. Has the writer thanked a number of people for looking at the manuscript at an early stage? Has she acknowledged support and suggestions made by others? Among women there is often tribute paid to significant others, and some women writers are so aware of that support they speak of it in glowing, appreciative terms. No two writers work in exactly the same way but most of us (particularly those of us who never thought we had it in us until we tried) have manufactured and maintained a necessary determination. What is it that you feel you need? Now might be a good time to think about that, to make plans or create a working programme.

Getting published

Anthologies

One good place to start getting your work published is in anthologies. Anthologies edited and contributed to by women writers have become an accepted part of feminist publishing since the 1970s. Articles and stories assembled around a theme, a subject area, or a common cause can play a part in shifting consciousness, adding to our awareness of the different points of view of so many women. I like to think of the anthology as the collective principle in print. This applies to non-fiction anthologies in particular. The emphasis here is on self-help, self-awareness, and a number of contributors offering a broad range of experiences, viewpoints, ideas and so on. I believe passionately in the importance and value of the anthology and my early experience as a writer came from contributing to and then later editing collections of writing, both non-fiction and fiction.

If there is more than one editor the work is shared, and so too is the learning experience. And if each editor brings to the project a different perspective in terms of race, class or sexual identity then the anthology can only benefit from such diversity. Another crucial issue around the editorial process is how to ensure the inclusion of women with disabilities. For so long disabled women have been seen in terms of 'disability' rather than as individual women who cope with a disability and the restrictions of living in a society that does not cater for their needs. To date, too few collections have addressed this challenge.

For most women writers, contributing to anthologies is the usual way of gaining publication experience and gradually (sometimes speedily) becoming known to women readers. By writing or phoning a publisher you can find out if an anthology is being planned. You may be pleasantly surprised to hear a voice on the other end of the phone asking if you would like to 'send something you've written for us to look at'. If it so happens that they are planning a short story collection, you may already have a story written (maybe two or three?) that you think appropriate.

How to approach publishers

Choose your publisher

Find the most appropriate publisher for your material, whether it is a story, novel, play or non-fiction. Your local library will keep directories such as the *Directory of Publishing* and *The Writers' and Artists' Yearbook*, a relatively inexpensive handbook giving information on publishers and the markets they cover as well as contracts, research, prizes, etc. Similar publications are also produced in the other English language-speaking countries such as the United States and Australia. Wherever you are your library should be able to help you find publications that give you this kind of information. Attic Press in Dublin have produced a practical guide to getting published, *So You Want to be Published?*, covering publishers in Ireland and the UK.

Phone magazines and ask them what sort of material they are interested in and how long pieces are expected to be.

If you are submitting a novel to publishers phone them first and ask them what material they would like to receive. Publishers much prefer in the initial stages to receive only a synopsis and sample chapters. It's a good idea to include a synopsis anyway. Publishers receive so much material that a synopsis will help them to decide at the outset whether your material is suitable for them. It is also useful to get the name of the editor in the company that deals with the specific area in which you are writing.

Publishing companies very often have an in-house style sheet that they can supply that details the layout and spelling that they use. Companies specializing in romance fiction have guidelines for authors that tell you in some detail what kinds of manuscript they are looking for and how to submit them.

Preparing and submitting manuscripts

The following guidelines apply to all kinds of manuscript, fiction and non-fiction.

Paper

Use white A4-sized paper of reasonable quality. Nowadays many authors produce their work on word processors. If this is the case, check with the publisher that the software you use is acceptable to them.

Layout

All manuscripts should be typed, with double spacing, on one side of the paper. On the left-hand side allow a margin of one and a half to two inches. This space is used by the copy editor and designer to give instructions to the typesetter. Begin each chapter on a new page. Number the pages throughout. You may also add to the page number your surname, initials or part of the title, for example 'Jones 8'. This is a safety measure to help identify loose sheets in case any of the pages of your manuscript get lost while at the publishers. Corrections should be written clearly in ink above the typed line. If you have more than just a few corrections then individual pages should be retyped. Avoid, as far as you are able, submitting a manuscript with spelling, grammar or punctuation errors. The work needs to be submitted in as finished and correct a state as possible. Italicized words should be underlined. Type a title page with the title, word length and your name and address. Also put in a copyright line as follows: © Christine Jones 1992.

Securing

Do not staple pages together. Use either paperclips or a rubber band to hold all the sheets together.

Word Counting

It's not necessary to be 100 per cent accurate in your word count. Add up the words on an average line and multiply that figure by the number of lines on the page. Multiply that by the number of pages.

Posting

Do not fold your manuscript. Buy an envelope large enough to fit it in flat. For novels, send the package by registered mail.

Keeping track

Keep a record of every piece of work you send to publishers or to any other publication outlet. First make sure you have a complete copy of what you are sending. *Never* send your original copy. Even writers who really ought to know better still make this mistake and then moan about it afterwards. There is never a good reason for posting off or loaning your only copy. Use a carbon if you cannot afford the cost of photocopying. Keep a record of what you send off, using a file-card system or a book that has categories. The categories would be as follows: the name of the story or novel or whatever, even if it's a simple title like 'Unnamed poem number 1'; a column for the date; and another column for updating information (for example, you might phone after a two-month period to check on what's happening). Record the information so that everything about this particular piece of work is current. This is especially important when you have more than one piece of work doing the rounds. Wherever possible write in the name of the person you've heard from or spoken to, so that you always have a starting point for further communication.

Waiting

Be patient. Given the volume of material that publishers receive there is often quite a long wait, three months or more, before they can reply. If you don't hear after a reasonable period of time write a follow-up letter. If you don't send the manuscript by registered mail enclose a self-addressed postcard so the publisher can let you know the manuscript has arrived.

Competitions

An organization called The Book Trust publishes an inexpensive book called *Guide to Literary Prizes and Grants and Awards in Britain and Ireland*. Address: Book Trust, Book House, 45 East Hill, London, SW18 2QZ.

Other organizations

The Society of Authors is an independent trade union for authors. It provides information on the book trade, journalism and the performing arts, and advises members on the business aspects of their work. It also publishes a number of *Quick Guides* covering copyright, libel, agents, contracts and tax. Address: 84 Drayton Gardens, London, SW10 9SB. In Australia the address is: The Australian Society of Authors, P.O. Box 315, Redfern, NSW, 2016.

The Writer's Guild of Great Britain is a trade union for writers in book publishing, film, radio, television and theatre. Address: 430 Edgware Road, London, W2 1EH.

There are also two women's organizations: The Society of Women Writers and Journalists, 2 St Lawrence Close, Edgware, Middlesex, HA8 6RB, and The Network of Women Writers' Association, 8 The Broadway, Woking, Surrey, GU21 5AP.

Publications

Directory of Publishing, Cassell, London.
So You Want to be Published? A Guide to Getting into Print, Róisín Conroy, Attic Press, Dublin, 1992.
The Writer's Handbook, Macmillan, London.
Writers' and Artists' Yearbook, A & C Black, London.

The last word

Some years ago during a period of grief and depression I searched the shelves of bookshops hoping to find words that would help make me feel better about my life and the world in general. I didn't know exactly what I was looking for but felt sure I'd know the right book if I saw it. I never did find it and walking out of a bookshop one day I muttered to myself that I'd probably have to *write* the book I wanted to read ... What was I saying? I hurried into a café and rummaged in my bag for pen and paper. I found my pen but there was nothing to write on. Fortunately, there were plain white paper napkins on the table. I used several to make notes. Not only did I have a new project to work on but I'd also found a way out of my miserable state. That was the beginning of *Through the Break*, an anthology that was published in Britain in 1987. The book evolved way beyond its humble beginnings but the point of this story was brought home to me recently when I read in a newspaper something Gloria Steinem had said after her latest book, *Revolution from Within*, was published: 'We teach what we most need to learn, we write what we need to read.' Good luck!

Appendix

Novel beginnings – a short history

The novel as a means of telling stories through the printed word emerged in seventeenth-century Europe. It was a form of expression that expanded rapidly in terms of both numbers produced and different types established. In the eighteenth century the most popular forms of the novel were those written as letters (the epistolary novel) and the Gothic. In the nineteenth century the Gothic gave way to the convention of 'realism', which predominates to this day. In the last half of the twentieth century we have witnessed the proliferation of the novel into a number of genres and sub-genres to the point where categorization has become almost impossible. The novel has comprehensively replaced poetry and plays as the major expression of fictional writing. This is a brief guide to the history of the English novel – an outline of the major developments of the last 300 years within the context of the wider economic, political and social changes of this period.

Recently it was announced on radio that Barbara Taylor Bradford, the writer of such blockbuster novels as *A Woman of Substance*, had been given a thirty-million-dollar advance against the royalties of her next three books by a large American publishing company. Barbara Taylor Bradford justified such payments by pointing out that the large sales of her novels enabled the publisher to take up works by lesser-known or new writers. It is ironic to reflect that when novels first appeared in the seventeenth century such a huge sum of money for an author would have been unthinkable, for the novel had a very low status. The novels produced then were criticized as 'escapist', much in the same way that romance fiction is criticized today. Far from being displayed proudly on the bookshelves of middle-class homes, they were furtively tucked away from public view. In the 1850s a friend of the novelist Charles Dickens was said to be surprised that Dickens' bookshelves contained little but fiction.[1] There were a number of reasons for this attitude, not least the fact that women were both the major producers and the main consumers of the novel in its early days.

Beginnings in prose

The term 'roman' is currently used in many modern languages to mean the novel, while the word 'novel' comes from the Italian word 'novella', which means 'small new thing' and which was first used in the sixteenth century to describe short tales. We now use the word 'novella' to describe a piece of writing that is somewhere in length between the short story and the novel (between 17,500 and 40,000 words). The word 'novel' first appeared in England in the mid seventeenth century, when it was chiefly associated with stories of illicit love. For this reason some authors described their fictions as 'history' because they wanted to be seen as 'serious' writers.

Although fictional narratives of one sort or another have existed for as long as there have been written records, they were traditionally either poetry or drama, written in verse rather than prose, and concerned with myths, mythical heroes, epic events and the gods. The modern novel can be traced to the romance narratives that were developed in twelfth-century France around 'courtly love'. These narratives were idealized representations of courtly life, framed by strict conventions of behaviour, and usually concerned with (although this seems paradoxical) adulterous love affairs. Stories were told by poets called troubadours, first in verse and then in prose. We would be hard pressed today to see a direct relationship between these narratives and the novel as we know it, but the courtly love poems were the first representations of the court and chivalry that did not rely on epic or mythical figures.

How then did the novel come about? A number of factors contributed to its development.[2] In the feudal period prior to the sixteenth century artists and writers had to rely on rich patrons to support them while they produced their work. Capitalism as an economic system based on the market-place emerged in the sixteenth century, and along with it a layer of society made up of mercantile traders and producers that we now refer to as the middle class. Among them were publishers who began to replace patrons as the supporters of writers. It is also important to recognize that the climate of ideas was changing. There was an increasing desire to understand the world by objective observation rather than by a reliance on systems of belief and religious dogma. This was the beginning of rationalism. Scientists like Sir Isaac Newton and the philosopher John Locke, who lived in the last half of the seventeenth century, began to investigate the ordinary physical world.

The development of printing was another factor that not only facilitated the novel but also had a profound effect on almost every aspect of life. Information through broadsheets and pamphlets could be communicated to larger numbers of people instead of being reserved for the elite. The greater availability of the novel no doubt contributed to its low status when it emerged – reading was no longer the preserve of the wealthy, upper classes. At the same time a rise in the literacy rate changed people's consumption of narratives. Individuals were able to read privately and the oral traditions of poetry and plays, performed within a communal or family setting, began to erode. It also must be said that this increased consumption was limited to the middle classes. The books were expensive and working-class families remained largely illiterate through lack of education, with little leisure time or adequate lighting to enjoy reading for pleasure. Nevertheless there was an increased audience ready to consume the newly printed books, although this too should be put in perspective. The average number of books printed for a first edition was about 500, and only when the author was very popular did the print run go as high as 2,000.[3] Today the first print run of a popular 'blockbuster' novel such as one by Barbara Taylor Bradford could be as high as 50,000 copies for Great Britain alone. Although obviously the literacy rate now is much higher than it was then, the thousands upon thousands of books currently printed each year means that there is tremendous competition in the market. In the eighteenth century, when buying and owning novels was not considered the thing to do, it was the circulating libraries (founded in the 1720s in London and the fashionable resorts, such as Bath) who determined the size of a print run, since it was in the libraries' interest to have a large selection of titles rather than large quantities of a specific title. Again, the subscriptions were not cheap and were beyond the average income of working-class families.

Last but not least, along with the rise of capitalism and the market system came the notion of individualism. People began to think of themselves less as members of a specific community, born to fulfil a certain traditional role in society, and more as individuals, concerned with their own inner, subjective experience. This is essentially what distinguishes the first novels from the narratives that had gone before. Instead of epic or mythic figures or allegorical types (characters representing some specific vice or virtue), there were representations of individuals who had both an outer and an inner life and a sense of creating their own destiny. Daniel Defoe's *Moll Flanders*, written in 1722, is a good example and is generally considered to be the first English novel. We have to look elsewhere for the actual prototype, which was the 'picaresque' novel developed in sixteenth-century Spain. 'Picaro' is a Spanish word meaning 'sharp-witted rogue' and these tales involved characters who lived off their wits while moving about from place to place. Picaresque novels are characterized by an episodic structure and perhaps the most best known is *Don Quixote* (1605) by Cervantes.

Moll Flanders is in the picaresque tradition and is the first novel to use a woman as a central character. Its full title is *The History and Misfortunes of the Famous Moll Flanders* and the preface warns 'The World is so taken up of late with Novels and Romances, that it will be hard for a private History to be taken for Genuine, where the Names and other Circumstances of the Person are concealed.'[4] It is claiming from the start to be *real* rather than fiction. It relates the 'autobiography' of Moll whose mother had been transported to Virginia for theft soon after Moll's birth. Moll is born in Newgate prison and, with her mother transported, she is left to live off her wits. She survives by prostitution, a number of marriages (one of which is unknowingly to her own brother) and by becoming a successful pickpocket and thief. She is finally caught and transported to Virginia with one of her former husbands, a highwayman. Between them they have amassed enough ill-gotten money to set up as planters and they end their lives honest, rich and penitent. Whether Defoe took his source for Moll Flanders from the life of any one woman is open to question but it has been suggested, and seems more likely, that he took his material from a number of sources. It is an extraordinary book for the kind of life that it represents, a woman abandoned at birth who must make her living in whatever way she can. It also offers a dubious but historically interesting moral. Moll is forced to fend for herself, which means she lives the life of a rogue, yet on another level she is a true individualist and capitalist. She ends up wealthy and happy and this seems to condone her previous life of vice.

Another fashionable form developed in the seventeenth century was the epistolary novel. The term comes from the word 'epistle' and simply means 'in letter form'. The first notable example in English, *Letters of a Portugese Nun,* published in 1678, was a translation from the French original. In 1683 Aphra Behn published *Love-letters between a Nobleman and his Sister,* and this spawned a taste for tales of illicit love. Aphra Behn was a woman who led a fascinating life and was probably the first English woman to earn her living by writing. She lived from 1640 to 1689 and was employed at one time by Charles II as a spy in Antwerp during the Dutch war. She wrote many plays, the most popular of which was *The Rover* (1677–81). Her themes often included the difficulties of arranged and ill-matched marriages. She visited Surinam in 1663, which was then an English colony, and subsequently wrote *Oroonoko, or the History of the Royal Slave* (1688), one of the earliest protests against the slave trade. This was later put into play form and attracted large audiences around the country. She was successful in her own time despite accusations of plagiarism and lewdness, criticisms she attributed to being a woman.

In epistolary novels it was common for an anonymous author to masquerade as an 'editor' and in the same way that novels purported to be 'history', epistolary novels purported to be *real* letters. It was a form rescued from the stories of illicit love and made 'respectable' by Samuel Richardson who wrote *Pamela* in 1741. *Pamela, Or Virtue Rewarded* and his subsequent novel *Clarissa* (1747–49) both tell a similar story of an innocent young woman ruthlessly pursued by a rakish young man. Pamela, as the title tells you, is finally rewarded for her resistance to Mr B's advances but tragically, Clarissa does not survive her treatment from Lovelace. The narrative in the epistolary novel is conveyed entirely though letters, mostly letters from the heroine or letters between lovers, and sometimes in responses from others, such as friends. *Pamela* and *Clarissa* were enormously popular and between the 1740s and the 1800s this type of novel flourished. Since then the epistolary form has ceased to be commonly used, perhaps for the obvious reason that letter writing is much less a means of communication in everyday life than it was. However, the general idea is still used, for example in the highly successful *The Color Purple* by Alice Walker which takes the form of letters written by the central character, Celie, to God and her sister Nettie.

A further type of novel that was very popular in the eighteenth century was the Gothic. This was at its height during the 1790s and early nineteenth century. The word 'Gothic' implied medieval and therefore looked back to a previous time in history. Walpole's *The Castle of Otranto: A Gothic Story* (1764) is generally accepted to be the first of this form. Gothic novels involved tales of the fantastic and supernatural or macabre set in haunted castles, graveyards, ruins and wild picturesque landscapes. Later the meaning altered until its emphasis lay much more on the macabre than on the original medieval element, which was sometimes dispensed with altogether. Ann Radcliffe, writing in the late eighteenth and early nineteenth century, was a leading author of Gothic novels and her book *The Mysteries of Udolpho* (1794) is often cited as a classic example. In this novel the heroine, Emily, is forced by Count Montoni to accompany him to the dark and mysterious castle of Udolpho where strange and threatening events occur. Emily is an exemplary heroine of great virtue, and in her stressful situation she repeatedly brings to mind her father's caution against succumbing to passion, first impressions or an over-active imagination. For the most part Emily adheres to this advice, faints only rarely, has remarkable fortitude and illustrates her own sensibility by her passionate response to nature. In its time the book was a great success. Gothic novels, many written by women, became the fashion and were the hit of the circulating libraries with such titles as *Castle of Wolfenbach*, *Clermont*, *Mysterious Warnings*, *Necromancer of the Black Forest*, *Midnight Bell*, *Orphan of the Rhine* and *Horrid Mysteries*.[5] Minerva Press in London, for example, specialized in the publication of Gothic fiction, publishing the top sellers of the day in the period between 1790 and 1820. The ten best-sellers in 1798 were Minerva books all written by, and largely for, women.[6]

Commentators on the participation of women in novel writing in the eighteenth century often ascribe their activity to the suitability of the novel form for the expression of inner thoughts and feelings – something for which, presumably, women had a 'natural aptitude'. Their motives, however, may have been more material. For middle-class women there was little scope for work outside the home, but increased wealth, education and leisure time provided the opportunity to write. Although it was still difficult to make a living from writing, it was possible to supplement the family income.

By 1800 women were writing a whole variety of novels. As well as the Gothic, there were romances like Fanny Burney's *Evelina* (1778), the story of a young woman's 'coming out' into society (the subject of many of Fanny Burney's novels), and novels detailing the lives of the fashionable and wealthy – a type named the 'silver fork school' – such as those by Susan Ferrier and Mrs Gore (who published about 70 of these). Maria Edgeworth (1768 to 1849) wrote a number of contemporary social novels based on different subjects, such as Irish life, and also wrote works for children. Her best known novel is *Castle Rackrent* (1800), which is credited with being both the first regional novel and the first historical novel in English. Historical and regional novels proliferated, with Sir Walter Scott the most prominent historical writer and the Brontës, Mrs Gaskell and George Eliot all later writing novels with a distinctly regional flavour.

Jane Austen (1775–1817), one of the well-known writers at the turn of the eighteenth century, is repeatedly quoted as saying: '3 or 4 families in a Country Village is the very thing to work on.'[7] In other words, she could write about what she knew – the upper middle-class world of rural southern England and, most often, a young woman's difficulties in finding an agreeable spouse. In this way Jane Austen's novels are essentially romances. Less acknowledged is the fact that she very often took particular types of novel writing to task. For example, in *Northanger Abbey* she parodies, sometimes directly, *The Mysteries of Udolpho* by Ann Radcliffe to warn young women not to take the Gothic novel too seriously. She also makes a larger point about the dangers of confusing fiction with reality. The novel as a more 'realistic' representation of human experience begins to come of age.

Development in the nineteenth century

In the nineteenth century the novel began to gain some respectability. Publishers and circulating libraries were keen to push the novel's literary merit. The libraries still served a middle-class clientele, but this was less to do with cost – the subscriptions had become relatively cheap – and more to do with the 'selection' of the audience. Mudie's Select Library, founded in 1842 by Charles Edward Mudie, introduced a strong moral tone to the whole notion of reading novels: 'No longer would the head of a Victorian family need to waste his time scanning circulating library works to see whether they were suitable for his daughters; no longer would the daughter ... have to throw her book behind the sofa at the entrance of her parents ...'[8] Novels could and should be morally 'worthy'.

The other change was the increase in male writers (presumably considered more able to write serious, edifying works), so that by the 1840s women no longer dominated the field. It is well known that women writers throughout the eighteenth and nineteenth centuries adopted male pseudonyms. This was an attempt to evade the inevitable bias against women writers (who were seen as only capable of writing 'romances') and to appeal to a wider audience. It is less well known that male writers of the late eighteenth century adopted female pseudonyms because the audience for the novel by and large consisted of women.[9] It is also notable that in the shift to attaining literary status, novels firmly adopted the 'realist' mode and the popularity of the 'cheap and sensational' Gothic fiction waned.

Paradoxically, however, when we look back to the nineteenth century it is the women writers, Jane Austen, the Brontës, Mrs Gaskell and George Eliot, who dominate the field of what we call 'literature'. And what were women writing about?

By the 1850s the scope of the novel had broadened considerably from the days of Jane Austen. Both Mrs Gaskell and George Eliot, for example, wrote regional novels about the rapid industrialization of society and the effects of this on the rural communities. They also wrote about the role of women in society and began to question the assumptions on which this role was based. Dorothea Brooke, heroine of George Eliot's novel *Middlemarch* (1871), is one of the first fully drawn heroines in the English language. George Eliot's characterization involves all the social, religious, historical, physical and psychological elements that make up an individual being. *Middlemarch* examines, among other things, the plight of a young woman who naively and idealistically binds herself in marriage to an unsuitable man whom she admires for his knowledge but does not love. Her husband, Casaubon, is a philosopher who wishes to write the definitive philosophical tract, 'The Key to All Mythologies'. Initially a willing disciple, Dorothea realizes by degree that this great work, to which Casaubon has devoted his life, is as arid and redundant as their marriage. One of the major themes of the novel is the question of the limited possibilities for women in society and the need for women to have a vocation. The novelist expresses her view on the inadequacies of female education: women are given a 'toy-box history of the world' and '... a girlish instruction comparable to the nibblings and judgements of a discursive mouse'. In the final pages of the novel a summary of Dorothea's life incorporates a question from the narrator concerning her fate:

> Many who knew her, thought it a pity that so substantive and rare a creature should have been absorbed into the life of another, and be only known in a certain circle as wife and mother. But no-one stated exactly what else that was in her power she ought rather to have done ...
>
> (Eliot, 1983, p. 894)

Realism

Many of the nineteenth-century women writers already mentioned, including George Eliot, are seen as the 'great realists'. It is worth pausing here to examine what is meant by realism. We can see by looking at the origins of the novel that in many instances there was an attempt to present a tale as if it were fact, by calling it the 'history of', or by a narrator's claim to be the 'editor' of an epistolary novel. Early novelists were keen to put a distance between what they wrote and the 'tawdry' novels of 'romance' that had gone before. However, these attempts to legitimize novels, as if they were solidly based in reality, soon became the conventions of fiction. Events occur with such pace in *Clarissa*, for example, that there would not have been enough time for the heroine to put it all down on paper!

We also need to put the question of realism into a wider context and look back again two hundred years to the seventeenth century's questioning, mentioned previously, of assumptions about the physical world. This new way of viewing the 'natural order' of things had been pursued by French philosophers of the eighteenth century as part of a movement known as the 'Enlightenment', which was characterised by a belief in reason and human progress. This philosophical school developed the concept of 'rationalism', a system of belief based not on tradition but on reason. In other words, religious doctrine, for example, which attributed the natural world to miraculous causes, was put under scrutiny according to the same critical methods as those used in science. This period, known as the 'Age of Reason', was very influential in the nineteenth century, and 'realism' in fiction, with its attempt to mirror reality, was a logical extension of this. In nineteenth-century France there was a specific 'realist school' of writers, including Honoré de Balzac and Emilé Zola, who attempted in their novels to represent the world as realistically as possible, down to the last detail.

But realism within the novel, as in any other art form, is still based on a set of conventions: there is a plot dependent on a story-line which has a cause and effect resolution; there are characters that have both an inner and an outer life; and there is an assumption that the world the characters inhabit is knowable and can be examined. The realist novel *seemingly* provides a window on reality.

Women campaigners

In the nineteenth century women began to organize and campaign around a number of issues including the slave trade, the right to enter professions, legal and educational reform and, of course, women's right to vote. The most well-known of these campaigns, championed by Josephine Butler, was the repeal of the Contagious Diseases Act which had essentially placed the blame and respon-sibility for venereal disease on women. Towards the end of the nineteenth century women writers began to echo these campaigns in their novels – writers such as Sarah Grand (the pen-name of Frances Elizabeth Bellenden McFall), Emma Frances Brooke, Menie Muriel Dowie, Mona Caird and George Egerton (the pen-name of Mary Chavelita Dunne). These women wrote novels challenging the institution of marriage and confronting, through open discussion of such issues as venereal disease, the prevailing censorship that condemned the treatment of sex in novels. In 1897 a literary magazine called *Blackwoods* stated that the 'sex-problem novelist' seemed to be '... forever examining her mental self in the looking glass ... the dominant note is restlessness and discontent with the existing order of things.'[10] Such novels were duly dubbed sensational and vulgar.

This sort of criticism did not prevent many of the novels from becoming commercial successes. In particular Sarah Grand's *The Heavenly Twins* (1893), which was directly concerned with venereal disease, sold 20,000 copies in its first year in England and five times that in the United States where it achieved the status of one of the overall best-sellers for the 1890s.[11]

Modernism and after

By the beginning of the twentieth century all the established art forms – music, painting and literature – had come under critical scrutiny from critics and artists alike. The novel was attacked again for not being true to life. Despite the French realists' attempts to represent life through minute factual detail there was still criticism that novels did not accurately portray experience. Joseph Conrad, writing to friends at this time, illustrates by his change of attitude this shift in opinion. In 1898 he wrote to a friend, 'You must have a plot! If you have not every fool reviewer will kick you because there can't be literature without a plot.'[12] Four years later in 1902 he wrote to Arnold Bennett, 'You stop just short of being absolutely real because you are faithful to your dogmas of realism. Now realism in art will never approach reality.'[13] A self-conscious movement in novel writing emerged, with a desire to 'make it new'. The interest inspired by Sigmund Freud in psychology, for example, had provoked new ideas about how to represent experience – sometimes in an attempt to become even more *real* – that is, truer to experience – than the conventions of realism can allow.

A style adopted at this time was the 'stream of consciousness' in which realist conventions of narrative (plot with a structure moving from beginning to end) are forsaken and the characters' thoughts and feelings are related in an uninterrupted flow. Dorothy Richardson pioneered the stream of consciousness technique and wrote a number of highly autobiographical novels, the first of which was *Pointed Roofs* (1915). Virginia Woolf, who also used this technique, criticized those writers still producing fiction in the realist mode and famously commented: 'Life is not a series of gig lamps symmetrically arranged; life is a luminous halo, a semi-transparent envelope surrounding us from the beginning of consciousness to the end.'[14] In her view, it was the writer's job to convey this inner illusiveness rather than the exactness of external material things.

We now live in what the literary critics and others dub a 'post-modern' culture. Modernism attempted to come even closer to representing the world as it is actually experienced by individuals. Post-modernism would question our very ability to express or represent experience *at all*. It is claimed we can no longer invent anything new but only borrow from different eras of the past, combining old elements and recycling them. Nevertheless, while some writers experiment with different forms of expression, realism continues to dominate fictional writing.

Looking at the history of the novel, it is interesting to note a number of things. Romance has always been at the bottom of the pile when it comes to ascribing 'literary value'. Certain novelists in the past have been keen to disassociate themselves from the idea that they are writing 'idle' romances. Yet romance, where it all began, remains the largest area of fictional publishing with millions of books produced each year. Despite the various shifts in thinking about how accurately we can represent human behaviour and experience, 'realism' as a fictional method has the greatest attraction for both authors and readers. We like stories to have a beginning, middle and end with characters that we can relate to. We like plots and resolutions. It's no good telling us that what we are reading isn't real because part of us knows that already and, on a feeling level, it may more closely approximate the real than a truly 'realistic' representation would. At the same time, the most unreal, the Gothic, now represented both in fiction and film, has had a revival and currently thrives.

As we can see, women have always participated strongly in the novel tradition, but many women writers of the past have disappeared from view because their books are no longer in print. Some have been revived by the Virago Press 'Classic' series that has brought back to light, for example, Sarah Scott's *Millenium Hall* (1762), an early utopian novel, and Sarah Grand's The *Beth Book* (1897). It is interesting to look back and think about why it was that women were so drawn in the eighteenth century to the Gothic, as both writers and readers. Perhaps the answer lies in the reason why women in our contemporary culture are strongly drawn to science fiction and fantasy. Not only do science fiction and fantasy offer opportunities to present life as it could be but they provide an imaginative escape from life as it is.

Notes

1   Cited in Terry Lovell, *Consuming Fiction*, Verso, London, 1987, p. 50.
2   In a now classic book, *The Rise of the Novel*, first published in 1957, Ian Watt outlines the rise of capitalism and the middle classes, the erosion of the patronage system and the rise of individualism.
3   See Terry Lovell, op. cit., p. 49.

4   G. A. Starr (ed.), Preface to Daniel Defoe, *Moll Flanders*, The World's Classics, Oxford University Press, 1981.

5   Bonamy Dobrée, introduction to Ann Radcliffe, *The Mysteries of Udolpho*, Oxford University Press, 1980, p. vii.

6   Terry Lovell, op. cit., p. 53.

7   Margaret Drabble & Jenny Stringer, *The Concise Oxford Companion to English Literature*, Oxford University Press, Oxford, 1990, p. 29.

8   Terry Lovell, op. cit., pp. 76–77.

9   Terry Lovell, op. cit., p. 82.

10   See Norma Clarke, 'A Forgotten Feminist Novelist', *Feminist Review*, No. 20, Summer 1985, p. 95.

11   Ibid, p. 95.

12   See Jeremy Hawthorn, *Studying the Novel*, Edward Arnold, London, 1989, p. 29.

13   Ibid, p. 29.

14   Virginia Woolf, 'Mr Bennett and Mrs Brown', *Virginia Woolf: A Woman's Essays*, Selected Essays, vol. 1, Rachel Bowlby (ed.), Penguin, London, 1992.

Sources

Clarke, Norma, 'A Forgotten Feminist Novelist', *Feminist Review*, No. 20, Summer 1985.

Defoe, Daniel, *Moll Flanders*, World Classic Series, Oxford University Press, Oxford, 1981.

Drabble, Margaret & Stringer, Jenny, *The Concise Oxford Companion to English Literature*, Oxford University Press, Oxford, 1990.

Eliot, George, *Middlemarch*, Penguin, London, 1983.

Hawthorn, Jeremy, *Studying the Novel*, Edward Arnold, London, 1989.

Lovell, Terry, *Consuming Fiction*, Verso, London, 1987.

Radcliffe, Ann, *The Mysteries of Udolpho*, Oxford University Press, Oxford, 1980.

Watt, Ian, *The Rise of the Novel*, Penguin, London, 1983.

Further reading

Austen, Jane, *Northanger Abbey*, Penguin, London, 1980.

Behn, Aphra, *Love-letters between a Nobleman and his Sister*, Janet Todd (ed.), *The Works of Aphra Behn*, vol. 2, Pickering & Chatto, London, 1993.

Behn, Aphra, *The Rover, Five Plays*, Methuen, London, 1990.

Behn, Aphra, *Oroonoko, or the History of the Royal Slave*, W.W. Norton, New York, 1980.

Edgeworth, Maria, *Castle Rackrent*, Oxford University Press, Oxford, 1981.

Grand, Sarah, *The Beth Book*, Virago, London, 1980.

Richardson, Dorothy, *Pointed Roofs, Backwater, Honeycomb* (in one volume entitled *Pilgrimage 1*), Virago Modern Classics, London, 1989.

Richardson, Samuel, *Pamela*, Dent, London, 1991.

Richardson, Samuel, *Clarissa*, Penguin, London, 1985.

Walker, Alice, *The Color Purple*, The Women's Press, London, 1986.

Index